AL MASH
A QUAKER TRAVE
IN THE LE

Al Mashrek
A Quaker Travel Journal in the Levant

by

Michael Thompson

best wishes
from
Michael.

William Sessions Limited
York, England

ISBN 1 85072 239 0

Printed in 11 on 12½ point Plantin Typeface
from Author's Disk
by Sessions of York
The Ebor Press
York, England

Contents

To my grandsons

Richard and Peter

Illustrations

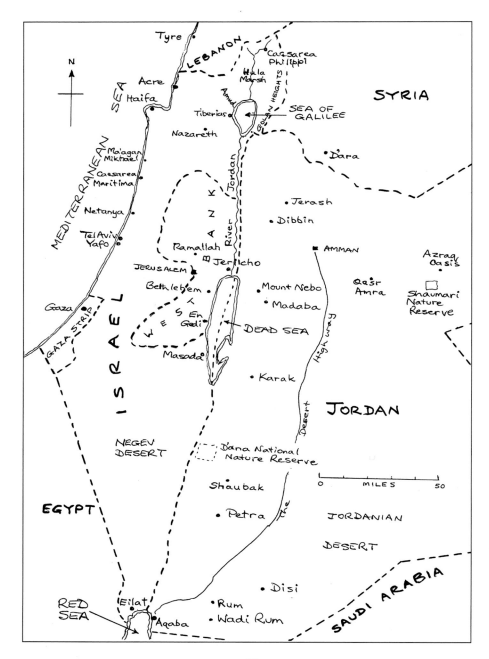

viii

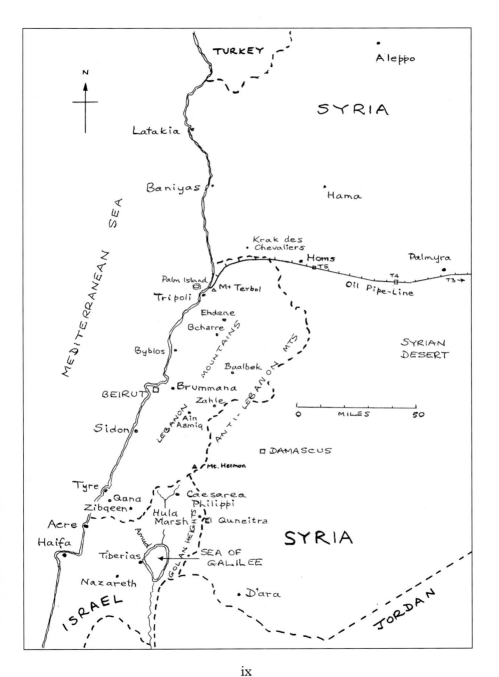

Introduction

SINCE I WAS AN INFANT in arms I have travelled. My first journey was at a few weeks, in a baby's wicker basket covered with a fine muslin net to keep the flies off. My parents, who were travelling from Haifa, Palestine, to Marseilles, took me aboard a sea-going boat in Haifa harbour, as the first part of their journey to England for home leave. Every two or three years they undertook that journey until the second World War broke out. Since those early days, I have travelled widely in Europe, parts of Africa and south-east Asia and extensively in the Near East.

My intention in writing this book is to share some of my experiences, in the hope that they will be of interest. I come from a long line of Quakers on my Father's side, and I was educated at Sidcot School, where my life-long interest in wildlife was nurtured. Although the book is partially autobiographical, I want, somehow, to bring together my travels in the Near East, my Quaker background and contacts with Quakers within the area, and my observations of its wildlife. I do not like the names Near East or Middle East, for they still have ring of western imperialism. The Near East or the Levant relates to those countries on the eastern seaboard of the Mediterranean, whereas those regions, such as the Arabian peninsula, which are further east are described as the Middle East. The name Mashrek was suggested to me by Phillippa Neave, the Quaker Peace and Service co-ordinator for the Near East, who is based in Beirut, Lebanon. Maskrek, I am told, is the Arab name for the Near East or the Levant, and is therefore appropriate.

Until the mid 1950s, along with my elder brother and younger sister, I visited our parents in Lebanon regularly. Then, for nearly thirty years, for family and professional reasons, I did not return until 1982, but there were several more visits during the last decade of the twentieth century. Most of these visits have been to Lebanon, but I have returned to Israel on three occasions. During these journeys I have made contact with Arab Quakers both at Brummana and Ramallah, and have been able to attend Middle East Yearly Meeting twice. One visit to Lebanese Quakers was for nine weeks, when I went out to Brummana under the auspices of the Friends' World Committee for Consultation (FWCC).

The descriptions of my travels in later years have been based on rough diaries I kept at the time. Some of these I have transcribed on to my word processor. In 1955 I kept a nature dairy, which has helped me to put together some of the chapter on my student days. After the death of my Mother in 1992, I found diaries of her journeys during the second World War, among my Father's papers. The collection also contains their love letters written in the War, when they were separated. With this information, I wrote about her journeys, of which there were eight, and they were then printed in 1994 as a private publication by Quacks of York under the title Travels of Tatah. Tatah is the Arab word for grandmother. My sister Jane and I were present on five of her eight journeys, but of some of them I remember little. I have used parts of the Travels of Tatah in the chapter on my early years. I have kept detailed records of the wildlife I have seen in the 1990s, and these I have used in the narrative.

My wife, Patricia, has questioned my need to publish my journeys, in that she wonders if I have anything important to say. I hope I do. I have lived, like others, through most of the twentieth century, and have watched the demise of the British Empire, especially in the Near East. My early life was affected by the second World War and I had a period when, with my mother and sister, I became an evacuee in South Africa. I have felt it was important to record the contacts I have made with many Quakers, especially with some of the delightful Arab ones. There has been a Quaker presence in the Near East for nearly 150 years, and, in spite of all the political and economic upheavals, it still continues to express itself. There have been several publications on Quaker Service in the Middle East, including a book of the same title by Henry J. Turtle published in 1975, and Christina Jones's book *Friends in Palestine* published in 1981. In 1955 the Friends' Home Service Committee published a booklet by Lettice Jowitt, in one of a series of Quaker biographies, called "Daniel Oliver and Emily, his Wife". I hope that my contribution, though limited, will add a little to the history of Quakerism in Mashrek. If nothing else comes of my manuscripts, I would like them to be part of the archival material at Friends' House Library, as a resource for more scholarly studies of Friends in the Near and Middle East. My journals do not contain the depth of historical, geographical and economic research that a professional like William Dalrymple might put into his writings.

I was encouraged to proceed by a number of Friends and family, and for this I thank them. Bob Sissons of Sessions guided me through the difficulties of publishing, and I thank him for his support. Without Kathleen Haines' efforts in reading and then correcting my manuscripts, this publication would not have been possible. I am for ever grateful to Kathleen. My thanks also go to my brother, John Thompson, and to David Gray and Ben Barman who kindly prepared maps and illustrations of the journeys in the Middle East.

Slingsby, North Yorkshire

2000

CHAPTER I

Beginnings

EMERGING FROM THE ENTRANCE of Jerusalem's
Ottoman-built station, a young newly qualified English
surgeon had his first views of the Holy City. It was to be one of
many, but that particular day, in the autumn of 1930, remained for
him a lasting memory. Many years later, my Father, John
Thompson, described to me his feelings. He had got off the train
from Port Said in Egypt, where he had disembarked from a P & O
ship, the S.S. Nankin, a few days earlier. Isolated and apprehensive
without his wife, Barbara, by his side, he made his way to the

Jersusalem Railway Station.

1

Department of Health of the Palestine Government in Jerusalem, where he had an appointment to meet Colonel W. Heron, the Director.

John Thompson, or Jack as he was known in the family, was born into a Quaker family in 1900. My paternal grandfather, James Atkinson Thompson, was a pharmacist by profession who owned several chemist shops in the East End of London; he had served his apprenticeship in Penrith. The Thompson family had lived in Cumberland for many generations, and around 1880, one member of the family, John Hall Thompson, became a convinced Friend. With John Hall's convincement, the whole Thompson family became Friends. James's wife, Florence (nee Watts), could trace her Quakerism back to 1820, when a member of her family, Joseph Watts of Bristol became convinced. Both James and Florence were actively involved in the Bedford Institute in the East End of London, and Jack was born near Hoxton Hall.

Father was educated at Saffron Walden and Bootham Schools, and, along with his best friend, Bedford Deane, went on to study medicine at University College and University College Hospital. Unfortunately, Bedford died from pulmonary tuberculosis just before he was due to qualify. Supported financially by his father throughout his medical studies, Jack qualified in May 1924. It was in 1926, while Father was a surgical officer at the Bedford General Hospital, that he met my Mother, the daughter of an Anglican clergyman, The Reverend William Sherrell. Later my maternal grandfather was to become a Canon of St. Alban's Cathedral. Mother and Father fell in love almost immediately, but were not able to marry for a number of years because of their medical and nursing commitments. Mother passed her State Registered Nursing examinations in 1926 and Father his Fellowship of the Royal College of Surgeons in 1928. All this time Father continued his involvement with Friends, and went annually on Neave Brayshaw's (Puddles) all male Young Friends' excursions to Normandy, as the party's doctor. My parents were married in 1928; the marriage that was to last over sixty years.

After a number of posts as a casualty officer and surgical officers, Father started to look elsewhere for the next stage of his surgical career. Mother, during this time, spent several months at

Woodbrooke, and nearly joined Friends by convincement, but did not do so because of the Quaker attitude to the Sacraments. Father applied for jobs in Birmingham and Swindon, but failed to get them, competition for surgical posts being keen. It was in May 1930 that he saw an advertisement in the medical press for medical officers to serve under the Colonial Office. He applied and was offered posts in Hong Kong and Palestine, and after much discussion with the family, he opted for Palestine. The appointment was for three years as its medical officer to The Palestine Railways. The post, as a civil servant, was on a salary of £750. He was required to take a course of instruction in tropical medicine before he departed. Once there he was allowed to build up a private practice, providing that it did not interfere with his duties with the Palestine Railways. Father received a letter from the Under Secretary of State in the Colonial Office confirming his appointment as from 28th August 1930. Thus it was that Father, Mother and their family came to be in Palestine.

In July 1930, Mother gave birth to my brother, John. She remained with John in England until March of the following year. Then, the two of them travelled out to the Near East on the S.S. 'Carnaro' from Trieste to Haifa, via Dover, Calais and Paris. They had a double sleeping compartment on the Simplon-Orient Express from Paris to Trieste, leaving Paris on the 23rd March. The whole journey, which had been booked by Thomas Cook's, cost £63, which included a night's stay in the Hotel Savoia Excelsior Palace.

The first family home was in Carmel Avenue, on the edge of a district of Haifa known as the German Colony. It was an upstairs flat on the corner of a busy crossroads. Later they moved to a detached stone built house in Hardegg Street in the German Colony. I was born on 30th April 1933 in St. Luke's Hospital and my sister, Jane, on May 21st of the following year. The whole family came to England on home leave for two or three months in 1933, 1935 and 1937, travelling to Mediterranean European ports before crossing the Continent by train. One such journey was taken in 1938, when it was decided that John, now aged eight, should go to Saffron Walden School.

That was the last time that John was to be resident in Haifa until after the war, when he went to Mount Carmel home during

O.M. 196.

№ 48583

GOVERNMENT OF PALESTINE.

DEPARTMENT OF HEALTH

Certificate of Registration of a Birth

Serial Number in Register	Place of Birth	Date of Birth	Name of Infant	Sex of Infant	PARTICULARS OF PARENTS							Permanent Address of Parents	Nationality of Father	Nationality of Mother	Name of Person Notifying Birth	Description and Address of Person Notifying Birth	Date of Registration	Signature and Designation of Official registering Birth
					Father			Mother										
					Name	Age	Religion	Name	Age	Religion								
5510	Haifa	30.4.33	Michael Mark James Atkinson Thompson	Male	John Herbert Thompson	33	Christian	Barbara Maxwell Thompson	29	Christian	%o Palestine Railways Haifa, Palestine	British	British	John Herbert Thompson	Father	8.5.33	Dr. Joseph T. M. Senior Medical Officer

Certified that the above is a true extract from the Register of Births kept at the Office of the Department of Health in the town of Haifa in the District of Haifa — Palestine.

Date and Office Stamp ....

8 MAY 1938

J. ....
Senior Medical Officer of Health.

Hafa District.

The Author's Birth Certificate printed in English, Arabic and Hebrew.

4

one of the school's long vacations. The newly-built house, of a modern design, was on the edge of one of Carmel's wadis (valley), and in a district known as French Carmel. The new Government Hospital in Haifa, in which both parents were much involved, was opened in 1938. It was an impressive building, situated on the waterfront near the harbour breakwater, and it was fully equipped. By then Father was renegotiating his position as Senior Medical Officer to the Palestine Railways to a Consultant Surgeon Specialist at the Government Hospital, Haifa, for which he was very well trained. Although downgrading his position with the Palestine Railways, he continued to work with them, as well as obtaining an honorary post with the Palestine Police.

In the two years leading up to the declaration of the Second World War, and later, my Mother undertook a series of extraordinary and courageous journeys. My sister Jane, and I accompanied her on five of them. The first of these was when she took John to England to start his schooling. They travelled together on an Italian ship to Trieste, before catching a train across Europe to London. Before she returned to Haifa, having left John at Saffron Waldon, the German armies invaded Sudenenland, which lead to the non-aggression pact at Munich. Mother found people in England, at that time very uneasy, for Germany was expanding and war seemed imminent, so she decided to return to Haifa. All went well until she reached Paris.

The French populace was in a tumultuous state, fearful of war and the bombing of Paris. On reaching the Gare de Lyon, Mother found crowds of people jostling and pushing to get on to trains to go south to Italy and the eastern states. She managed to get on a train, but had not booked a seat. She was sitting on her suitcase in a crowded corridor, when a lady in a neighbouring compartment said, "Are you English? We thought you were French". They then offered her a seat, taking their young daughter to sit between them. The lady and her husband, who had been on annual leave, were trying to get back to Istanbul, where he was the British Ambassador. Apparently, due to the deteriorating international situation, he had been recalled to Turkey. There Mother sat all night, unable to move or to sleep and she became very thirsty. However at dawn, at the Swiss border town of Valour, the train stopped; the Ambassador managed to get three mugs of very welcome cold water. Mother said good-bye to the Ambassador and his family, and was met at Trieste by the Cook's agent, who had booked her into a hotel. She was stranded for the best part of a week and spent her time wandering round the city. There was a wine festival on at the time. She recalls, in her diaries, how she ventured into a main public square where there was a political meeting. The mayor was addressing a large crowd, telling them how Hitler and Mussolini had brought peace to the world. To her amusement the crowd disappeared rapidly during a violent thunderstorm. From Trieste she flew down to the Adriatic port of Brindisi. It was the first time that Mother had flown and, and to her surprise, she was the only passenger on board. At Brindisi she changed planes, but this time flew in a red flying boat straight to Haifa harbour.

In spite of increasing nervousness about the political situation in Europe, Father and Mother prepared to go on leave to England in 1939. I was then six years old and travelled with Jane, ahead of our parents, accompanied by our nursery governess, Betty Clutton, to Marseilles. Betty Clutton's parents, who were English, lived in an old farmhouse just outside Carcassonne, her father being a retired mining engineer. We stayed on the farm for a month, blissfully unaware of the strife that was coming to Europe. Mother and Father joined us eventually, having travelled by car from Marseilles. Driving across France and Belgium, accompanied by Betty Clutton, the family reached Ostend. Along the route, according to Mother's diaries, people were fearful of war. Once in England we met John, our grandparents and other members of the family. At that time they were all living at the grandparents' country cottage at Wittering in Sussex, but it was not a happy time. Grandpa Thompson had developed heart failure and within a few days he died. Not long after, war was declared by Neville Chamberlain on 3rd. September 1939. Following Grandpa's death the family moved to Bournemouth, having closed down the cottage. John, Jane and I, along with our parents, then went to Stondon to visit Mother's parents; Grandpa Sherrell being the incumbent of the village of Stondon in Bedfordshire. Travelling cross country was difficult, because of military movements on the roads. At the rectory, Mother's family had come together, her brother Campbell, her

6

sister Ursula and her husband Hugh, along with Ursula's brother-in-law, Osmond. Hugh and Ursula were also on home leave from Malaya, where Hugh was a rubber planter in Johore Estate. As we sat round the large circular dining room table one evening, the telephone rang. It was for Osmond, calling him up to join his regiment, the Black Watch. The company fell silent as they then knew that war had come. A few days later, Father was informed that he had to return to Palestine.

Along with other women whose husbands also worked in Palestine, Mother saw Father off at Victoria Station, not knowing when she would see him next. Back at Stondon, she pondered her next move. John returned to Saffron Walden and I was to join him, in spite of my young age. She went to London to arrange a passage to Haifa for Jane and herself. That evening, after returning from London with their tickets, she told me her plans. I apparently was so distressed and tearful that she changed her mind, and agreed to try and get another child's fare from the Messageries Maritimes office in London. Next day she returned to London and succeeded. That night of tears was for me a turning point in my life.

Having been seen off by Grandpa Sherrell, we reached Folkestone in the early afternoon, but passengers were not allowed on to the boat until dusk. Thus, after a lengthy stay on the train, wearing our life jackets, and with gas masks hanging round our necks, we were eventually allowed aboard the ferry. Everywhere was in darkness. Then, with little warning, the Channel steamer sailed as fast as it could to Calais; it was the 21st October 1939, over a month after war had been declared. At Calais the Paris bound train was about to depart, and Mother just managed to find two seats in a third class carriage. Jane sat on her knee, and became more and more miserable. The wooden seats situated over the wheels, became increasingly uncomfortable. Fortunately, two English-speaking Roman Catholic priests on the other side of the gangway, made space for Jane between them. She immediately fell soundly asleep. On reaching Paris around midnight, a kind taxi driver found us a quiet hotel, where we were offered a bowl of soup and some bread by the woman owner, before turning in for the night. The meal was most welcome for we had not had anything to eat all day.

SENIOR MEDICAL OFFICER
PALESTINE RAILWAYS

8

Next day, Mother contacted a long-standing friend of the family, Emile Guttman. He showed us round part of Paris, which was very much on a war footing, and we saw some of the bunkers being built for the defence of the city. We later learned that our host, a Jew, had committed suicide before the fall of Paris. That evening we caught the night train to Marseille and the rest of the overland journey was uneventful. Boarding the Messageries Maritimes liner, we found a number of others making their way back to Palestine, via Port Said in Egypt. Arriving at Port Said on 1st November 1939, we were met by Father, who was very surprised to see me. From there we were taken by taxi to El Quantara on the Suez Canal to catch the train to Haifa. Being the Senior Medical Officer to the Palestine Railways meant that Father got certain privileges, one of which was to have his own special coach, with its serfagi, an Egyptian servant wearing a long white robe and a red fez on his head. We travelled in style back to Haifa overnight, reaching it next morning. Of this third journey I recollect little, not even the day in Paris.

As elsewhere in Western Europe, this was the period of the 'phoney war'. Then came the rapid advance of the Axis Powers across Europe followed by the Dunkirk evacuation in May 1940.

Palestine Government's Hospital in Haifa, 1938.
Now called Rambaum Hospital.

All this time British forces were building up numbers in Palestine. Father, as usual, went on working at the hospital and with the Palestine Railways, whilst Mother joined with other expatriate women to run a canteen for the British soldiers. Italy declared war on 10th June 1940. The war zone had extended into the Mediterranean basin and the oil refinery at Haifa was now being bombed by German, Italian and Vichy French aircraft. The Vichy French had taken over Lebanon, the border of which was only some twenty miles north of Haifa. The situation deteriorated even more in 1941. Both Greece and Crete fell to Germany in June, as the result of the first airborne landings in modern warfare. The Arabs in Iraq revolted against British rule under Rashid Ali in May, and German aircraft were attempting to land in Iraq. Although Tobruk in the Western Desert remained in Allied hands, they were retreating eastwards towards Cairo. Tension in Palestine was, according to Mother, rising. German airborne landings were expected in Palestine at any time, so that they could take control of the oil refineries and pipelines. Mother, during those days, continually watched the skies looking out for parachutes. It was against this background, that Mother and Father made a stupendous decision, that we, Mother, Jane and I should be evacuated to South Africa. Again, of this period of my life I remember little, other than going regularly to the Government primary school in Haifa, swimming at the beach next to the Haifa harbour breakwater, walking in the woods on Mount Carmel, and, on one frightening occasion, watching the refinery being bombed. The sounds of sirens and aircraft triggered fear in me as they must also have done to people at home.

By 5th June 1941, Mother had a strong conviction that we should go to South Africa, even though Thomas Cook held out no prospect of a passage. By now, the Palestine Government was encouraging the wives and children to leave, and they were prepared to pay for their passages. Male government civilian personnel had to stay. On 8th June, the Free French and British Expeditionary forces started the invasion of Lebanon. All day the big guns could be heard firing. Hundreds of people were trying to get away, including our best friends, the Webbs. At home, trunks were packed, passports and visas were ready. Father pleaded with Mother

The Author with his Sister who travelled on their Mother's Passport, 1939.

not to go, but she insisted, so that all four of us, along with our luggage, caught the train to El Quantara on Monday 9th June. That night Haifa received its heaviest bombing raid of the war. Jane was particularly upset that she was leaving Father behind and left him her favourite doll, Polly. On arriving in Cairo the following day, the family made for the Victoria Hotel and stayed there for a week. It was time to wait. Father made contact with various friends and acquaintances, so that we were amply entertained in Cairo. Eventually, a message came through the Thomas Cook's agent that we were to leave Cairo on 16th June for Suez. Father saw us onto the train and here we said our good-byes. Jane was very upset and cried and cried. I, apparently, thought it was all very exciting. Our luggage, which included some of the family silver, went ahead of us. Mother, at that time, thought she would never return to Haifa. By now I was 8 years old and can remember vividly many of the events of that journey. When we arrived at Port Tawfiq there was no sign of our luggage.

Scattered around the bay at Port Tawfiq were numerous ships of all shapes and sizes, including the Empress of Russia. Most were decked out in battleship grey, all part of the Allied war effort. Mother stayed back to find our luggage, whilst Jane and I were put onto a launch, accompanied by some friends who were also going to Durban on the Empress. She describes vividly in her diaries her acute anxiety at losing our luggage and being separated temporarily from her children in a war zone. The ships were constantly being subjected to aerial bombardment. She remained on the quayside from midday to early evening in the awful heat at that time of the year. She became increasingly dehydrated, her thirst only being relieved when she boarded the last launch to the Empress, having located the luggage. Once on board, Mother soon found Jane and me sitting cheerfully on our hand luggage in the middle of a stairwell. We had not been allocated a cabin, and, in fact, we had been double booked. The ship's bursar found temporary accommodation for us in the ship's hospital and there we remained until alternative arrangements could be made. Once settled, Mother had the opportunity to write to Father, the first of a series of love letters I have in my possession. Using Quaker language, she wrote, 'My dearest best beloved. I have missed thee greatly and God only knows when we shall meet again, but I pray that thee be spared to me'. At that distressful time, she thought she would never see him again.

Besides the escaping expatriate families aboard the Empress of Russia, the main passenger cargo was hundreds of Italian prisoners of war captured in the Western Desert campaigns. They were cramped into the ship's holds, in that searing heat and humidity. Mother took pity on them, in their shabby and dirty uniforms. They were only allowed on deck during the early evening, at the time that the ship was blacked out. The Empress, a Canadian Pacific liner launched in 1913, was fitted out for trooping in April 1941 in the Clyde, and was now on its return journey to Britain, via the Cape of Good Hope. As one of the last coal burning ships, she had to make stops to refuel. We sailed away from Port Tawfiq the following afternoon. Next night, the Port received a heavy raid, in which the ill-fated Georgic was sunk. The Webbs were aboard, but luckily they escaped with their lives in their night clothes, but lost everything else. Back on board the Empress, life settled down, especially as we were allocated a cabin. Within a few days we arrived at Port Sudan. The temperatures were 110 degrees F in the shade, with a high humidity. The ship started loading, and there was coal dust everywhere. Individuals, including me, quite quickly developed toxic skin boils and became ill. Our blackened skins were also covered with prickly heat. Leaving Port Sudan, we sailed on to Aden and stopped there for a few days to take aboard more coal, but by then the climatic conditions had eased. We were given the opportunity to go ashore and explore some of Aden. The Canadian crew, according to Mother, were most helpful, especially during their celebrations of Dominion Day. We eventually sailed out into the Indian Ocean, circumnavigating Madagascar because of increasing U boat activity. The weather became rough, with high seas, but, by 5th July 1941, we were anchored off Durban. The prisoners were put ashore immediately, much relieved to get away from their cramped conditions, but those expatriates without prearranged accommodation, like us, had to remain aboard. It was then that Mother learned that escaping members of the Albanian royal family were also aboard, along with hundreds of gold bullion blocks belonging to the Albanian state. After five days we were left on the quayside at Durban, with our luggage, but with no where to go. So ended Mother's fourth epic journey.

Our sojourn in Natal, South Africa, is another story, which is told in the Travels of Tatah. However, briefly, Mother managed to find a hotel at Umhlali Beach, with the help of Anne Robertshaw, a friend who had arrived in Durban a few weeks earlier. From there we moved on to Salt Rock Hotel, a smart fashionable place where the residents dressed for dinner. Salt Rock was not really suitable for the family's needs. It was then that mother heard of Hildray Farm at Kloof, a small township between Durban and Peitermaritzburg. Mr. and Mrs. Young, the owners, agreed to take us in, as they had done for other expatriate families. We moved in on 6th August 1941. By then Mother was beginning to absorb the peaceful situation in South Africa, and life on the farm for Jane and me became idyllic. We both started at local schools. Kloof was a beautiful place, with tree-lined roads and a small shopping centre. All the time, through the news bulletins and Father's frequent letters, Mother was aware of what was going on elsewhere in the world, especially in England. Through Father's letters we got constant news of John and the family at home. I was involved in a bicycle accident and had to be admitted to the children's ward at Addington Hospital in Durban with concussion and a suspected skull fracture. Fortunately, I made a complete recovery.

With the war situation easing in the eastern Mediterranean, Father was granted leave to come to Natal. He arrived at Durban by ship on 23rd December for what was a most joyous family reunion at Christmas, but, unfortunately, without John. Father stayed at Kloof for two and half months, during which time he and Mother went off on holiday together to the Drakensburg

Mountains. On 13th January Mother received a telegram from Ursula, who had escaped from Malaya before the fall of Singapore. She asked if she, along with her children, Anne and Tony, could join us in South Africa. She had travelled to Australia with her three young children, one of whom, Timothy, had died on the journey. Hugh joined the Johore Volunteers, and was taken prisoner on Singapore Island. He spent the rest of the war working on the death railway in Burma, which he miraculously survived. Eventually, on

The Author's Mother, Barbara, in Nurse's uniform, 1942.

14th May 1942, Ursula and her two children arrived at Durban. Father, meanwhile, had departed by boat to Suez on the 12th March. On the following day, Mother, who felt strongly that she should get a job, was offered a staff nursing post at Grey's Hospital in Pietermaritzburg, so the family moved further inland.

With the help of distant cousins of Father's, Muriel and Wallis Wells, both Friends and members of Pietermaritzburg Meeting, Mother and Ursula were able to find a detached bungalow in the Scotsville district. There the two sisters, with their offspring, settled down to family life. We were all sent to different schools; I went to Murcheston School next to Grey's Hospital. I felt happy enough, but, in retrospect, I doubt if I learned very much, because of all the upheavals in my life at that time. Unfortunately, I became seriously ill with broncho-pneumonia and was admitted to Grey's. It took me over a month to recover. Mother resigned her nursing post at the end of November.

At the end of October 1942, El Alamein had come and gone and the German forces were retreating in the Western Desert.

Father then felt it was safe enough for Mother to return to Haifa to be with him. She was to take up a nursing post at the Government Hospital in Haifa. Leaving us in the care of Ursula, she set off on 6th January 1943 on her first journey through the whole length of Africa, a journey she was repeat, with slight variations, on two more occasions. It took her a month, passing through East Africa to the source of the Nile and on to Aswan in Egypt, where she met Father again. She remained in Haifa for over a year, before returning to South Africa up the Nile again, to collect Jane and me. The last piece of her second journey was by air, flying with Imperial Airways over the Rhodesias to Salisbury. All her adventures and mishaps during these two journeys are amply described in the Travels of Tatah. Her third journey started on 1st May 1944, which was a replica of her first journey. Having said good-bye to Ursula, Anne and Tony, who were to return to England soon, Mother set off with Jane and me to Durban.

Although I was only 11 years old at the time, encouraged by Mother, I kept a diary of this exciting journey, the grammar and spelling of which was appalling. Much of it remains in my memory today. I lost sight of my diary for many years, but I found it among her papers and travel diaries after her death. The description of this journey back to the Mashrek comes from both sources.

Taking off at dawn on the following day from Durban in a British Overseas Airways Sunderland flying boat, we headed north. This was the first time that Jane and I had flown; we were very excited as we looked down on Durban disappearing in the distance. Conditions aboard were not very comfortable and flying at 13,000 feet, without oxygen and no heating, we initially became very cold. We landed at Lorenzo Marques in time for breakfast, before flying on, following the Portuguese African coastline, to Mozambique. There we spent the night in a hotel overlooking the bay. Next day was another early start, with breakfast at Lindi, a stop off at Dar es Salaam and, finally, Mombasa for an overnight stay in what I describe as a 'dirty hotel'.

The next stage of our journey was by train to Nairobi, where Mother had booked us into the Salisbury Hotel. From the train I recall seeing some of East Africa's wild animals.Unfortunately, on reaching Nairobi I went down with another chest infection, but

15

Mother was carrying one of the new sulphonamide antibiotics M & B 693, she had obtained from Father. It did the trick, but it delayed our departure on the next stage of our journey into the interior by three days.

Going by train to Mbulamuti in Kenya, after a steep climb through bushland and with plenty of wild game to observe, we reached our next destination. At the border we changed trains and moved onto Namasagali in Uganda. To cross Lake Kyoka, we had to board a flat-bottomed, paddle steamer called 'The Grant'. So on to Port Masindi, Masindi overnight, Packwach on Lake Albert and the Albert Nile. Initially, on Lake Albert, we were aboard the 'Robert Corridon,' before changing to the flat-bottomed 'Luggard' our next steamer, which took us to Numili on the Uganda-Sudan border. I can well remember the drive from Nimuli to Juba in a convoy of estate cars, and, although we came across no big mammals in the shrub-like bush, we saw plenty of evidence of them, particularly elephant. During the night in Juba I can remember the roaring of lions, which often roamed the streets, we were told.

Next morning, we departed from Juba in another flat-bottomed paddle steamer, the 'Gedid'. The next seven days were spent navigating through the reed beds of the Sudd, bumping from side to side of the banks of the White Nile, which changes course from one year to the next. Being the hottest month of the year, the Nile's water level was low, so that the steamer stopped at Kosti instead of its destination, Khartoum. Passengers had to transfer to cars and be driven across semi-arid country to the Sudanese capital. Within a few days the family was in Cairo, reunited with Father, having completed the last part of the journey by train. By 31st May we were all back in Haifa and the family home on Mount Carmel. There we stayed for six months before moving on again. I had returned to the Mashrek.

By the age of eleven I was already ' well-travelled.'

Hippos in the Nile. Drawn by JOHN THOMPSON

CHAPTER II

Student Days

FOR JANE AND ME to start our formal education, we had to return to England. Up to that point our education had been somewhat fragmented, but we had had an education of a different sort in that we had seen some of the world. So, in March 1945, along with our parents, we sailed from Haifa to Liverpool in a Dutch cargo ship, the Straat Soenda. The ship was loaded with Jaffa oranges for the British market, some of the first to be moved through to Britain at the end of the war. The journey was not without incident, for, by the time we reached Gibraltar, the Javanese crew had mutinied; only the cook remained loyal! Leaving Gibraltar in a convoy of thirteen ships, accompanied by an escort of five destroyers, we sailed out into the Atlantic. On reaching the inner docks of Liverpool, we watched the oranges being off-loaded before setting off to London late one evening. There to greet us at St. Pancras Station was John with other members of the family. It was obviously a very emotional occasion. Thus ended the last of Mother's war time journeys.

Following a prolonged period of leave in England, Mother and Father returned to Palestine in the autumn of 1945. Jane and I were enrolled as pupils at Sidcot School in the summer term of that year, thus joining John who had been a pupil there since 1940, having been moved from Saffron Walden. After four terms at Sidcot, Jane moved to another school specialising in ballet, whereas I remained there until 1952. For most of my time at Sidcot David Murray-Rust was headmaster, and by the time I left, after a third year in the sixth form, he became a personal friend and one of my mentors. Our parents remained in Palestine until the British Mandate was handed over to the United Nations Organisation in May 1948. Only

John visited them during those post-war years, for there were dangers. Father had witnessed, and could describe, many of the 'terrorist' activities carried out by either the Stern Gang or the Irgun Zwei Leumi during those years. As a senior medical civil servant, he remained in his post in Haifa until 14th May, when the Union Jack was lowered for the last time. He, along with Mother, was one of the last to leave and they both did so with great deal of sorrow for they had come to love Palestine, in spite of its insoluble problems. Almost within hours of the withdrawal of the British, full scale war broke out between the Arabs and the Jews, Palestine was partitioned and the state of Israel came into being.

In October 1948, Father joined the Iraq Petroleum Company and became the Medical Director of the Company's Hospital in Tripoli, in northern Lebanon. The hospital mostly served the local Lebanese population, but particularly the employees of the Company. There was a small population of Europeans, predominantly British, based on Tripoli, which was where the oil pipeline from Iraq terminated on the eastern Mediterranean coast. Large ocean - going tankers were moored off the refinery north of Tripoli, where they loaded up with oil for Western markets. Many of the British residents were long-standing friends, who had been in Haifa prior to 1948. Against this background, our parents created another home for us in the Maskrek. For the next decade, until 1958, the three of us visited them on a regular basis for our long summer holidays; but we were not always there at the same time. I visited them on four occasions, the final being in 1955. Of all these summer holidays, I remember best the last one.

On 20th July 1955, when I was twenty two years old, I flew out, with Jane,on a British Overseas Airways Argonaut aircraft to Beirut. These were some of the last of the civil airline propeller-driven planes to be used on that route prior to the onset of jet flight, of which the Comet was the first. I remained in Lebanon until the end of September, before returning to Britain to start my clinical studies at King's College Hospital. John, who had just been awarded his Slade Diploma, was already in Tripoli and was teaching art at the Friends' School, Brummana, under the headship of Herbert Dobbing and the guidance of Edith Baker.

Life in Tripoli soon settled into some sort of pleasurable routine.Mid-week mornings, for me, were spent observing and helping Father in his sixty bedded hospital. I found this an eye-opener and it helped to break me in to the clinical work I was about to start when I returned to London. Father always joined us for lunch, before returning to the hospital in the middle of the afternoon. One day, on one of our earlier visits to Tripoli, Father brought a visitor home to lunch. He was Daniel Oliver, a tall elderly Scotsman, with a large walrus moustache and an infectious laugh. Daniel Oliver was a well known and much loved Quaker missionary, who ran, along with his wife, Emily, an orphanage at Ras-el-Metn in the hills above Beirut. He had come to see one of his ex-orphans, who had been admitted to the hospital. Father being a Friend at that time, told him of our Quaker background. We had a most entertaining meal, as Daniel related some of the amusing incidents in his life. Daniel died in October 1952 and was buried in the small Friends' burial ground at Ras-el-Metn. Emily died two years after Daniel and is buried alongside him.

At the height of the summer, the afternoon heat, along with the high humidity, was sometimes unbearable The only thing to do was to have a prolonged siesta. So, like other members of the family, stripped to my underclothes, I lay on my bed and sweated! However, by mid-afternoon, the worst of the heat was over and I was able to go by bus to the tennis club next to the Company beach, north of Tripoli. There, along with my peer group, I played several sets of tennis, before taking a swim in the warm waters of the Mediterranean. The tennis proved to be an excellent training for the K.C.H. tennis team. Back home and after an evening meal with the family, I would listen to music, or read or work on my reptile collection. Sometimes, especially at weekends, dances, out in the open, were put on for the teen-aged expatriate children. Life, so it seemed to me, was idyllic, but very superficial and out of touch with reality. I suppose, as I reflect on those days in Tripoli, I was part of a way of life associated with British imperial attitudes and behaviour, although we were living in independent Lebanon. That way of life ended with the Suez crisis in the following year, for after Suez, the power and influence of the British Empire in the Near East was no more.

It was during my 1952 visit to Lebanon that I collected insects for the Sidcot School collection. Miss Raistrick, who taught me A level biology, encouraged me to add to the school's collection, and she equipped me with a collecting box and various other items. Quite quickly I caught and set various butterflies and insects, and among my peer group I acquired the nickname the 'Prof'. Much to their amusement I used to take my butterfly net to the evening dances because large hawk moths, such as the oleander hawk *Daphnis nerii* and various large beetles, were flying around the lights surrounding the dance floor! By the end of that particular visit to Tripoli people thought I would collect anything.

One day, at the end of my visit, I was given a small dead snake, with alternating black and white ring markings. When I got back to London I took it to the Herpetological Department of the Natural History Museum in South Kensington. It proved to be a rarity and was identified as *Micrelaps mulleri* by the Curator, Mr J.C.Battersby. At that time this species was thought to be found only around the Sea of Galilee, and with only one other record from Syria, my coastal plain specimen indicated that little was known about its distribution. Mr Battersby asked me, if I should ever return to Lebanon (as I did in 1955), to collect reptiles for the Museum's collection. Thus, the reference earlier to my reptile collection.

Father equipped me with some chloroform and a 'killing' jar, along with some disused plaster of Paris tins to make into lizard traps. In our garden I trapped 56 individual green lizards *Lacerta laevis*, and, after marking them with poster paint, I released them and studied their movements. By the time I returned to England my collection contained 60 specimens, which was made up of 12 different species of snakes, lizards, skinks, a species of slow worm *Ophisaurus apodus* and the Mediterranean *Chamaeleo chamaeleon*.

The collection, which is still in the South Kensington Natural History Museum, was eventually classified by Professor George Haas of the Hebrew University of Jerusalem, when he was visiting London in 1955. Although some of the specimens are still used as type-specimens, there was nothing unusual in my collection. Professor Haas told me that they were a valuable contribution to the understanding of the distribution of some of the more common reptiles in the Near East, especially as biologists were limited in their movements in the area because of political boundaries. Nowadays, with such emphasis on conservation, I would not collect reptiles by killing them, but would send colour photographs to the Museum instead.

It was at weekends that Mother and Father would explore Lebanon with us. Father's medical duties at weekends were often covered by his deputy, Dr. Ibrahim Ayoub, a Palestinian Arab and a life-long friend of the family, who eventually settled in London. I was to meet his brother, Charles, in Beirut in years to come. We mostly went up into the mountains behind Tripoli, often taking a picnic lunch with us. On one occasion, they arranged for us to explore the vaulted cave system in a rubber dinghy. The cave is the Jeita Grotto, out of which flows the Nahr el Kelb or the Dog River. The Dog River, just north of Beirut, has played an important part in the history of invasion, for nearly every army, from Alexander the Great to the British, used it as a means of gaining a foothold in the country. We visited the Cedars of Lebanon on several occasions, which in the 1950s was a thriving ski resort. Remnants of the forest, from which it is said King Solomon obtained cedar wood to build the Temple in Jerusalem, are struggling to survive. The wood was exported through the port of Byblos. Initially using the ski-lift, John and I went up and over the ridge known as the Col des Cedres at nearly 9000 feet and looked down on the Bekaa Plain, which separates Lebanon from the anti-Lebanon. In the distance we could see Baalbeck, the site of the famous Roman ruins, which I had last visited in 1944. Lebanon is full of historical sites and well endowed with Crusader Castles. The family managed to get to Krak de Chevaliers, probably the best preserved Frankish Crusader in the Near East. The Castle, just over the Syrian border, is perched on a hill in an arid landscape. On the day I was taken to the Krak we lost our way, and never arrived, although we could see it in the distance. Tripoli Castle, the domain of the Crusader, Raymond of Toulouse, was easily accessible, but had become the home of hundreds of Palestinian refugees since partition.

Of all the Crusader castles I visited, my favourite was Byblos. One Sunday morning, Father suggested that he and I should visit the site of Byblos, the metropolis of the Phoenician world. Driving south along the coast from Tripoli, we soon reached our destination. We got there early, well before any other visitors had arrived. Passing through the main gate, we came to the Crusader castle. Built into its massive walls were parts of the old Roman columns, and lodged in the walls were canon balls from a bombardment by the British in 1840. Scampering around the ancient masonry I spotted several

21

grey, horny lizards, known as the starred agama *Laudakia stellio*. Looking round we could see the various Phoenician walls and ramparts, and, beyond them, Greek and Roman ruins. Centrally placed, but moved from its original site, was the Temple of the Obelisks. The Temple was thought to be associated with the religious rites of Adonis and Astarte. Visiting potentates, including Egyptian pharaohs, sometimes left a small obelisk when they came to Byblos. It was here that I learned something about the origins of the Greek word bulbos, which means papyrus, hence the name Byblos, from which is derived book or scroll, thus the name Bible, a collection of books. The Phoenicians were some of the first to ship papyrus, as a writing material, from Egypt to Greece. Using a purple dye, extracted from the common eastern Mediterranean shellfish *Murex truncalis*, which they processed in large vats. They dyed their clothes, particularly for ceremonial and religious occasions. Recently excavated purple-stained vats were there for us to see, displayed in their original buildings. Beyond the vats we came across some recently excavated Neolithic burial jars, many of which contained skeletons, all in the embryonic position, buried under the crushed limestone floors of their circular, primitive stone houses. The skeletons, now in Beirut's Museums, indicated how long Byblos was occupied by man, dating back to the stone age. The Phoenicians, like the Lebanese today, were the commercial intermediaries between the West and the East, and at Byblos every civilisation which had conquered that part of the world has left its mark. That day with Father was one I would always remember, for we so rarely did things together.

A few miles north of Tripoli is a small 2000 foot mountain called Jebal Terbol. Between it and the sea is a small coastal strip on which the refinery and the large oil tanks were situated. Every summer, and 1955 was no exception, I would climb Terbol before dawn, accompanied either by our parents or John. From the summit we could watch the dawn over the Lebanon range, which at its highest point, Kornet es Squda, rises to nearly 10000 feet and is snow-capped all the year round. Enjoying a picnic breakfast, we watched the changing colours of the dawn, from deep purples through to light pinks and, finally, to the whites of the chalk mountain range, from which the word Liban, or white, is derived. Before returning home, more often than not, we had a swim in the sea at the Company's club. For me, those morning vigils on Terbol had a spiritual dimension to them, which I was to retain for many years afterwards.

Father was a keen fly fisherman. It was his relaxation when off duty. Mother often joined him, but seemed to spend her time unravelling fisherman's knots! The result was that we often would go north, particularly on a Sunday afternoon, to the Nahr el Kebir, which is the boundary between Lebanon and Syria. I was never interested in fishing, but was always willing to go on the expeditions. I was attracted by the natural history of the river. Besides seeing several species of bird and numerous dragonflies, it was the small turtles that I remember. Being a fresh water habitat, for we fished well away from the sea, I suspect I was watching the Nile soft-shelled turtle *Trionyx triunguis*, a common freshwater species in those days along the eastern Mediterranean coastline. I saw this species again in the Dalyan estuary, Turkey, in 1997. Another fishing trip, over a long weekend, was a much more elaborate affair. It was a camping expedition along the upper reaches of the River Orantes, a river that emerges from the slopes of the north-eastern Lebanon range and flows north into the Bahr el Houmous (Lake of Homs), a large freshwater lake in southern Syria. It re-emerges north of the lake to flow through Hama and on into northern Syria. The Orantes carries the melting snows of Lebanon and flows all the year round, and is rich in wildlife, particularly fish, including trout. We camped by the riverside, with all the paraphernalia of modern western living, such as refrigeration and kitchen equipment, all suitably manned by servants. For me, it was an experience never to be forgotten, not only for the beauty of the river, with its winding gorge of densely green vegetation coursing through some very arid landscape, but also the 'colonial way of life' aspects of the trip. Again, I did not fish, but observed the wildlife.

We ventured into Syria on several occasions. One such visit, along with our family friends the O'Connors, was to Aleppo in the north. Setting off by car along the coastal road to Banias in Syria in August, we passed its Crusader castle, known as Tortosa. Unfortunately, there was no time to explore the castle, for we had to reach the Company's compound at Banias for lunch. Banias, like Tripoli, was another outlet point for the I.P.C. pipeline from Kirkuk in Iraq. Around the bustling Banias jetties supplying the ocean-going tankers, the expatriate staff had a thriving sailing club. We were invited out for an afternoon's dinghy sailing. In spite of the setting sun and a light breeze, it was still very warm. From the sea, I remember appreciating the beauty of the coastline, dominated by its fine Crusader castle.

Next day we drove north again as far as Latakia, before taking the road north-eastward to Aleppo. The scenery, as far as I can remember, changed dramatically to a treeless rolling country, dry and arid for the most part, with few signs of human habitation. We noticed the conical, bee-hive shaped houses of the Alawi people that are found in this part of Syria, and the womenfolk dressed in colourful clothing. President Asad of Syria, who came to power in 1970, is an Alawi, a minority Muslim sect. We eventually arrived in Aleppo thirsty, dusty and tired from our long car journey. We made for the home of Dr. Altounyan.

Dr. Altounyan's father was Armenian and his mother English. Like his father before him, he was the physician superintendent of the British Hospital in Aleppo, one of two such hospitals in Syria at that time. For many years, Dr Altounyan was the secretary of the Middle East branch of the British Medical Association, of which Father became President in 1957. Father gave his Presidential address to the B.M.A. at Basra in Iraq in November 1957, and, through his membership of the B.M.A., he got to know Dr.Altounyan. Father was further honoured when he received the Lebanese Republic's Order of Merit medal for his medical services to Lebanon in 1958.

Our host was an expert in bronchoscopy, and had an international name in this field of medical research. In those days the bronchoscope was a large rigid instrument which was difficult to use without a general anaesthetic, unlike the fibro-optic instrument of today. Dr.Altounyan's younger son, Roger, was also a doctor and worked at Fisons for many years on asthma research. Of Mrs Altounyan, I remember little. After a meal, we all sat on their balcony overlooking Aleppo and Father and Dr. Altounyan had a lot to say to each other, as the ageing doctor puffed away at his hubble-bubble or hookah. They told us about their family of four children. They were all keen sailors and each winter and spring, outside Aleppo, there was a shallow lake of sufficient depth to sail a shallow-draft dinghy. The family were friends of Arthur Ransome,

24

the children's author, and they became the children of Swallow and Amazons and other books.

Next day we were taken on a guided tour of Aleppo, starting with its famous mediaeval souk. This was followed by a visit to the Citadel situated on a mound overlooking the city. The massive ruin, mostly well preserved, dominates its surroundings. Built of local ochre coloured stone, it had a fortified entrance gate and rampart that strode over the glacis of smooth stones before the main high walls were reached. It was, so we were told, almost impenetrable, in spite of various invading armies, such as the Crusaders, trying, by siege, to overcome it. Aleppo and its Citadel had a long history, going back to the Hittites, followed by other invasions and civilisations, such as the Assyrians, the Persians, the Mongols in CE 1260 and, finally, the Arabs. During the Crusades, Aleppo's Citadel became the centre of Salad ad-Din's political and military power.

We were shown the Arab features of the Citadel, built mostly during the reign of al Malik al-Zahir. The inner courtyard was large because the Citadel supported a sizeable population. The spectacular and almost intact throne room contained Byzantine arches of alternating black and white stones. I also remember the minaret and the mosque built in the thirteenth century, which, according to Arab tradition, was where Abraham milked his cow. The whole visit is, still today, etched on my memory.

After a few days, we moved off south towards Hama. Hama needs to be visited in order to be appreciated. Situated along the River Orantes, which is quite a sizeable river, the old town is renowned for its water wheels or norias. These great wheels, some of which are over 60 feet in diameter, are made entirely of wood. They are continually creaking due to friction, which produces an almost musical sound. Apparently they have been there for centuries, and have supplied the town and its local orchards with water, in spite of being inefficient. Half the water picked up by the bucket blades is lost and falls back into the river, whereas the remainder reaches the aqueducts and irrigation canals. We watched many small boys being carried up to the highest point on the wheels, before jumping off into the river. Hama was severely damaged in 1982, when President Asad quashed a rebellion of the Muslim Brotherhood, but, I am told, the water wheels are still there.

Finally, we had to stop at Homs on our return journey, because Hanny, who had been our domestic help in our Haifa days, had married one of the I.P.C. Arab engineers. They had moved to Homs, which was then an important I.P.C. Syrian staging post, some years previously. It was great to see Hanny, and her several daughters, after loss of contact, following the end of the Mandate. So ended, I thought, my first venture into Syria. However, Father had other plans.

Towards the end of my 1955 visit to Tripoli, Father announced that he had made arrange-

A Wooden Waterwheel at Hama, Syria, 1955.

ments for all three of us to be flown out to T3, the I.P.C. pump station on the pipeline in the middle of the Syrian desert. He had come to know the manager of the station, who had been admitted to the Company's hospital in Tripoli, and it was the result of hospital admission and the gratitude expressed, that our trip was arranged.

According to my nature diary, we flew at midday from Tripoli airport in a nine-seater Dove aircraft owned by Airworks, the air company contracted to the I.P.C. for internal flights along the pipeline. There was a full complement of passengers aboard, and the Canadian pilot kept us informed. By the time we were airborne, hot air rising from the ground below produced large air pockets. The result was that the light aircraft bounced about all over the place, dropping several feet at a time. However, for me, this did not detract from the excitement of the flight, for we got excellent views of the northern Lebanon range and the Bekaa Plain, and, in the distance, the Anti-Lebanon. We passed directly over Crak de Chevalier, and viewed it in all its splendour. It was not long before we landed at Homs, our first port of call.

On taking off again, we flew due east, stopping off at T4, before finally landing at T3, our destination. The aircraft flew directly over Palmyra, the city in the desert from classical times. The endless Syrian desert, when viewed from the air, was gently undulating and covered with pock marks, which, we were told, were dried up wells from east-west caravan routes of the Roman era. It seemed that in former centuries there was more vegetation, which mankind had gradually destroyed.

Like other desert pump stations, T3 had its own small landing strip near to the residents' compound. Having touched down, we were taken to the visitors' guest house, a comfortable apartment overlooking the central grassed area that was maintained by constant water sprinkling. The whole atmosphere of the place was very British, including their attitude to the local wild life. I had not brought my binoculars with me, thinking, before we set off, I would not see any birds. How wrong I was, for T3 was an artificial oasis and contained more bird species than I had seen in all my visits to the Mashrek. Once we had been introduced to the manager, Mr Walters, a burly Scotsman, we were left to our own devices.

I recorded that we played tennis, swam in the open-air swimming pool and generally mooched around the place. I spent time watching some most spectacular birds. As I lazed about on the edge of the swimming pool, sunning myself, I noticed the swallows *Hirundo rustica* swooping down to pick insects off the water's surface. On the grassed area there was black-winged stilt *Himantopus himantopus*, with its long red legs and straight black bill, walking in an ungainly manner picking up insects. I had never seen a stilt before, and it, along with the hoopoes *Upupa epops*, the black-headed yellow wagtails *Motacilla flava feldegg* and the blue-cheeked bee-eaters *Merops superciliosus* that flew constantly around the tennis courts, was entirely new to me.

Arrangements were made for me to spend a morning with the station's resident doctor, a Syrian. I found what he told me most instructive. Besides looking after the I.P.C. employees, the

Company provided medical assistance to the predominant, wandering Bedu tribe, the 'Anaza, whose tents we could see pitched out in the desert beyond the compound. The Bedu, according to the doctor, had four common conditions that he had to deal with on a regular basis. Some of them suffered from chronic progressive corneal scarring, called trachoma, which was due to a viral infection, as well as corneal abrasions from dust and sand. There was a predominance of digestive ailments from eating too spicy foods, producing peptic ulceration, and, from inadequately cooked beef, the beef tape worm, although the true Bedu are not great meat eaters.

During our stay, Mr. Walters had to visit Palmyra to see the local police chief. He invited us to come with him. Nowadays, I suspect, there is a modern road from the station to Palmyra, but in 1955 we drove across the desert on earth tracks created by vehicles. We seemed to be following a line of telegraph poles, on which occasionally I spotted a long-legged buzzard *Buteo rufinus*. The desert, according to my diary, was not altogether barren, for amongst the stones, boulders and sand, I noticed dwarf, succulent spiny shrubs, species of feathery grasses and low aromatic plants. In this steppe-like terrain, the cars threw up clouds of dust and would frequently disturb desert wheatears *Oenanthe deserti*. Eventually, we could see Palmyra in the distance, with its dominating Arab castle, its palm trees and nearby Bedu encampment.

With the formal part of the manager's visit over, we were invited into a room in the local prison, where we sat cross-legged on a carpet. The company was all male, except my sister, Jane, and her companion. Except the prison governor, who was in uniform, the Arabs were dressed in their traditional keffiyehs and black baggy trousers. Several dishes were placed before us, mostly of meat and rice mixtures. We were encouraged to take something from every dish, for not to do so was considered impolite. Using the fingers of our right hands, which was the Arab custom, we dipped into every dish as it was passed round. The food, although very spicy, was acceptable. Like others, I wondered if we would be served up with a sheep's eyes, but they were not on the menu. Instead, following the Syrian doctor's information, I found myself worrying about uncooked meats and, thereby, contracting beef tape worm. Time proved that my fears were unfounded. When the meal was over, a finger bowl and hand towel were provided for our sticky fingers. None of our party spoke Arabic, so we did not understand the conversation, but, for me, the meal was a most wonderful, never to be forgotten, experience.

Emerging from our meal, we found our hosts had provided us with two Arab guides, who both spoke English. They took us to the ruins. Unfortunately, we were being shown round in the early afternoon, when the sun was still high in the sky and the glare from the white masonry was almost unbearable. My first impression was of the great colonnade, with its associated arches running on an east-west axis. There were numerous tombs, dominated by the Temple of Baal. The ruins, we were told, had remained in the desert since Queen Zenobia's empire had collapsed in the late third century CE, and in places the sand had preserved them. It was whilst I was exploring some of the tombs that I noticed various reptiles. I recorded seeing Menetries's lizard *Ophisop elegans*, the bridled skink *Maybuya vittatus* and, running around on the inner walls of a tomb, the Turkish gecko *Hemidactylus turcica*.

Our guides informed us that the paintings of the sanctuary to the Temple of Baal were early Christian, indicating that the sanctuary

The Author with two Syrian Guides at Palmyra, 1955.

was used in the fifth century CE as a Christian church. I thought this was a remote place to find a Christian church and wondered who had brought the faith to Palmyra. It was later to become a mosque. We wandered amongst fallen statues, Corinthian carvings and sarcophagi of various sizes. We only got a passing impression, but it was enough to see its importance to the caravan trade of those days, with Palmyra halfway between the Euphrates and the Mediterranean coastline. With the defeat of Queen Zenobia's armies by the Romans, her empire collapsed and no other civilisation took its place. We travelled back to T3 along the same route.

I had a few remaining days in Tripoli in 1955, after our visit to Syria. During that time I packed up my reptile collection in a large biscuit tin, each one wrapped up in cotton wool soaked in surgical spirit within a plastic bag. I boarded the B.O.A.C. aircraft at Tripoli airport, and had no difficulty in taking my collection through customs. The return journey was uneventful. I took up residence at King's College Hall on Champion Hill, within walking distance of King's College Hospital where I started my clinical studies.

The narrative of this chapter makes little mention of Mother, but she was very much in evidence, supporting us all, in our various activities. Away from home, Mother, in her capacity of a nursing sister, helped with the Save the Children work among the Palestinian refugees at Tripoli Castle and the camps along the road to the I.P.C. terminal. Besides running a beautiful home in Tripoli, with the help of Rifka and Nifie, Rifka's niece, Mother's great love was her garden. Out of nothing she had produced a sea of colour; though it was dependent on constant watering with a sprinkler. The flowers attracted numerous insects, particularly butterflies, such as the common swallowtail *Papilio machaon* and the tiger swallowtail *Papilio sinon*.

Train Journey in the Kenyan Highlands. Drawn by JOHN THOMPSON

30

CHAPTER III

The Land of my Birth

LIKE MOTHER AND FATHER, I thought I would never return to the 'Land of my Birth', which had become the State of Israel. Both had decided that to go back would not be a good idea. However, I was keen to go, so that when in 1982 an opportunity arose, they asked me to make arrangements for such a visit. I was asked not to make the journey too strenuous, for Father, in his 82nd year, had angina, whereas Mother, who was several years younger, was in good health. Both John and Jane, for family reasons, were unable to join us.

I had been in contact with Mother and Father several times on the telephone before we set off on our sentimental journey. Their excitement was palpable. Father, in his diary, comments about the current political unrest between Israel and its Arab neighbours, but I told them not to worry. I have always taken the attitude that there is never a right time to go to Israel, for armed conflict can flare up at a moment's notice, and that we should take a calculated risk. On April 21st I drove from York to Sturminster Newton in Dorset and we set off next day for Heathrow. Security and customs checks were, as expected, most thorough, for there had been a recent spate of aircraft hijacking incidents in the region. After a long wait in the departure lounge, it was time to walk up the gently sloping covered way into the Boeing 747, bound for Ben Gurion Airport. Suddenly, Father complained of tightness in his chest due to his angina; so we stopped and he took a puff of his sublingual nitro-glycerine spray. The pain went and we moved on. For a moment, I wondered if his angina was going to be problem, and realised what a responsibility I had taken on. We both thought his excitement was the cause of his symptoms.

By late afternoon, we were airborne and were soon flying above the clouds. Our fellow passengers were mostly Israelis, with a good number of pale-faced, male ultra-orthodox Jews dressed in their black trilby hats, long black coats and curly sideboards. There was a lot of noisy chatter, mostly from children. We all settled down to a four hour flight to Ben Gurion, and landed there at 9.30 pm Israeli time. It took us an hour to get through all the necessary passport and customs baggage checks and collect our rented car.

The car drive north to Netanya was one I will always remember. Cramped into the small, four seater 800cc Fiat, with all our luggage, I drove off in the dark, not quite knowing where I was going. I had to have all my wits about me, for I was driving on the right-hand side of the road in strange surroundings. From time to time, we passed through army check points, but were not stopped. Eventually, we saw a road sign post to Netanya, and, after much searching, found the Hotel Topaz in not the most expensive part of the seaside resort. We got there well after mid-night, and the night porter, who had given up expecting us, gave us a warm welcome and showed us to our rooms. Mother and Father were obviously very tired and were pleased to get to bed.

I awoke next morning, with the sun pouring into my room. As I knew that Mother and Father were slow in getting up, I slipped out of the Hotel and made for the beach before breakfast. Netanya, so it seemed to me, was no different from seaside resorts found in the western world. According to Mother, in the 1930's it consisted of two small hotels, a few beach huts and miles and miles of unspoilt sandy beaches. I didn't linger, but returned to the Hotel for breakfast. Walking back through the municipal gardens, I sighted two species of birds I had not seen before. Flitting amongst the flower beds was a male Palestine sunbird *Nectarina osea*, with its spectacular metallic, dark blue plumage. Then, suddenly, I came across an adult white-throated or Symyrna kingfisher *Halcyon smyrnensis*, perched on some arched trellis work. Unlike our European kingfisher, this bird was feeding on small lizards and insects, and not fish. Making for the dining room at the Hotel, I found it bustling with holiday makers, mostly secular Jews of all shapes, sizes, colour and nationality. Mother and Father were already sitting at a table, having helped themselves to the buffet breakfast of hard boiled eggs, yoghurt, cheeses, bread and coffee or tea. Over the meal we discussed what we should do with the day. There was an air of impatience and expectation among us, for we were all eager to get to Haifa to see our old haunts.

With Mother as my navigator, we set off for Haifa along the main highway going north. The first thing we noticed was a long convoy of low-slung tank carriers, all with tanks on board. It was not until we got back to Britain that we realised the significance of the convoy, for it was part of the military build-up for the Israeli invasion of Lebanon in the weeks to come. Occasionally, either singly or in pairs, I saw spur-winged plovers *Hopopterus spinosus* standing hunched up on the roadside completely oblivious to the passing traffic. Much had changed along the approaches to Haifa.

On entering Haifa, we soon found the lower end of Carmel Avenue, now named Ben Gurion Avenue. Several of the municipal buildings of the Mandate, such as the Government Offices were still there, but looking rather dilapidated. The view up the Avenue to the Persian Gardens had not changed, but the dome of the Bahai Shrine was now gilded with gold and stood out brilliantly in the sunshine. Having located the still functioning Italian Hospital, we came across our second home in Haifa in Hardegg Street, now named Radak Street. The beautiful old stone building, now over a hundred years old, was basically the same, but was unkempt in appearance. We knocked on the door, but got no reply. However, some people from a second floor flat opposite noticed us and invited us in for coffee. Our hosts were Mr and Mrs Scheraan, who both spoke English, and were emigrants from Czechoslovakia in 1948. We got on well with them and learned a great deal from them.

Returning to Ben Gurion Avenue, we parked the Fiat and walked up to the first major crossroads. There, on the corner, was Prosser's Restaurant, much enlarged, but now under Chinese ownership, with a Chinese name. In former times, Prosser's had been a successful German restaurant, that Mother and Father visited frequently. On the opposite corner was their first flat, which they acquired in 1931. It was unchanged, but obviously had seen better days. For old times' sake, we entered the restaurant for an early lunch. The lay-out was still the same, with its parquet floor, on which, as a young couple, they used to dance the night away. The Chinese waiters served us with an excellent chicken curry.

Besides Prosser's, there was the Windsor Hotel, still retaining its name and set back with its massive bougainvillaea climber in full bloom. Mother pointed out the primary school, which we all attended. We returned to the car and drove past Allenby Street, a name still retained from the Mandate, to the upper end of Carmel Avenue. They soon located St. Luke Street, and I parked the car next to the Anglican Church of St. Luke. Next to the Church, in the early 1930s, was a series of adapted buildings that made up the first Government Hospital in Haifa. In these very buildings Father began his surgical career in 1932 as a Surgeon Specialist. We walked across to the main building and introduced ourselves. There we met the German warden of the Church of England conclave and students' college, Wolfgang Steiffert. He dropped what he was doing, and made us most welcome. He showed us round the well-cared for church, which had not changed since Mother and Father left Haifa in 1948. It was here that Jane and I were baptised into the Anglican Church, and it was here, I realised, that I had my Anglican upbringing. John, however, was baptised in London soon after his birth. At the time of our baptisms, our parents had registered us as Birthright Friends at Stoke Newington Meeting, which was where the Thompson family worshipped.

Wolfgang then took us across to the old hospital, of which Father, in his diary, comments, 'It all looks so small and confined'. Mother suddenly stopped opposite a wrought iron gate, set in a high wall of a small garden. It was the old maternity unit. She pointed out a lower floor front room and said, 'That room, Michael, was the one in which you were born in 1933 and Jane a year later'. The building was now a private residence. A flood of happy memories overtook them both, as they surveyed the scene, and I was glad to share the memories with them. The old surgical wards and operating theatre were completely transformed, for they now provided sleeping accommodation for the students, some of whom we met as we were shown round. The tour over, we thanked Wolfgang and said we hoped to meet him again on Sunday.

With Father's guidance, I found no difficulty in going up Mount Carmel. The steep road, renamed Zionist Avenue, passed close to the Bahai Shrine. We stopped at a lay-by and looked down on Haifa. There, for the first time, we could see the Government Hospital, with several new buildings round it. The breakwater of the harbour, built by the British in 1933, had not altered. Father's Palestine Railways office had disappeared under a large grain silo. Reaching the junction at the top of Zionist Avenue, we drove into Hatishbi Street, where we knew we would find the 'house on stilts'. However, the area had been further developed since 1948, and the trees had matured considerably, so locating the third family home in Haifa proved to be more difficult than we had anticipated.

I knocked on the front door and introduced myself. The owner, a distinguished, tall, elderly gentleman, came to the door in his dressing gown. He said that he had been expecting us all the week. I was taken by surprise, but he explained that our visit had been reported in the local Haifa papers by the hospital authorities, and he knew that Mother and Father had been the first owners of the house. Mr. Shalom Fickman, a Russian Jew and a leading notary advocate, now retired, had lived in the house for 14 years. He immediately welcomed us in.

The decor and furnishings were very similar to our family home, and the sitting room had changed little since I was last in it 38 years earlier. I walked over to a shuttered window, which he kindly opened. There below me was the wadi, unchanged since my boyhood days. I suddenly realised that it was in this setting that my interest in wildlife was triggered; here, in the past I had watched golden jackals *Canis aureus*, and crested porcupines *Hystrix cristata* and listened at night to the striped hyaena *Hyaena hyaena*, with its unearthly laughing cry. The valley, in the spring, was covered with red and blue anemones and, in the shady parts, cyclamen.

Originally the house, which was built on stilts because of the sharp fall away of the land, was completely isolated and surrounded by pine woodlands. Neighbouring houses could be seen, but they were some distance away. Now it was all different, with massive infilling of the area. Before we left, Mr. Fickman served a glass of Benedictine liqueur and wished us luck in our journey. We thanked him for his kindness and left. On turning back for one last look at the house, I noticed swallows were nesting nearby; they were the red-rumped swallow *Hirundo daurica*, another new species for me.

We returned to Netanya for a very welcome evening meal, along with a bottle of Mount Carmel wine. During the evening, I managed to contact Professor Yehudah Werner, Professor of Zoology at the Hebrew University of Jerusalem, who had replaced Professor George Haas. We had been previously in contact over a number of reptile species, and had arranged to meet a few days later at his home in Jerusalem. Meanwhile, Father arranged for us, on the same day, to visit Mohammed Jaber Ghesth and his family, who lived north of Jerusalem in the West Bank. Mohammed, with whom Father had kept in contact with since 1948, was his ex-clerk from his Palestine Railways days. The owners of the Topaz Hotel discouraged us from going into the West Bank, because of recent violence, but we were not put off, and booked in to the Church of Scotland Hostel near the Jaffa Gate for one night. So ended a most extraordinary day, one which passed all our expectations.

As the previous day had been so demanding, we decided to be more leisurely in our activities. I had been told, prior to our visit to Israel, that the Israelis had a very positive attitude towards wildlife conservation. With this in mind, I decided that it would be a good idea to visit one of their nature reserves, of which the nearest to Netanya were the fishponds at Ma'agan Michel. My long-standing friend, Dr. Tom Lawson of York, a British ornithologist of repute, had recommended the site. Driving north again, we soon reached our destination. On arrival we could find no warden, so I drove in, in spite of the unhelpful attitudes of the locals. We could only assume it was because it was the Shabat. I parked next to one of the disused, overgrown fishponds that still had some water in it. It was full of birds, mostly waders presumably moving through on migration. I immediately identified avocets *Recurvirostra avosetta*, black-winged stilts *Himantopus himantopus*, along with little stints *Calidris minuta*, curlew *Numemius arquata*, redshanks *Tringa totanus*, turnstones *Arenaria interpres* and numerous dunlin *Calidris alpina*. My attention was attracted by three hovering lesser pied kingfishers *Ceryle rudis*, which were easily identified by their black and white plumage. We remained in the one place and took in the wealth of wildlife about us. As I was photographing some of the

36

birds, a female sand lizard *Lacerta agilis* crossed on the sandy soil at my feet. I lost all sense of time and, as there was so much more to see, Mother and Father suggested we moved on. Unfortunately, we could not visit Athlit's Crusader Castle and its beach, which, during the days of the Mandate, was a favourite family picnic site. The whole area had been wired-off as a military zone. Instead of driving on towards Haifa, I took a minor road up to Mount Carmel. We stopped in a lay-by for a picnic lunch, opposite some quite large caves, not dissimilar to the caves in which an Anglo-American archaeological team uncovered two skeletons of Neanderthal man in the 1930s. Both Mother and Father had been invited to the site when one of the skeletons, known as Carmel Man, had been uncovered. Eventually, we reached the Carmel National Park situated at the southern end of the Mount Carmel range. To get there we had to pass through two Druze villages, which Father described in his diary as being 'rather drab and untidy; interesting but depressing'. The National Park, was well wooded with the umbrella pine *Pinus pinea*, but with plenty of open spaces and picnic sites. Having lingered for a while, we returned to the coastal road and so back to Netanya for the evening.

The little of Church of St. Luke's in Haifa was packed with worshippers. We were welcomed by a few of the faithful and sat down on a hard, wooden bench near the front. The electric organ was played, with a great deal of feeling, by an elderly Arab gentleman. The litany and hymns were all in Arabic, but, in spite of that, we entered into the spirit of the service. The sermon, however, was given in English by two black South Africans. Their inspired contributions on getting to know Jesus were given in short sentences, and then immediately translated into Arabic. The translations doubled the sermon time, which, for me, seemed endless. The whole atmosphere was very evangelical and fundamentalist, but it obviously went down very well.

The service over, the congregation gathered round us and, through an interpreter, discovered that Mother and Father had worshipped for 18 years in their little church, starting in 1930. Some remembered them and they found they had several mutual friends. The small Anglican community was entirely made up of Arab members, with no ordained clergy. Once a month an

Anglican clergyman came over from Jerusalem to administer communion, and, on occasions, the Archbishop of Jerusalem himself came. This community, so it seemed to me, was a legacy of the British Mandate, and how self-sustaining it would be in years to come, was anyone's guess. We said our farewells and made for Central Carmel for lunch.

Over lunch, taken on a cafe pavement table, Mother decided that she would like to look up her hairdressing establishment. Before the meal was over, I looked up into the sky to see a large flock of common cranes *Grus grus* flying in formation, heading north to their breeding grounds in eastern Europe. Their call and flight excited me, for I had never seen anything like it before.

Using Haifa's equivalent of Yellow Pages, we found Madam Kopito's hairdressing salon still existed. Walking into the reception, Mother found that the business was now run by Madam Kopito's daughter, who immediately recognised her. Overcome with emotion, the daughter rang up her mother, now aged 87, and arranged for us to visit. On reaching Madam Kopito's flat, we received a tremendous welcome. We were invited to take tea with the old lady and stayed with her for over an hour. Out poured a welter of memories and talk about bygone friends. Madam Kopito found an old photograph album, which contained some photographs of her previous clientele. In it she found a photograph of Mother having her hair done in the early 1930s. We could not believe our luck. It had been an extraordinary experience and a most moving occasion. So, once again, we said farewell and returned to Netanya.

The day we visited the Rambaum Hospital at Bet Galim in Haifa was, I suppose, the most important day of our visit to Israel. The Hospital is named after a famous Jewish rabbi. I had written to the Medical Director several months before our journey, stating that we would like to visit the hospital. I received a reply from Dr.Z. Ben-Ishai, the Deputy Director, informing me that they would be delighted to receive us as their guests. Father had written extensively in his diary, so I have depended entirely on his description for the events of the day. He was now aged 82 and had not practised medicine for nearly two decades, so he was rather overcome by the some of the medical technology we were shown.

He wrote, *'This was one of those special days of our tour when we were invited by the Director of the Rambaum Hospital, the successor of the Government Hospital from 1948, to pay a visit to the Hospital and to meet some of the old associates. He had advertised our coming in some of the local papers and invited those who knew us to come. We arrived at the Hospital gates around 10.00 am to find the gate guards and folks milling in and out - we were told later an average of 1,000 people pass in and out during the day'.*

'The Hospital now consists of the old blocks as we knew them, along with a new huge square concrete block giving the total bed capacity of about 500. We were soon greeted by the Deputy Director, Dr. Ben-Ishai, with a very smiling welcome and handshakes all round. He first conducted us to his office through corridors where doctors and nurses were going about very purposefully. He greeted me as the Director from 1938 to 1948; not quite true, but very flattering. In the archive of the hospital he found the visitors' book with the signatures of the High Commissioner, Harold MacMichael, Keith Roach, Dr. Heron and others, including Barbara M. Thompson, on the occasion of the opening ceremony on 22nd December 1938. He also had a copy of the Civil List detailing particulars of my appointment, salary etc.; I was handed copies of these documents. We then went on a tour round the two hospital blocks, where I saw my old office and consulting room'.

'Dr. Ben-Ishai was concerned about the bed accommodation, which we had thought was pretty marvellous in our time. Certainly now the wards and rooms were overcrowded and even some of the corridors had beds in them. The Orthopaedic Department was having to accommodate its casualties here. The work is all in specialities now, with separate staffing of each and some 300 medical staff to sustain it. Anyway, it was a mouth-watering experience to see all the sophisticated apparatus, perhaps especially in the Infant Department with each baby attached to complicated monitoring apparatus. The Oncology Department and Nephrology with its self-administered dialysis machines was also impressive. Everybody looked busy and purposeful and it was all most encouraging to think that this had developed out of our 'new hospital' with its humble equipment and small staff. We enjoyed seeing it all and our host, I think, was understandably proud to be able to demonstrate it to us. We noted that there were no private beds, and the aim is of no more than three patients to a room'.

'Then, we went down in a lift and waiting for us was a group of about 20 people, and the Director himself, Professor Joseph M. Brandes MD, a large, cheerful man, who conducted us into a room with chairs at one end and a table and some chairs facing. Our group and Professor Brandes sat at the table and the rest opposite. We were given a very flattering speech of welcome, making this an auspicious occasion after 34 years. As souvenirs I was handed a handsome book or atlas of Mount Carmel, a coloured framed picture of the hospital and copies of the Civil list and opening day signatures. I made a reply as well as I could and I hope satisfactorily, but seeing all those friends there, doctors, nurses and others, was too moving an experience, and at the closing of my words, I fear I was reduced to a few tears. I suppose we had an hour's get-together, before they all dispersed. The press also was there in great numbers. Dr. Ben-Ishai stayed with us throughout and finally waved us off from the gates'.

My own impressions of the day were of intense interest in all that was going on in the Rambaum Hospital. What had been small beginnings in 1938, had developed into a large hospital complex, with its associated medical school, from which 60 students graduated every year. We were shown what had been the Palestine Police wards, which were not different in outward structure, but had now become the neonatal intensive care and paediatric wards. The day was not without its humour, for we entered the back door of the hospital, which in former times had been its front door, only to approach the reception party, with its red carpet, from behind! Besides the good humour, there was a high emotional content, which, at times, was too much for both Father and Mother, especially Father. He shed a few tears; I had never seen him cry before.

Before leaving the immediate area of the hospital, we looked briefly at the old bathing club beach, which the expatriate population used between the hospital and the Haifa harbour breakwater. Peering over the wall, brought back vague memories of my boyhood days, for at this beach I learned to swim, between ages 5 and 6. Also, near by, was the Palestine Police cemetery. Father walked among the gravestones, seeking out the names of some of the injured or seriously ill policemen he had cared for. He was much distressed by the lack of care given to the Police cemetery, compared to the neighbouring British servicemen's cemetery. We eventually got back to the Topaz exhausted, but happy with the day's events.

It was a cloudy, windy and rather cool day when we set off for Jerusalem. I had been in contact again with Professor Werner, who had kindly arranged for us to stay overnight at the Church of Scotland Hostel, opposite the Jaffa Gate in Jerusalem. We were quickly onto the main highway, climbing eastwards from the coastal plains to Jerusalem, the route passing through typical Eastern Mediterranean terrain of small rocky outcrops, scrub and pine trees. From time to time we passed a rusty tank, left in memory of the battles fought in the 1967 conflict. Approaching Jerusalem, we became aware of the fortress-like, new settlement housing blocks in the occupied West Bank, that stood out starkly against the skyline.

On reaching the centre of Jerusalem, having passed the old Ottoman railway station, we eventually found Professor Werner's flat. I spoke briefly with him and made arrangements for us to visit him and his family in the evening. Finding the St. Andrew's Hostel was not difficult, but I found driving in Jerusalem a nightmare, for I had to contend with cars, cyclists, buses, donkeys and humans!

Walking through the main entrance to the Hostel was, for me, like walking backwards into a bygone age. We were back in the days of the British Empire. The marble-floored entrance hall, with its potted plants and portraits of Queen Elizabeth II, Winston Churchill, and General Allenby, was designed, I suppose, to make me feel British and to remember that at one time this part of the world was under British influence. We were made most welcome by the Arab male staff, all wearing red tarbooshes, and dressed in white tunic coats and white trousers. They showed us to our rooms, which were comfortably, but simply furnished. After a quick wash and a brush-up, we decided to make for the West Bank and seek out Mohammed Jaber Ghesth and his family. Mohammed had been Father's faithful clerk in the Palestine Railways office in Haifa, and since the ending of the Mandate they had kept in constant contact.

We knew that the Ghesth home was in the village of Beit Hanina, just over the border in the occupied West Bank. Passing through two army-manned road blocks, we saw no signs of civil unrest. It took us some time, but eventually we saw Mohammed

41

himself waiting at a street corner. What a welcome! There were kisses on both cheeks and never-ending hand shakes. The family lived in a three-storeyed house built into a hillside. They lived on the lower floor, the other two floors he rented to U.N. personnel. We were introduced to Mrs. Ghesth, and the wife of one of their sons, along with several of their grandchildren, who were shy and slightly suspicious of us.

Sitting in a row on a long settee, in a spacious sitting room, we talked to Mohammed and his eldest grandson. Madam was completely silent, but soon disappeared to prepare a meal. The grandson, an intelligent and well-mannered person, was ready to go on to higher education. He very much wanted to go on to study medicine, but access to Israeli medical schools was almost impossible. The American University at Beirut used to be available for Palestinian Arabs, but, because of the current political situation, it too was barred. Britain was no longer giving grant aid, through the British Council, for higher education in medicine, and Britain would have been the family's first choice. His only options were Yugoslavia, East Germany, Russia, India and Brazil. Father was much saddened by this revelation.

Eventually, we were ushered into the dining room to have an immense meal set before us. Tea or coffee was offered, along with 'minced burgers' or kibbabs, cheese cakes, bread of all sort of shapes and sizes and egg dishes. Madam piled up our plates! We were overwhelmed with typical Arab hospitality. Mohammed pleaded with us to stay on until the evening and we had great difficulty in convincing him that we had to get back to Jerusalem. We finally left the Ghesth household in the late afternoon, and, after saying our fond farewells, we were guided back to the Hostel by Mohammed's brother. We got back to St. Andrews just as the evening meal was being served. It was all a bit of an effort, but the meal, served by waiters with their bow ties and cummerbunds, was very tasty.

It was mid-evening when we reached the Werner's flat in west Jerusalem. Yahudah Werner, a large man of European extract, welcomed us at the door. Quietly spoken and with a whimsical, if sceptical, sense of humour, he spoke perfect English. We were introduced to his young wife, his mother-in-law and two of his older sisters. Theirs was a cultured home, with numerous full bookcases and paintings on the walls. I was soon into conversation with him about Israel's reptiles, particularly the small snake *Microlaps mulleria*, that I had in my 1955 collection. He told me that Professor George Haas, his predecessor, was still alive and was now retired. Mother and Father conversed with the other members of the family, whilst we were offered cups of tea and further eats! It was getting quite late by the time we left the Werner's home, after what was, for me, an exciting and fruitful evening. We thanked them, before returning to St. Andrew's Hostel. Mother and Father turned in quite quickly, but I decided to wander about the grounds of the Hostel that looked out over Jerusalem's floodlit walls, with the Dome of the Rock in the background. I tried some night photography, before eventually retiring to bed.

The following day dawned cold, but sunny. Mother and Father took some time getting up, so I took the opportunity to walk around the Hostel's spacious gardens. Originally an Arab house, with later British additions, it included a bell tower. The fortress-like buildings, several of which were covered with flowering bougainvillaea, were in a superb position overlooking the City walls. I came across a memorial tablet on a wall, laid by Viscount Allenby, to commemorate the liberation of Jerusalem on 9th December 1917 by British Forces. I pondered on the implications of what was stated, for here was established the fact that the Holy Land was now in the hands of a Christian occupying power, which had not happened for over 600 years since last Crusades.

Having said good-bye to the Hostel's staff, and paid for our overnight stay, which was more expensive than we had anticipated, we decided to spend the morning in the Old City of Jerusalem. Parking next to the Jaffa Gate, which had been much restored, we wandered down into the old souk. It had been many years since I had been in a souk, so I found the whole experience vibrant and exciting. There were all sorts of people of different ethnic groups, bustling up and down the narrow and sometimes covered ways. There was noise, different smells and so much to see and take in. The shops were small by western standards, with groups all selling the same products bunched together, such as shoes or jewellery. We haggled and bargained for a few small items, such as olive tree

43

wood carved into camels, small pieces of pottery and a brass tray. Eventually, we found our way to the newly surfaced, but rather slippery, Via Dolorosa. From there it was a short distance to the Wailing Wall, which had changed considerably since Mother and Father had last seen it. They remembered the Arab houses built in front of the Wall, which the Israelis pulled down in 1967 after the whole of Jerusalem was captured by them. In its place there was now a large plaza, with better access to the Wall. As we watched the Wailing Wall, pious orthodox Jews were going through their bowing rituals and stuffing small pieces of prayer papers into the Wall's fabric. The sexes were segregated, men on one side and women on the other. We returned to Netanya in the afternoon, to find the local population, in family units, out in the Municipal Gardens picnicking to celebrate Independence Day.

On the remaining two days of our visit to Israel, we took things more easily. The hectic rushing about was no longer necessary, as we had, by then, seen most of what we intended. On one of those days we drove over to Nazareth, taking the road over Mount Carmel to get there. Nazareth was full of visitors and motor cars, but we were able to find somewhere to park for an early lunch at an Arab restaurant. The meal over, Mother decided she wanted to paint, so we headed for the hills. The hot khamsin weather brought with it dry dusty winds. We found a suitable spot by the roadside, with a view over Nazareth. Mother settled down with her easel and paints, whilst Father retired to the car for an afternoon nap. I decided to go off and explore the area, armed with my camera and binoculars. What immediately struck me was the sheer diversity of plant life, most of which was coming into or was already in flower, especially the poppies with their deep red colour, quite unlike those we get at home. There seemed to be butterflies everywhere, including species of clouded yellow *Colias sp.*, grizzled skipper *Pyrgus sp.*, and marbled white *Melanargia sp.* As I walked up the narrow path, wearing sandals only, I began to think of one of my favourite parables - the Parable of the Sower (Matthew 13v 4 - 9). I became aware of the four habitats described in the Parable, the rocky terrain, the footpath, the thistles and the good soil. Not far away I could see an Arab farmer, with his horse-drawn plough, ploughing a small patch of 'good soil'. Small areas like this one, I thought, had not changed much since Jesus of Nazareth walked this earth. For me, that moment on the Nazarene hillside, was a moment of Eternity.

We rounded off our holiday by visiting Caesarea, which is north of Netanya on the coast. We found it quite easily and parked next to its ancient aqueduct. The sea was whipped up by the wind, producing waves with great white plumes running off their crests. In spite of the warm dusty wind, Mother settled down for another painting session. Father and I explored the ancient ruins. The massive Herodian buildings, built in a Roman style, dominated the site, with remains of Byzantine and Crusader additions. The Crusader Castle, perched on the end of a promontory, was built with stone from the metropolis. Little remained of the central palace buildings, but the massive ramparts were still intact. Everywhere there were fallen Roman columns and shattered statues. The amphitheatre, recently restored, was too far for Father to walk. As on other ruins in the area, starred agamas lizards *Laudakia stellio*, some quite sizeable, were scampering over the masonry. I was pleased to have visited Caesarea, with its New Testament associations with Herod the Great and later, Pilate. We had lunch in a restaurant overlooking the sea, but in sight of a massive cement factory spewing out white smoke from its tall chimneys, which seemed to settle everywhere.

So ended a remarkable and exciting journey, beyond our wildest dreams. Having safely delivered Mother and Father to their home in Sturminster Newton, I returned to York. Before departing, they thanked me profusely, saying the whole experience had been a wonderful 'rounding off' for their lives. For me, it was an encounter with the past which I would never forget and it had the effect of increasing the bonds of love between us.

CHAPTER IV

Woodbrooke on the Road

A S ALWAYS, I THOUGHT my recent visit to Israel in 1982 was to have been my last, but life's circumstances change. Patricia and I married in 1985, Father died peacefully in 1989 and, by 1990, Mother was more settled in her widowhood. In that latter year, an opportunity to return to Israel arose and, after much discussion, Patricia agreed to come with me. We responded to an advertisement in the Friend, placed by David Gray. He asked if any Friends would like to join him on the fourth Woodbrooke on the Road Holy Land Tour. I had known David from the time we had served together on Young Friends' Central Committee in the late 1950s, so I contacted him and expressed an interest in the coming Tour.

With all our fares and tour payments completed by the beginning of 1990, David asked all Holy Landers, as the Group came to be called, to come together for a weekend at Woodbrooke to learn something about the area to be visited. Over the weekend we heard a series of lectures from Woodbrooke director, Tony Brown, who spoke about the Biblical content of our coming journey, and Bert Bremer, an American lecturer on Islam, in which he tried to remove some of our prejudices about the Moslem world and, finally, from Samir Khalil, a Lebanese Coptic Christian, on his interpretation of the Christian message. The ultimate contributions were from Kurt Strauss and Harvey Gillman, two Friends with Jewish backgrounds, on the Jewish experience. They, along with Marion MacNaughton, who added her thoughts on anti-Semitism, were to be participants in the tour. There was plenty of opportunity, along with much laughter, to meet and get to know some of our fellow travellers, especially Hugh and Daphne Maw, known from Sidcot days, who were leaders with David. It became apparent how much planning had already been put in by the leaders. We departed Woodbrooke after lunch on Sunday, having stayed over the two nights with David and Margaret. Margaret was not on this occasion coming with us. We thanked them both for their kind hospitality and looked forward to our journey.

No sooner had we reached London to stay overnight with Sue, our daughter, than Patricia learned that Sheila, her sister-in-law, who was ill, was not expected to live much longer. In spite of that knowledge Patricia decided to carry on the journey, hoping that Sheila would still be alive when we got back. Sue drove us over to Gatwick in the morning, and the Woodbrooke Holy Land Tour for 1990 departed by Dan Air for Ben Gurion Airport, Israel, late on the afternoon of 25th March. We arrived well after midnight, and, by the time the party had gone through customs and passport checks, it was well into the early hours of the morning. Friends were then bussed to the Holy Land East Hotel in Israeli-occupied East Jerusalem, to snatch, they hoped, a few hours' sleep.

Patricia and I were given a downstairs room, overlooking the playground of a neighbouring Arab boys' school. Like others, we did not sleep well, and were woken early by the call to prayer from the local minaret, followed by crowing cocks and baying donkeys, and, later, the loud chatter and laughter of the boys in the playground. We decided to get up early and join Friends on the roof of the Hotel for a pre-breakfast Meeting for Worship, which was held in a small conference room. Climbing the stairs to the top of the building, we emerged onto a flat roof to see a large part of East Jerusalem, with its busy narrow streets below, coming alive with people going about their daily business. In a cloudless sky, the dawn sunlight, casting its yellow rays made the gold plate Dome of the Rock glow. Within the old Ottoman city walls, this famous mosque, which seemed a stone's throw away, is the third most important holy site in Islam. As far as I was concerned, this first experience of dawn over Jerusalem was something I would always remember. It was simply beautiful and, being in Jerusalem, the experience had, for me, a spiritual dimension, which helped me and others in the gathered Meeting for Worship that morning.

Meeting over, we ascended to the dining room, to join the bustle of other visitors for a buffet breakfast.

Waiting in a bus was Yael. Yael was to be our constant companion and guide during the first week in Israel. As a young Israeli, she was full of enthusiasm for what her young country had achieved since its creation in 1948. We accepted her point of view, but we felt that she found Friends' attitudes difficult, especially as they wanted to know the other side of the story, namely the Arab experience. Her first move was to take us to the Israeli Holyland Hotel in West Jerusalem, to look at a scaled-down model of what Jerusalem looked like at the time of the Roman occupation, nearly two thousand years ago. The centre piece of the model was the Temple, destroyed in 70 C.E. Patricia, writing in her diary, thought we had too much Jewish history and culture to absorb in one session. From there, the party was bussed to the Holocaust Museum and the Memorial to those millions of Jews, who had lost their lives in the Holocaust, at Yad Vashem.

Situated in an area of incredible beauty, the Memorial is built into the hillside, surrounded by pine trees and spring flowering wild cyclamen. Following a brief visit to the Museum, Patricia and I, along with other Friends, entered the Memorial. We passed through a chamber of boulders, covered with huge blocks of concrete slabs. Inlaid in the floor were the names of the extermination camps. There was an everlasting flame burning in memory of those who died. We passed on into a recently constructed chamber in memory of the children who had died. In this chamber there were six candles and a series of reflective darkened glasses, each reflecting one of the candles. The overall effect was to produce thousands of dancing flames, each representing a child. The effect was shattering. Some members of the group were reduced to tears, particularly our Jewish Quaker participants. Emerging into daylight, Friends moved over to a low wall, under some trees, to sit, reflect, and pass into a period of Worship. 'How could humans be so cruel to each other?' I kept asking myself. That morning, man's inhumanity to man was very real. Some felt the Memorial left them with negative feelings, for the whole presentation lacked an element of forgiveness. Maybe for some, in such a situation, forgiveness is not possible. I felt there had to be an Israel, but an Israel with compassion. The Israelis in creating their homeland, often by conquest, needed to consider the needs of the Palestinian Arabs, whom they had displaced in their thousands. Friends, silenced by the experience, climbed aboard the bus to be taken to the Old City.

Dropping Friends off at the Zion Gate, Yael guided the party through a series of back streets to the Jewish quarter of the Old City. We reached the Cardo, the 2,000 year old Roman street surrounded with reconstructed houses and shopping precincts. There we settled for a falafel lunch, after which Yael was keen to show us the Wailing Wall (or Western Wall), at the base of which are the remains of the Temple's surrounding walls, destroyed in 70 C.E. by the Romans. Nothing had changed, as far as I was concerned, since my visit with Mother and Father in 1982. Friends watched the worshippers and mingled with the crowds of visitors in the plaza, including loud speaking Germans, diminutive Japanese, local Arabs and secular Jews. We were then shown the two routes of the Via Dolorosa, along which Jesus walked on his way to his execution, one Catholic the other Protestant. This experience again highlighted for me the divisions within Jerusalem. The Stations of the Cross, often marked by a modern sculptured plaque on appropriate walls, were pointed out to us. Passing a number of small Arab shops, packed full of merchandise, the party reached the Holy Sepulchre, one of the oldest churches in Jerusalem and much venerated by countless Christians from all over the world. The Church was packed with visitors, and, what little we saw of it, Patricia and I found far too ornate. I suppose it was the Quaker puritan streak in my personality that questioned its validity. Yet, for millions of Christians it was, and still is, very meaningful. Friends lingered for a while, before Yael led them back to the Jaffa Gate. We joined Daphne and Hugh Maw, who took us back to the Damascus Gate. As we approached the Post Office, situated outside the walls, we witnessed a scuffle between some Israeli soldiers and a small crowd of Arabs. It showed us, once again, that tension between the factions was only just below the surface.

No one can visit Jerusalem in a day, so next morning Yael took the party to the Wailing Wall again. It was the time of Ramadam, so some shops en route were closed. Through a well-guarded gate in the Wall, Friends entered the precincts of the El Aqsa Mosque and the Dome of the Rock. The whole area was, and still is, sacred to Islam and Judaism, but since the Diaspora it had been under either Christian or Islamic control. Some of the women members of the party were inadequately clothed, and had, therefore, to put on long flowing, ankle-length gowns. Without shoes, cameras or handbags, Friends entered the El Aqsa Mosque, which was built on the site of Justinian's basilica by the Moslems in the eighth century. Recaptured for Chritianity by the Crusaders, it was restored to Christian worship until 1187, when it returned to Islamic control with the final defeat of the Crusaders. Unlike most mosques, the El Aqsa is square, with two central marble columns separating various naves. The entire floor area was covered with full-sized Turkish and oriental carpets, on which small groups of worshippers, their heads bowed to Mecca, could be seen. The whole scene made a tremendous impression on me.

The group then moved over to Dome of the Rock, climbing a flight of stairs, below some beautiful Mameluke pointed arches, to reach the entrance. This building, the third most important shrine in the Islamic world, is octagonal and is covered with many multicoloured mosaics in symmetrical patterns, and on which is placed the gold plated Dome. Once inside, I became aware of the central rock from which Mohammed ascended into heaven and the massive marble pillars that supported the Dome. Again, I marvelled at what I saw and could only think that in the past, Mother and Father had brought me there, but I could not remember the experience.

Emerging into the bright sunlight, Friends moved on, past the site of the Second Temple of Herod the Great, to St. Anne's Church of undressed stones and simple design, which was built by the Crusaders. Sitting quietly in the nave, with few visitors about, the group started humming a well known hymn. The period of reflection and worship was much needed in the prayerful atmosphere that pervaded the place. Nearby, was the Pool of Bethesda, a deep chasm at the bottom of which there was some stagnant green water. The Pool's surrounds had been excavated, showing layer upon layer of subsequent civilisations and is the supposed site at which Jesus cured the paralytic man. (John 5)

Boarding the bus again, the party was taken to the top of the Mount of Olives, passing the Hebrew University of Jerusalem. After taking in the view and observing some Israeli troops on manoeuvres, Friends walked past the Jewish cemetery towards the Church of All Nations and the Garden of Gethsemane. Entering the Garden through a wrought-iron gate in a high wall, Friends found a place of peace and tranquillity, quite unlike the hustle and bustle of the streets of inner city Jerusalem. I was surprised how small the Garden was; it contained a number of very old, gnarled olive trees, surrounded by well-kept flower beds. All settled spontaneously into a period of silent worship. For me, this was the only place, so far on the tour, which one could describe as being part of the 'Jesus experience'. Time, again, was pressing. The party moved out into the alleyway next to the Garden's gate, only to be confronted by a platoon of shouting, fully armed, young Israeli conscripts jogging towards the street below. The contrast of the silence in Gethsemane and the conscripts was too much for some Friends; many of the women in the party were in tears. On reflection, maybe, the young soldiers were all part of the Gethsemene experience, for that is what, according to the Gospel narratives, occurred nearly two thousand years ago when Jesus was taken away by the Temple guards. (Mark 14 v 43).

By now, some of us were beginning to tire. We were shown other places of interest by Yael, but finally the party arrived at the Garden Tomb. The place was crowed with visitors, often in small groups singing hymns and taking communion. Cared for and run by the Anglican Church, the Garden Tomb was the supposed site in which Jesus's body was laid after his death. Overlooking the neighbouring bus station, and completely uncared for, was the Place of the Skull, Golgotha, which, according to General Gordon, was the site of the crucifixion. Patricia commented in her diary,' The Garden was too full to be beautiful'. As I looked round, I was distracted by a green lizard *Lacerta laevis*, which I had not seen since my reptile collecting days in 1955.

That very full day ended, after the evening meal at The Holy Land East Hotel, with a meeting of Friends with a number of the Quaker Peace and Service field workers. Present were Kate Lock and her husband Tim, along with Graham, an ex-student from

Edinburgh, and Jo, the physiotherapist. Kate, a trained nurse, worked at a Palestinian clinic for women in the West Bank, a clinic which some of the health professionals in the party were to visit later in the week. Tim was the QPS Near East co-ordinator at that time. Each was able to tell us a little bit about some of the valuable work they were undertaking, all of which seemed helpful and highly commendable. Graham, for instance, who spoke fluent Arabic, worked on the legal aspects of Palestinian dispossession and arrest. Living in the Moslem quarter of Jerusalem, he expressed very pro-Arab sentiments.

The visit to the Gaza Strip was an occasion I would always remember. Leaving Jerusalem very early, our bus took us past the Monastery at Latrun, before joining the coastal road going south. South of Ashkelon, the party reached the border post between Israel and the occupied zone of Gaza. There we were all rapidly transferred to a white-painted United Nations UNRWA bus, having been asked not to take any photographs. An UNRWA official joined us to act as our guide; he was a Palestinian Arab who spoke excellent English. Driving further south, everyone noticed the contrast between the affluence of Israel and the poverty of Palestine. By the coast, well-watered Israeli settlements could be seen. Eventually, the party arrived at Jabaliya refugee camp, a sprawling mass of run-down shacks and mud houses. Passing along an unmade road and by an Israeli army lookout post, the bus stopped out side a clinic.

Everywhere there were cheerful smiling children, who added to what appeared to be chaos, in which a dedicated staff were trying their best to cope with overwhelming demands and limited resources. We talked to a young Palestinian doctor, who, sitting at a table, was running an infant welfare clinic. Not only was he giving advice to the women, often dressed in traditional Palestinian dresses, but also immunising some of their infants. The high infant mortality rate, which is an indicator of health and social welfare, was many times above that of neighbouring Israel. Both Patricia and I were saddened by what we learned and observed; the injustice of it all was very apparent.

I had read about Mary Khass, so to meet her was an added pleasure. Friends were driven to the Gaza Pre-school Resource Centre, situated in a refugee camp south of Gaza City. We were welcomed by Mary, a remarkable Quaker lady, who stood up to the Israeli occupying authorities whenever she experienced injustice. Her little school, supported by several international agencies, including Friends, was in much need of help. Friends, on the advice of David, had brought a number of small teaching aids as gifts for the school. Having thanked Friends for their gifts and after meeting some members of the staff, Mary told us a little about life in Gaza. The intifada was at its height, with young Palestinian youths, all over the Israeli occupied areas, throwing stones at the occupying forces. Mary, at times, would join the youths to try to persuade them to not to throw stones. Then, almost immediately, she would go and see the local army commander and tell him precisely what she thought of his actions and the behaviour of his troops. Like others, I thought Mary was a person of immense courage, wisdom and hope. She died in her mid-sixties in 1995.

Lunch was arranged at Sun Day Care Centre in the centre of Gaza. With a pending curfew, Friends had no transport, other than a series of taxis. However, Patricia and I, along with another Friend, were taken in Mary's small, white car, with its Quaker Star on the side. The car had been provided by American and British Friends. I sat in the passenger seat next to Mary. I discovered that she was born in Haifa and was brought up as an Anglican at St.Luke's Church. Being a similar age, we decided that we both had been members of Haifa's Anglican community at the same time. Soon after partition, Mary found herself working alongside American Friends in the Gaza Strip, helping with the massive Arab refugee problem created by the foundation of the State of Israel. The American Friends' Service Committee had been asked by the infant United Nations to take on the initial task of caring for the refugees. It was this contact with American Friends that convinced Mary of the Quaker message, and she joined the Society in 1986. However, she had now become increasingly isolated as a result of the restrictions placed on her movements. For me, it was a privilege to have been with her for those few hours.

Dr. Abu Ghazaleh was a big man in every sense of the word, with numerous contacts in the Arab and western world. He was the medical director and founder of the Sun Day Care Centre for handicapped children, and had, at one time, been at Woodbrooke.

He was effusive in his welcome and showed Friends around his Centre, explaining some of the difficulties he had to face under Israeli occupation. He blamed a lot of the problems of the Palestinians on the Americans, who had not been even-handed in the conflict. Along with the facilities for the mentally handicapped children, some of whom we met, the Centre ran a training programme for young women to work in the community with individual families, helping mothers to become educators. This had become necessary because of the intifada. The Israeli authorities had closed the schools in the area. Finally, on the top of the building, Friends met a group of Palestinian graduates, who had taken their degrees in either Jordan or Egypt. However, because of the high unemployment problems in the Gaza strip, they were now being instructed in an MA medical course. The tour of the establishment ended with a simple meal and an exchange of gifts, before being bussed back to the border and then on to Jerusalem. For Patricia and me it had been a most memorable day, but we were glad to get back to the hotel. On reaching Jerusalem, some Friends joined the 'Women in Black' demonstration opposite the King David Hotel. These women, both Arab and Jew, are united in their plea for peace and they held up placards reading ' End the Occupation.'

It was at Gaza that I realised, more than ever, how helpless the Palestinian cause had become, against the military might of Israel. There seemed to be no future for the people we visited, but many seemed to be making the most of what they could in a very difficult and unjust situation.

No Holy Land Tour is complete without a visit to Bethlehem. Yael was keen to take us there on what Patricia described as a 'whistle-stop' tour. As we found in other parts of the Holy Land, Bethlehem, an Arab town, was crowded with pilgrims and tourists. To gain entrance to the Church of the Nativity, the party had to go through a low arch, purposely built in a bygone age to prevent riders on horses from entering the precinct. The Church itself represented three Christian traditions, Roman Catholic, Greek Orthodox and Armenian. I was immediately struck by it ornateness and the upward drifting incense, through which shafts of sunlight penetrated to the stone-flagged floor. In a grotto, below the high altar and the supposed birth place of Jesus of Nazareth, an Orthodox priest was chanting his prayers. It seemed to me to be unreal, and +what it had to do with Christianity I do not know, especially as modern historical research suggests that Jesus was born in Nazareth. Eventually, when the grotto became vacant, Friends descended the narrow stairs to look at it. A star marked the site of the birth. Emerging again into the sunlight and the neighbouring cloisters of the Roman Catholic Church of St. Catherine, I found more peace.

South-east and not far from Bethlehem is the Shepherds' Fields, one of the three claimed sites where the angels proclaimed the birth of Jesus. Whatever the authenticity of this site, Friends were taken into the garden of the site's Franciscan Church, that the monks had kindly let them use. Sitting among some its ancient masonry, a Meeting for Worship was held, during which Denise Neale of Birmingham read an appropriate passage from the New Testament (Luke 2). I sat and absorbed the warm sun, the spring flowers, the bird song and a view across rural Palestine. In the distance I could see an Arab farmer ploughing a small field, using a wooden plough and a mule. We all absorbed the peace of the scene.

We returned to Jerusalem where, parting company with Yael, we acquired another guide and driver, named Jo. By contrast, on the same day as we visited Bethlehem, David arranged for Friends to visit Neve Shalom or Wahat Al Salam, to give it its Arabic name. On a site leased from the monastery of Latrun, south of the Jerusalem-Tel Aviv road, there is a special community, devoted to finding peaceful solutions to the Arab-Israeli conflict. In the community equal numbers of Arab and Israeli families lived side-by-side in harmony, each keeping the other's Holy Days and festivities. Whilst keeping their own cultures and religious identities, the families, particularly the children, learn each other's language and are taught about Judaism, Christianity and Islam. We were introduced to Carol Aron, whose late husband was a co-founder in 1972 of Neve Shalom with a Dominican monk, Father Bruno Hassar. Along with all their community activities, there was a Peace School and numerous Peace Posts, some of which we had seen on our travels. This successful experiment in communal living, which seemed to stand the test of time, was, for me, most

55

impressive. Like others in the party, I marvelled at the courage of Carol Aron in what was a difficult political situation. Indicative of the success of the project was the attendance of over 20,000 people, when the community held an Open Day in 1987. Following a brief tour around the grounds, Friends returned to Jerusalem.

My visit to En Gedi, along with Patricia, Hugh Maw, Anne Fletcher and David, was, for me, a very special occasion. I had often read in books about natural history of the Middle East and how En Gedi was rich in wildlife along with its Biblical associations. Thus, when David suggested we should go there on 'Land Day', I jumped at the opportunity. Land Day was the day when the whole of the Arab business world closed down in protest against the illegal occupation by the Israelis of Arab lands.

Whilst other Friends had different plans, the five of us got up in the early hours of the morning, and, while it was still dark, drove east in a hire car. Initially we got lost, but eventually found ourselves on the road to Jericho. Passing through several military road blocks without stopping, we descended from the heights of Jerusalem to below sea level. The night was very cold, as we plunged over 3000 feet through the Judean wilderness and on to the bottom of the Rift Valley. At an old ruined Palestine Police fortified station, we turned south towards the Dead Sea. By the time we reached En Gedi, dawn was with us, silhouetting the Mountains of Moab on the Jordanian side of the Rift, all in deep purple and rose-red colours. I was struck by the sheer beauty of the place. On reaching the locked entrance gate to the Arugut gorge, one of the two making up the National Nature Reserve, we hesitated. However, it was possible to circumvent the surrounding fence, which we did. We were immediately confronted with a notice, written in Hebrew, Arabic and English, telling us what to do if we should meet one of the light-furred leopards *Panthera pardus* in the gorge. Leopards, it seemed, had re-established themselves in the upper wilderness reaches of the reserve, and Israeli conservationists were doing all they could to protect them, and thus increase their numbers.

Moving forward quietly along a well-trodden path, we immediately became aware that the whole area was rich in wildlife. We saw two male bluethroats *Luscinia svecica* on migration north, and soon after that a pair of little green bee-eaters *Merops orientalis.*

By now the sun was rising, changing the gorge's high cliffs from rose-pink, through to ochre-yellow and finally a dazzling chalky white. The rich vegetation of reeds and willows, associated with the stream bed, became denser; small semi-desert plants, often in flower, eked out an existence on the rock faces. Quite quickly we were all seeing birds we had not seen before, such as the male blackstart *Cercomela melanura* and a small party of Tristram's grackles *Onychognathus tristramii*. High above us, circling on thermals, were white storks *Cinconia cinconia*, along with lesser spotted eagles *Aquila pomarina*, Egyptian vultures *Neophron percnopterus* and griffon vultures *Gyps fulvus*. It was an ornithological feast, with birds in abundance. Scurrying among the boulders in the gorge were numerous rock hyrax *Procavia capensis*. These rodent-like mammals, more related to the elephant, were often sunning themselves in small family groups. They are obviously an important food source for several of the mammalian and bird predators to be found in En Gedi.

By mid-morning it was becoming very hot in the gorge, so when the small party came across a shallow pool, full of croaking edible frogs *Rana esculenta*, each one of us stripped to our underwear and went in. Fully refreshed, it was then time to retrace our steps to the entrance gate, where we were asked for our entrance tickets. Being unable to produce them, we were duly ticked off by the park warden. Apparently, no human beings are allowed into the gorge during the early hours of the morning, so that the animals can feed undisturbed; an attitude I fully support. The car park, by now, was full with Israeli families enjoying a day's outing. The return journey to Jerusalem was uneventful. But what a day it had been! En Gedi had come right up to my expectations. The whole trip had had a spiritual dimension; it was a place in which God could be found, a place at which I could feel at peace and unity with creation. I like, for instance, the Old Testament story of Saul and David, in which Saul when searching for David in En Gedi takes shelter in a cave. David is also in the same cave, but deeper in. While Saul is asleep, David cuts off a piece of Saul's clothing to prove to him later that he, David, was also there. Although there were caves visible to us on the cliffs, we didn't venture into them.

The next day we were all back in the bus, again travelling south in the Rift Valley. David had arranged a tight schedule, but for some, such as Patricia, bus travel was becoming irksome. Accompanied by our guide Jacob, wearing an Israeli army hat, we stopped first at a viewing point overlooking Wadi Qilt. The Wadi, which is part of the extensive Judean wilderness, is a deep, mostly inaccessible, gorge and is best known for the Greek Orthodox Monastery of St. George. Supplied by spring waters, the monastery buildings cling to the gorge side and are easily visible from where we all stood. Unfortunately, the community of monks is dwindling in numbers.

Back on the road, and passing many Bedouin settlements with their traditional black tents, we reached the Kibbutz Almoc, one of the illegal Israeli settlements in the occupied West Bank. Kurt Strauss arranged the visit for he had some relatives living there; Kibbutz Almoc was the nearest Jewish community to Qumran. Once there, we were all ushered into a fortified underground shelter containing fragments of the Dead Sea Scrolls and other excavated items from Qumran. Some Friends felt uneasy at the visit, but it proved to be very helpful, especially the short film on the Scrolls. The visit to Almoc was a brief one, for it was intended that we went on to Qumran itself. After a short ride, we reached the ancient excavated site. As Jacob, our guide, showed us round Qumran, he explained how important the Scrolls were in Jewish culture and heritage. We learned a great deal about the Essenes, who arose as a sect, along with the Pharisees and Sadducees, in the century before Jesus' birth. Concerned with purification, the Essenes made a great deal of personal cleanliness and washing, and this could be seen in the structure of their domestic buildings. In the distance we could see the caves in which the Scrolls had lain hidden and unharmed for nearly nineteen centuries, until they were discovered by a Bedouin boy in 1947. I was most impressed with the whole area and felt sure that, in the future, what I had learned would help me in any historical reading about the times of Jesus.

Because of David's tight schedule, we could not linger at Qumran, but had to continue on our bus journey south along the bottom of the Rift Valley. We soon reached En Gedi again, but this time, instead of going into the gorge, the party stopped at its Dead Sea resort and one of its many swimming places. The Dead Sea was choppy, which made floating on the back difficult. Patricia ventured in, along with other Friends, but it was too cold for me. Patricia wrote in her diary, 'It is a strange sensation of buoyancy and inability to control oneself in the usual swimming position. I kept on trying to turn on to my tummy'. The dip, not to be missed by the majority, ended with a fresh water shower to get the excess salt off the skin and out of one's hair.

There are two ways up Masada, either visitors walk up from the coach park, along the zigzag path to the top, or they use the cable car. Most opted for the cable car. The view from the top is stupendous, for Masada is a plateau hill, of massive dimensions, on the edge of the western Rift escarpment. In spite of the haze and increasing midday temperatures that were becoming almost unbearable, Friends could see north up the Rift and the southern end of the Dead Sea, as well as the Mountains of Moab on the Jordanian side of the valley. Jacob took the party on a conducted tour, pointing out the fortress buildings and the palace built by Herod the Great, along with an early example of a synagogue. We had no time to visit the north-facing palace, built on the edge of the plateau; that had to wait for another occasion. Surrounding Masada, at the base of the fortress, the outlines of several Roman encampments were visible. The whole site was taken over by the Zealots following the destruction of the Temple in Jerusalem in 70 CE. Soon after that the Roman legions laid siege to Masada, finally overcoming resistance of the Zealots in 73 CE, by building a ramp up to the fortified walls. On entering the fort, the Romans discovered that resistance had ended with the mass suicide of its occupants, except for two women and three children who survived to tell the tale of extraordinary courage and fortitude. Masada symbolises, in their current culture, the deep-seated, fortress attitude of present day Israelis. Descending the ramp, we rejoined the bus and drove back to Jerusalem, but not before seeing both the brown-necked raven *Corvus ruficollis* and the fan-tailed raven *Corvus rhipidurus*. The return journey was long and tedious, for we had to avoid the West Bank because of the intifada.

Bundled into seven taxis, Friends set off from East Jerusalem to the Friends' Boys' School at Ramallah. Founded by American Friends over a hundred years ago, both the Boys' and the Girls'

Schools were still functioning in spite of the difficulties of the occupation of the West Bank by the Israelis. We had to pass through an Israeli army border check point before reaching Ramallah. Once in the West Bank, Friends were very much aware of Israeli troops, some in riot gear, patrolling the streets. On reaching the school, we found the pupils were trying to snatch what schooling they could before the afternoon curfew limited their activities. Over a cup of tea, the headmaster, Khalil Masdi, welcomed Friends and then addressed the group for nearly an hour about some of the educational difficulties he had under the occupation, along with some of the draconian regulations laid down by the authorities. He was directly accountable to a military man, who, more often than not, had no idea about educational needs. Khalil had recently published an educational manual, much against the military authority's wishes. It became apparent that Palestinians on the West Bank had a basic infrastructure for an independent state, and that some of them were very well educated. Following his talk, Friends were shown briefly round parts of the Boys' School before being taken in small groups to the Friends' Meeting House in the middle of Ramallah.

A number of Ramallah Friends were gathered at the Meeting House, mostly from three families. However, there were also expatriate American and French Friends present. Yvette, a French Friend, was well known in the area and ran an 'open house' hostel for those in need. Our party outnumbered local worshippers. The Meeting House was cold and the roof leaked; the garden was overgrown and uncared for, with graffiti covering the outside walls. Several of the windows were broken.

The Meeting for Worship, which was partially programmed, was one of the most memorable I have ever attended. We had vocal prayer in Arabic and sang 'Dear Lord and Father of Mankind', before ministry was offered. Kurt Strauss rose to his feet and was just starting his contribution, when there was a loud bang outside, along with a lot of noise and civil disturbance in adjoining streets. Unperturbed, Kurt carried on. The noise and the worship reduced some of the company to tears. Outside there had been a mini riot, with a rubber bullet being fired and hitting a youth in the face. Meeting over, Yvette hurried to the local hospital, for we had all heard the arrival of the ambulance. The boy had been seriously hurt and he later died from his injuries.

Emerging from the Meeting house, we found the whole area swarming with Israeli troops. Friends were escorted through the crowds to the Girls' School in twos and threes, to be served with a simple Arab meal by local Friends. This meal was much appreciated, for we knew of their limited financial resources. The party was then addressed by Abla Nasir, the acting head of the Girls' School, who, after explaining the difficulties she faced, thanked British Friends for the gift of £100,000 to keep the two schools open. The gathering over, Kate Roberts and Patricia went with Ellen Mansour to see some of the work of a small co-operative doing Palestinian embroidery.

Returning to Jerusalem, we found we had time on our hands. Patricia and I decided to walk the perimeter walls of the Old City to the Citadel. The partially restored Citadel, with its Crusader tower, is now a museum of the history of Jerusalem. On entering the building, we were confronted with a pile of automatic weapons left there by young Israeli soldiers, who were going round the museum. Ironically, the pile had been placed under a Biblical quotation on the entrance wall that stated, ' And in this land there shall be peace'. We looked at some of the exhibits, but were mainly attracted to a short, but excellent, animated film on the history of Jerusalem. As soon as the film was over, the museum closed. We emerged into failing daylight to find we were next to the Anglican Evangelical Church, which has a mission to the Jews. The current leaders of the community were The Reverend John Bulman and his wife, Joan. Both had been patients of mine when John had been the incumbent at the Anglican Church on Leeman Road, York. We met Joan, who was pleased to show us round, before we finally returned to our hotel.

On the last morning of our stay in Jerusalem, we awoke to two inches of snow and large snow flakes still falling. Few of the party had brought warm clothing, but the snow did not last long and the day warmed up. The plan was to go to Tiberias, via Jericho, but the bus was stopped at an army road block because of military activity just outside Jericho. By a devious route, the party eventually arrived at Nazareth. It had been a tiring day's journey.

Guided through the narrow streets of Nazareth, bustling with traders, Jacob took us to the Anglican Church. There, we were to meet an extraordinary character, Canon Riah Abu el Assel, the Anglican Vicar of Nazareth, who was also the secretary of the Israeli Peace Groups. He later was to become the Anglican Bishop of Jerusalem In a most moving address, given in his church, he told Friends that he had a personal problem of identity. He was an Arab, but not a Moslem, an Israeli citizen, but not a Jew, a member of the Anglican Church, but not an Englishman. He asked Friends to pray for the small Arab Christian community, whom he considered to be under great disadvantage in higher education. He explained about other difficulties his community had to face, and for his outspokenness he had been under country arrest for the previous four years. The ban had been lifted at the beginning of the year, which allowed him to travel abroad again and explain the Palestinian Arabs' case. Canon Riah read a passage from the Old Testament indicating that the Arabs, also, could lay claim to some of the disputed lands. He felt that things were changing and that enlightened Israelis could see what was happening in the Occupied Territories, and that the peace activists were both Jews and Arabs. I came away from the gathering much more aware of the problems and the political undercurrents in Israel at that time. We thanked the Canon for giving up his valuable time and wished him well in his efforts. Standing at the back of the Church and listening silently was Jacob, who, on getting back into the bus, told us how much he disagreed with what Canon Riah had to say. Our visit to Nazareth ended with entering a second or third century CE synagogue, which in its lay-out and furnishings, would be very similar to the one that Jesus might have attended. In this simple setting, we sat in silent worship, which was in complete contrast to the Church of the Annunciation, a new Basilica built in the 1960s.

Arriving at the Church of Scotland's Hostel at Tiberias, after the hustle and bustle of Jerusalem, was like inhaling a breath of fresh air. Immediately we entered the Hostel's precincts we became aware of the peace and tranquillity of the place. In former times these Victorian buildings were a Church of Scotland missionary hospital, run for tuberculosis and malaria patients. For many years the hospital was served by the Torrance family, and in the Mandate days Father used to send some of his patients there to be under the care of Dr. Torrance, the last of the missionary medical superintendents. Before finally closing as a medical unit, it served as a maternity hospital and eventually was converted into a visitors' hostel. Patricia and I were allocated a room overlooking the Sea of Galilee; its high ceilings, simple furniture and mat-covered stone floors all added to the atmosphere of the place. We stood on the adjacent balcony to absorb our surroundings and the beautiful views across to the Golan Heights. When it was dark, we took a stroll along the foreshore and were delighted to see the ghost-like shapes of many night herons *Nycticorax nycticorax* appear from out of the darkness to settle in some nearby trees.

Dawn over the Sea of Galilee is a beautiful experience. In front of the dawn, the mauve coloured hills of Golan, and shafts of yellow light from the rising sun, reflect off the water's surface, and add to the intensity of the experience. We were both up for the dawn to witness it. On our first morning in Galilee, David had arranged for Friends to visit most, if not all, of the historical New Testament sites on the Sea's western shores. For me, on reflection, one site seemed to merge into another, leaving me a little confused.

Standing on the traditional or supposed site of the place where Jesus delivered the Sermon on the Mount, there is an eight sided Basilica built in 1937 (Matthew 5). Each of the rich, mosaic sides represents one of the eight Beatitudes, the dome symbolising the ninth Beatitude, 'for great is your reward in Heaven'. To get to the Basilica, the bus had to negotiate a narrow farm road, after which Friends had to walk up a muddy path. As elsewhere, the place was swarming with visitors. I did not venture far inside, but, after a cursory glance, wandered round outside taking in the area's natural beauty. It seemed to me that it would have been more meaningful, as far as the New Testament narrative was concerned, to have left the area unspoilt.

So on to another basilica at Tabgha, the site of the first feeding of the Multitudes. Here again, to illustrate the message, the floors were covered with mosaics from the original 4th century church, including one depicting the loaves and fishes. At Simon Peter's Landing Place or Mensa Christi, there is a small Franciscan chapel, built on a stony outcrop. Next to the chapel, situated on the foreshore, there is a small shell-covered beach. Adjacent to the beach, there is a life-sized bronze statue of Peter kneeling, and Jesus is asking him to feed his sheep (John 21). Now, the sun was still high in the sky, but, at dawn the statue would have made a moving sight. By now Friends had had enough of crowds, so they ascended a small hillock behind the chapel for a Meeting for Worship. Sitting out in the open, among a wealth of spring flowers, and along with a reading from John's Gospel on feeding sheep, the party experienced a most moving period of worship. I certainly did so. Suddenly, round the headland, two small Arab fishing boats came, fishing in a traditional manner. It seemed to me to be most appropriate, and, in a way, an authentic 'Jesus experience'.

Capernaum was a disappointment to us both, except that among the ruins of the third century synagogue, a pair of hoopoes *Upupa epops* was nesting. After we had looked at the excavations of Peter's house, we made for a ferry jetty. By pre-arrangement, Friends were taken across the Sea of Galilee to En Gev. Friends had to share the boat with a party of German Lutherans and Dutch Christians, who, in their own ways, were celebrating the crossing. David asked the skipper to cut the engines half way across, so that we could have a Meeting for Worship. This he did, and for half an hour the boat drifted silently on a mirror-calm Sea. During Worship, Anne Fletcher read an appropriate passage from the Gospels, as did a member of the German party in German, who ended their period of Worship quietly singing a hymn. Some of them appreciated the silent Worship, which had been, for some of us, a moment of peace that 'passeth all understanding'. With the engines restarted, it was not long before Friends disembarked at En Gev for a picnic lunch. There on the foreshore, groups of little egrets *Egretta garzetta,* all in their breeding plumage, were feeding in the shallow waters.

From then onwards, we had further bus rides to Hamet Gadar, a small Israeli enclave surrounded by Syria and Jordan and, finally, to the baptismal site on the River Jordan. The site is no longer at its original position, because, over the years, water extraction from the Sea of Galilee for irrigation purposes had lowered the outflow of the River Jordan on its way south. From there the party returned to Tiberias, and on the way witnessed one of those rapid storms that can turn the Sea into a towering rage.

On the way to the Golan Heights, an Egyptian mongoose *Herpestes ichneumon* was seen on the edge of the River Jordan, a mammalian species which is quite common in the area. By contrast, somewhere along the route going north, a soldier, with his rifle slung over his shoulder, flagged down the coach for a lift. The Arab driver, with Israeli citizenship, stopped and, after a conversation in Hebrew, invited the soldier aboard. His presence immediately caused a great deal of tension among Friends, especially as he was armed. Some said he should not be allowed on board, as his presence could compromise the Quaker Peace Testimony; others allowed it to happen. I wondered how the situation could be resolved. We were told that there was a tradition in Israel that members of the armed forces should always be given lifts whenever they are requested. The soldier took a seat at the back of the coach, and was soon joined by Anne Fletcher, who tried the best she could to explain to him the Quaker attitude to armed conflict. After a few miles, the bus stopped and the soldier got down; the tension eased. Jacob, of course, being an ardent patriate, did not understand the Quaker position.

By now we had reached the occupied territory of the Golan Heights, captured from the Syrians in the 1967 war. The party immediately became aware of the heavy military presence and were taken to a partially manned military base at Kibbutz Ein Zivan for a convenience stop. The distance from Ein Zivan to the U.N.I.F.I.L. hill-based, observation post, overlooking the flattened and uninhabitable Syrian village of El Qunaytirah, was short. The post was bristling with electronic early warning detection equipment. The bus pulled up underneath the observation post and Friends got out and surveyed the scene. The heavy barbed wire border of the demilitarised zone stretched either way into the distance, and was designed to prevent Syrian infiltration into the Golan. To the east and beyond was an endless semi desert land, with little, if any, evidence of human habitation. The destruction of El Qunaytirah, so we were told, was necessary for Israel's security. To the north we could see the snow-capped Mount Hermon, and flying around

Mount Avital to the west were several short-toed eagles *Circaetus gallicus*.

Moving north again, we reached the Druze village of Mas'ada and an extinct volcanic lake at Birket Ram. Sitting not far from the lake for a falafal lunch, some of us watched an osprey *Pandion haliaetus* perched on a pole sticking out of the lake. By now, we were in the foothills of Hermon, and all around us were numerous orchards, mostly of apple trees. Stretching in the distance were several small Druze villages; prominent in the foreground was a white mosque, with its simple dome. A Druze farmer, dressed in his traditional baggy trousers and white turban, trotted by on a donkey. Several women were working in the orchards spraying or picking fruit. We were tempted to photograph some of them, but were discouraged by Jacob, for to do so would offend them. I marvelled at the beautiful tranquil scene before us.

David decided that Friends should go further into Druze country, so we moved on to the village of Majdal Shams. In the central square is a memorial to those who lost their lives in the struggle for Druze independence. Friends, on getting off the bus in the square, were immediately surrounded by school children. In wandering round the village, we got a flavour of what life in a Druze village was like. They are an interesting people, having broken away from mainstream Islam many centuries ago.

The tour had become a 'whistle stop' tour, for no sooner had the party stopped at one place than it was time to move on. David, in arranging the itinerary, had decided that we were to see as much of northern Israel as possible. I had visited a number of Crusader castles in my life time, but none so impressive for its position and size as Nimrod. Overlooking northern Galilee, but still within the Occupied Territory, this castle, which was named after an ancient Graeco-Roman God, was built in the twelfth century. It did not remain in the control of the Crusaders for long, before it was captured by the Moslems. From the heights of its ruined keep, we got a magnificent view of the surrounding countryside, including south Lebanon. The local mountain scenery consisted of rocky outcrops and mostly Mediterranean umbrella pine trees. It gave me a particular thrill to see the Lebanon again, albeit under Israeli occupation; the buffer zone extended up to the Litany River.

Below Nimrod is Baniyas. From a large cave in a vertical rock face behind the settlement of Baniyas emerges a spring, which soon becomes a stream flowing into a series of artificial pools, before becoming one of the sources of the River Jordan. In New Testament times Baniyas was called Caesarea Phillipi after Herod's son, Philip. Jesus visited Caesarea Phillipi and it was there that he asked his disciples who they thought he was (Matthew 16). There was little time to explore, but the visit remained in my memory. Not far away from Baniyas was the border crossing between Lebanon and Israel, known as the 'Good Fence'. The road ran parallel to a high, barbed wire border fence. It was at this point that many Palestinians and Lebanese with work permits in northern Israel could cross to get to their work. In the past it had been a flash point, but now had become a tourist attraction, with the flags of both countries fluttering in the wind. It pleased me to see the Lebanese flag again, with the Cedar of Lebanon motif in the centre of it.

It was now late in the afternoon and time to return to Tiberias, but on the way David suggested that we went see the National Nature Reserve at Hula. However, when we arrived, the Reserve was closing for the night. A visit would have to wait for another time.

Built into the 1990 Tour were two 'free' days, one we already had at En Gedi and the other was taken in the middle of the time we were staying at Tiberias. Friends were able to organise various activities for themselves, but five of us, at David's suggestion, decided to spend the day exploring the National Nature Reserve at Nahr Amud. Besides David, the party consisted of Kurt Strauss, Janey O'Shea, an Australian Friend with an interest in biology, Patricia and me. Having purchased a picnic lunch, we were driven to our destination by Richard Baxter, one of the hostel wardens, in their mini-bus.

On a previous visit to Nahr Amud, David and others had discovered a cave in the Amud valley, not far from the road, in which there were a number of fruit bats. David was keen to show me the cave. On clambering up the steep slope to gain access, we came across two Greek or spur-thighed tortoises *Testudo graeca*, the first I had seen in the wild since my boyhood days on Mount Carmel. On entering the vaulted shallow cave, we soon became aware of the bats. There, high in the roof, was a struggling mass of them all audibly chattering; some were flying round obviously disturbed by our presence. Littering the floor were piles of guano, among which were seeds of various fruits. Janey, who knew something about bats, immediately recognised them as fruit bats. They were, in fact, the Egyptian fruit bat *Rousettus aegyptiacus*, which, according to various sources, was endangered in Israel because of the citrus fruit industry. David Makin, one of Israel's leading bat experts, who I had met at an international bat conference in Prague in 1987, once told me that large numbers of bats are destroyed every year, but the Israeli conservation lobby was trying to do something about it. This colony was between 100 to 200 individuals. We left the bats, hoping we had not disturbed them too much.

Emerging from the cave, we found a pair of blue rock thrushes *Monticola solitarius* nesting nearby, with a golden eagle *Aquila chrysaetos*, a number of white storks *Ciconia ciconia*, and a pair of griffon vultures *Gyps fuvus* circling above on rising thermals. Progressing up the Amud valley, with its vertical, canyon-like cliffs towering over us, we noticed several other caves and high isolated pinnacles of limestone rock. One of them reminded me of the Old man of Hoy. In the distance we watched a Bonelli's eagle *Hieraeetus fasciatus* collecting nesting material. Alpine swifts *Apus melba* were circling round their cliff nesting sites, and a pair of hoopoes *Upupa epops* was mating. There was an abundance of spring flowers, most of which we were not able to identify. We walked on until we came to the massive water conduit that takes water from the Sea of Galilee to the citrus growing areas of southern Israel. The water had to be pumped across Nahr Amud, but from then onwards it reached its point of delivery by gravity. At the time of our visit the pump was not working, due, we were told, to over-extraction from the Sea of Galilee. David and Patricia scrambled up the side of the conduit, while the rest of us sat and waited for them. A mixed nationality patrol of armed Israeli youngsters, out on military exercises, passed us, singing and shouting. We retraced our footsteps through a beautiful valley of outstanding wildlife, before having a long walk down to the main road, where we caught a bus back to the hostel at Tiberias for a welcome rest and a meal. So ended another memorable day for our small party, and for other Friends, with a period of silent Worship.

Our time at the Church of Scotland Hostel had come to and end. For all of us it had been a most restful, and at times exciting, visit, in which we appreciated the calm atmosphere that pervaded the place. Having thanked the wardens for their kind hospitality, Friends set off in the bus to Haifa. It had been planned for the party to meet Elias Chacour, the Arab Melkite priest and author of the best-seller, Blood Brothers, but he was not available. Elias had struggled tirelessly for reconciliation between Arab and Jew for a long time. Disappointed, Friends accepted the idea of stopping off at Acre instead. On reaching this ancient town, with it old multi-arched caravanserais and Crusader castle, Friends were able walk through the narrow alleyways, grapple with the many street hawkers and look round the multitude of small shops. Some went round the castle, for Acre had been an important sea port for the Crusaders. In the distance was the Ahmed Jezzar Mosque, with its emerald-green dome and imposing minaret. Eventually, Patricia and I joined the party, who were relaxing at a cafe on the newly created promenade overlooking Acre Bay. On the opposite side of the Bay I could see Haifa, the place of my birth.

The route to Haifa went past Acre's Ottaman 17th century citadel, which in the days of the Mandate had been a prison. Father, as the Medical Officer to the Palestine Police, visited the prison frequently, often to see Arab or Jewish terrorists wounded in the troubles at the end of the Mandate. We soon reached Haifa and travelled up Ben Gurion Street, past several places I had visited with Mother and Father in 1982, including my old primary school. At the viewing point next to the Carmelite Monastery on the western tip of Carmel, there before us was a panorama of Haifa, with its British-built harbour breakwater and the Rambaum Hospital complex, which was opened in 1938 by the Palestine Government. It gave me a great thrill to see these places again and point them out to Patricia as well as Friends.

Leaving Carmel, we drove south along the coast road and stopped near Kefar Gallim for an inadequate lunch and a walk along the sandy shoreline with bare feet. Following a brief visit to Herod the Great's coastal port, Caesarea Maritime, it was generally decided that there had been enough bussing, so we moved onto our final destination of the Tour - Shefayim.

Shefayim, situated just north of Tel Aviv, was one of the earliest kibbutzim to be established. The first Jews settled there at the time of the British Mandate, and we were immediately aware that it was a settled and long-established community. Many of the original principles of the community had been abandoned, families were now living in their own homes and parents were looking after their own children. It had a tourist block, catering for many visitors who would come for the swimming pool and other sporting facilities. Neat rows of red-roofed bungalows were surrounded by numerous gardens, mostly of flowering shrubs, such as hibiscus. There was an old windmill, which residents had converted into a museum, the contents of which showed the difficulties that Jews, arriving at the end of the Second World War from Europe, had in entering the Mandate. Anti-British feelings were paramount in the displays. Patricia and I were shown to our room in the tourist block; it had a balcony overlooking the Mediterranean. The day ended with a meal.

Tucked into one corner of the kibbutz was Amos's bungalow. We met him, however, at the community centre, as one reason for coming to Shefayim was to meet Amos. He had been a member of the community since boyhood and told us a great deal about it, as well as his fears and hopes for the future of Israel. He expressed very liberal ideas about the 'Palestinian problem', so much so that the authorities, from time to time, had suppressed his voice. He had been placed under house arrest, but now was more free to move around. He recognised, like some of his fellow Jews, that the Palestinian Arabs had rights just as valid as those of the Jews. He had been instrumental in setting up an organisation to help those Arab families, in which the man of the household had been temporarily arrested for breaking curfews imposed at a moment's notice. Such men, according to Amos, lingered in jails for days, leaving their families vulnerable and without a source of income. After speaking for over an hour, he showed Friends round the kibbutz, including the clinics and the museum. We were most impressed to see the care given to the elderly; the footpaths were wide enough for them to travel in battery-driven buggies. The whole place seemed to us to be happy.

After enjoying lunch and a swim in the kibbutz's beautiful freshwater swimming pool with its large water chute, Friends gathered together again to be shown round the orange groves by Amos. For many years Amos worked in the groves, but, because of his political views, he was transferred to the printing press situated in the small plastics factory, where he was isolated from his fellow workers. Citrus fruits were a major source of income for the kibbutz, and fruit was picked almost the whole year round. On entering the groves, we noticed they were extensively irrigated, with water, we assumed, coming from Galilee along the conduit. Some of pickers kindly offered us oranges. Our full day at Shafayim ended with further discussions with Amos about the Israeli-Arab conflict and how he saw the situation. The stay at Shafayim had added another dimension to the Tour, one that all agreed was important.

The return flight to Britain was late in the evening, thus giving us all one more day in Israel. The Tour I had looked forward to, was rapidly coming to an end. David gave us two options, either to stay on at Shafayim and join the main party at Ben Gurion Airport later that day, or to return to Jerusalem for the last time. Patricia and I opted for Jerusalem. We boarded the bus, which unfortunately was delayed because of a road traffic accident. We reached the Holy Land East Hotel much later than planned.

By the Jaffa Gate, the Church of Scotland had a gift shop, which Patricia and I reached just as it closed. Thwarted, and thinking we had plenty of time, we decided to make our way across the Old City to the Hotel, via the Via Dolorosa. We had to get back to the Hotel, as David had arranged for us to go round the clinic at which Kate Locke worked, north of Jerusalem. What we had not bargained for was Palm Sunday.

Leaving the Jaffa Gate, we walked down the gentle slope of David Street, looking at the various trinket and souvenir shops, hoping to find one or two small gifts for those at home. Suddenly, we were caught up in a religious procession. We discovered we were on the regular Palm Sunday route, and whether we liked it or not, were being sucked along by it. From nowhere, another procession appeared going in the opposite direction. I could see Patricia drifting away from me. For a moment I felt my feet giving away under me and I thought I was going to fall. Somehow, I managed to get into a small shop front and waited there until pressure of the crowd abated. I only hoped that Patricia was all right. Then, before I realised it, the crowd had gone and I hurried forward to find Patricia safe and sound a little way ahead of me. As we reflected on the experience, we realised how it must have felt at Hillsborough when a large number of football fans died in the crush from trampling and suffocation. Had Jesus been in a similar crowded narrow street, when his garments were touched by the woman taken in haemorrhage and he felt that something leave him.(Luke 8 v 43)? With the pressure easing, we made our way rapidly to the Damascus Gate, to reach the Hotel just in time to go to Kate's clinic.

The party of Friends going to the clinic were all the health professionals on the Tour, and to reach the clinic two seven-seater taxis were hired. The clinic was like a health centre, dealing mainly with female and children's health issues. Kate taught simple first aid, so that the adults could go back to their villages and help. As a project, it seemed to be working well. Friends were then shown a video of the current difficulties and restrictions the Palestinian medical services had to face in the present political situation, which was introduced by a Palestinian consultant gynaecologist. He told us that the cervical screening and family planning programme were being introduced locally, but not without some resistance from the local womenfolk Illustrating his talk, he showed also some of the injuries sustained by Palestinians as the result of the intifada. Palestinians, according to the doctor, were very much second class citizens in Israel when it came to medical care. We all admired the way Kate managed under such difficulties.

It was time to return to Jerusalem and this time we returned in the Centre's mini-bus to the Damascus Gate. Kate took us to a small cafe just inside the Gate, but it was closed by the military authorities while we were there. We watched an Israeli soldier arrogantly dealing with a wayside stall holder; tension was high because of the intifada. Thus, returning to the Hotel, we joined the rest of the party aboard the bus for the last time and set off for Ben Gurion Airport. From a late start, the uneventful flight ended at Gatwick too late for us to reach York that evening. Patricia rang York as soon as it was feasible, only to discover that her sister-in-law, Sheila, had died two days earlier. So ended the 1990

Woodbrooke Holy Land Tour. For both of us, for different reasons, it had been a most memorable visit. I had been moved by many of the events and places we had visited, and I was very grateful to David for his leadership and the encouragement he gave us to come.

Entrance to Friends' Meeting House, Brummana. Drawn by BEN BARMAN

CHAPTER V

Lebanon Re-visited

I RETIRED FROM GENERAL PRACTICE in York at the end of 1992, and quite soon afterwards I was asked if I would like to serve on the Middle East Committee of Quaker Peace and Service. I jumped at the opportunity, feeling strongly that this was the sort of activity I would like to get involved in during retirement. I had only attended a few meetings of the Committee, when the Clerk, Jocelyn Campbell, asked me if I would like to represent London Yearly Meeting at a reconvened Middle East Yearly Meeting, which was to be held at Brummana in March 1994. Jocelyn and her husband, Duncan, had been the Principals of the Friends' High School at Brummana in the late 1950s. I was delighted to have the opportunity and agreed to go, provided Patricia could come with me. She agreed to come, although she was apprehensive as to what her role would be.

We travelled out to Beirut on 24th March on an Olympic Airways airbus, stopping off at Athens for five hours en route. Our travelling companion was Andrew Clark, the General Secretary of QPS, who had not met Patricia before. I had known him at various Committee meetings. At Athens we were joined by Heather Moir, an American Quaker and Clerk of the Friends' World Committee for Consultation (FWCC) and Jan Ramaker, a Dutch Quaker representing the European and Middle East Section of FWCC. While waiting at Athens and Beirut airports, I got into conversation with Heather Moir, who I discovered was educated at Sidcot and the Mount Schools, before moving to the United States. Her father, Jack Catchpool, also educated at Sidcot, was the founder of the Youth Hostels Association. I met Jack during my last year at Sidcot in 1952 and he encouraged me to come to a YHA work camp in Israel, but my Father would not let me go because of passport difficulties and the possibility of compromising his position working in an Arab state.

It was a short haul from Athens to Beirut and it was not long before the lights of Beirut's coastline were clearly visible. Coming down the stepped gangway from the aircraft, I quietly said to Andrew that it felt strange to be back on Lebanese soil. He responded by saying, "Why don't you kiss the ground!". We laughed. We were met at Beirut's airport by several members of Brummana Monthly Meeting; Andrew and Sabah Baz stayed on to sort out Jan Ramaker's visa difficulties, while the rest of us were driven up to Brummana by Sami Cortas.

We had not driven far along a sodium-lit boulevard towards the centre of Beirut, when we were stopped at a Syrian Army check point. Sami uttered some words in Arabic and we passed through it without incident. In the darkness it was impossible to see any of the massive damage caused by the civil war that had ended three years previously. Crossing the 'green line' that had separated the warring factions, we headed for the hills and Brummana. Tired and pleased to reach our destination, we were taken to Renee Baz's home, the matriarch of the Brummana Quaker community. Introductions were made all round, before Tony Manasseh, who had stayed with us in York, came to take Patricia and me to his home, where we were going to stay for our time in Brummana.

On reaching the Manasseh home, which was built into the hillside, there were further introductions. Present were Tony's wife, Jocelyn, and their two children, Joya aged 5 and Philip aged 4. Staying for Yearly Meeting were Jean Zaru, the only Palestinian Quaker present, who was representing Ramallah Monthly Meeting and the West Bank. We soon discovered that she was a remarkable person, who had a real depth of understanding of the problems of the Middle East. John and Marjorie Scott of Lancaster Meeting were also there; we had met them briefly in Jerusalem in 1990 when we were on the Woodbrooke Holy Land Tour. They were both, at one time, much loved members of the staff of the Friends' School at Ramallah. It was their first visit to Brummana. The final guest in the Manasseh household was Henry Selz, an American Quaker who had spent nearly all his working life in service for Friends in India and the Middle East. Henry was a delightful character, with a marvellous sense of humour. He used the English language to great effect and we all warmed to him. He lived on his own in the Turkish part of Cyprus, his Indian wife having died some years previously.

It was late when we eventually retired to bed. We, with the Scotts and Henry Selz, were accommodated in the basement of the house, with shared facilities. Our twin bedded room, with its high, arched ceiling of typical Arab design, was comfortable. So ended our first day; we were in much need of sleep.

We woke early after a disturbed night. Emerging into the morning air, I made for the terrace outside our bedroom, overlooking Beirut. The City, in the morning light, was covered with a dense haze from an offshore mist, combined with belching smoke from the power station to the north burning crude oil. From this vantage point at Brummana, situated at 2000 feet. I could look north up the coastline to Jounieh. It was spring time and wild cyclamen *Cyclamen persicum* were everywhere, growing in the terrace's supporting walls or in small clumps below the few umbrella-shaped Mediterranean pines *Pinus pinea* in the Manassehs' unkempt garden. I could just make out alpine swifts *Apus melba*, flying over Beirut, and in the warming sun, scrambling over the garden walls were two species of lizard, the starred agama *Laudakia stellio* and the green lizard *Lacerta laevis*.

The Manasseh household and guests gathered round a large circular table for an ample Lebanese breakfast of libani (a Lebanese yoghurt), Arab bread, various seeds, cheeses and coffee. It was then time to go over to the High School for the first sessions of the Middle East Yearly Meeting. Tony took us down the short, uneven lane, past the dispensary of his late father, Dr. Philip Manasseh, which had been destroyed by Druze shellfire in 1985, to the School's main gates. There we were welcomed by staff, scholars, and members of Brummana Friends' Meeting, including Albert Abu Khalil, who had been on the staff of the school for many years and remembered my brother, John, from the time he served on the staff. Also present was the Principal of the School, Shukri Husni, whose father worked for the Iraq Petroleum Company, and who, like me, had learned to play tennis on the Company courts in Tripoli. We had a lot in common and I felt almost immediately I had returned to my second home.

76

There were about 30 participants at Yearly Meeting, which was held in the School's reception room. Besides local Friends and Jean Zaru from Ramallah, there were those we had met the previous evening. We were then introduced to Ralph and Jean Wadge from England; Ralph and Jean, as the QPS representatives in Lebanon in 1985, were signatories to the agreement transferring the management of Brumanna High School from Friends to the Cultural Society. Also present was Anna Kennedy, an American Friend from East Jerusalem who was working for QPS, Corrine Johnson from Philadelphia, who was director of the International Programme of the American Friends' Service Committee (AFSC) and Paul Lalor and his Greek wife, Floresca Karanasou. Paul and Floresca were the AFSC representatives in Amman, Jordan. In due course, I got into conversation with Paul, who obtained a post-graduate degree in Middle East studies from the Middle East Centre at St. Anthony's College, Oxford. He told me that Derek Hopwood, the Director of the Centre, had recently published a book entitled *Tales of Empire - The British in the Middle East.* Based on archival material and personal diaries, Paul felt that this book would give me a great deal of information about the kind of society Mother and Father lived in during the Mandate days. He thought the Centre would be pleased to receive a copy of Mother's Travels of Tatah.

This was the first time the Yearly Meeting had met for nearly twenty years, and expectations were high. On settling down to a meaningful Meeting for Worship. God's guidance was sought. Tony Manasseh was appointed Clerk and Jean Zaru assistant Clerk, along with recording Clerks. An Epistle Committee consisted of Andrew Clark, Renee Baz, Jean Zaru and Henry Selz. Following the reading of Letters of Introduction and Travelling Minutes of visiting Friends, Yearly Meeting settled down to consider a variety of topics pertaining to the Middle East. Sessions were high in emotion and often controversial, though held in a spirit of worship. Reports were received from the respective Clerks of Brummana and Ramallah Monthly Meetings. It soon became apparent that Brummana Friends felt very hurt and bitter about the fact that the School was no longer run by Quaker Peace and Service, and they, like Ramallah Friends, felt the isolation created by the civil conflicts in their respective countries.

During the midday break there was an opportunity to walk up the hill to explore parts of Brummana. Patricia did this on her own on one occasion and found it a daunting experience. Pedestrians had to dodge cars roaring up the hill, often sounding their horns and pouring out polluting, black exhaust fumes. There were few pavements. The Lebanese economy is based on the car and the lorry, with little, or no, public transport. The pollution problem is augmented in Beirut, where over half of Lebanon's 800,000 cars are to be found. Asthma is prevalent among children, and thoughtful Lebanese are worried about what is happening. Rubbish was being dumped everywhere and we felt there was a lack of civil planning and authority, but then they had just come through a prolonged civil conflict.

Brummana was becoming Americanised; the women were chic and well dressed, and the shops full of glittering gold ornaments. The resident population at that time was around 8,000 and was predominantly Maronite, but the numbers swell to 70,000 when there is a large influx of rich Arabs, mainly from the Gulf States. The scenery inland and beyond is stunning, with the mountains still covered with snow. The 6834 foot mountain, Jabel el Knisse, to the south-east of Brummana dominates the scene. Across the valley I could see Aley, much destroyed in the civil war. Somewhere beyond Aley, which is in Druze country, is Ainab, where in 1944 Father, Mother, Jane and I spent a holiday in the Lebanon.

Yearly Meeting sessions came and went. At the end of one such session, Nasib Lahout, a member of the Lebanese parliament and a financial expert, addressed Friends. Mr.Lahout, a Maronite Christian, gave Friends a wide ranging and refreshingly honest picture of the current political situation, and the social changes occurring in Lebanon since the end of hostilities. He was a lively and highly articulate person, who gave some very informative answers to questions at the end of his contribution. We noticed that he had a paralysed arm and a limp, from a stroke he had suffered 10 years earlier. Friends felt it had been a privilege to listen to this courageous politician, who seemed to be making some attempt to put right some of the deep divisions that had occurred in Lebanese society. Whether he would succeed was another matter.

We had reports on the work of FWCC by Heather Moir and that of QPS by Andrew Clark, as well as those on the two schools, Ramallah and Brummana. Sami Cortas, who was very much the go-between for Brummana Friends and the Cultural Society, read a statement about the future of Quakers in the Middle East. The contents of his statement was added to the Yearly Meeting minutes. Sami, who is a member of the Cultural Society, made arrangements for Friends to meet other members of the Cultural Society after Meeting for Worship on Sunday. The Cultural Society was the management committee set up in 1985, at the height of the civil war, to run Brummana High School after QPS departed. With the agreement of other Friends, I was asked by Andrew Clark to accompany him to the American University Beirut (AUB), for further discussions with the Cultural Society about the future of the School. British Quakers were in an unenviable position in 1985. It was difficult to get expatriate staff to work at the School, and the Lebanese government could not guarantee their safety. There was also an enormous budget deficit, which would jeopardise Q.P.S. work elsewhere.

Patricia sat patiently through most of the sessions taking copious notes. These, I felt sure, would help me when I came to write my final report to Meeting for Sufferings. She was not a Friend and this was her first experience of a Yearly Meeting. At times the atmosphere was electric, with emotional outbursts from some, no doubt due to the pent-up emotions from years of frustration and isolation.

The final day of Yearly Meeting was Sunday, which, according to the Latin calendar, was Palm Sunday Friends gathered together in the Meeting House, which is on the right immediately on entering the School gates. Built at the turn of the century, it was a large building, too large for the current membership of Brummana Monthly Meeting. They normally met in the School's reception room on Sunday mornings. On this special occasion some 30 persons were present, including Nasri Khattar, a poet and retired academic from the School of Architecture at the AUB. Nasri, a life-long Friend, had become isolated in Beirut and was rarely seen in Brummana, so his appearance at Meeting that morning was a delight to local Friends.

Sitting in a square at one end of the Meeting House, with shafts of sunlight falling upon the worshippers, the Meeting for Worship soon settled down, in spite of a nearby noisy road and the sound of neighbouring church bells. As expected, there was a lot of ministry, from both local Friends and visitors. It centred on the meaning of Palm Sunday and Jesus' mission. I found it very helpful and was pleased I was there and was able to share the experience with Patricia. Meeting over, Friends poured out on to the Meeting House steps for group photographs, before starting the final session of Yearly Meeting.

Before the final session started, coffee was served. During it Brummana Friends presented their visitors with a number of gifts, including John Turtle's book *Quaker Service in the Middle East; Brummana High School*, which was published in 1975 and now is out of print. The book gives a vivid picture of life at Brummana and in the School, as well as the Quaker contributions at the orphanage at Ras el Metn and the psychiatric hospital at Asfuriyeh, Beirut.

The final session ended on a 'high note', with the reading of the Epistle. It tried to capture the flavour of this gathering, in which God's guidance was sought, but not always achieved Yet, in spite of the obvious diversity, along with the tensions and hurts, there were times of joy and unity. For me, it was an experience not to be forgotten. Visiting Friends thanked Brummana Friends for their kind hospitality, especially Tony Manasseh, who had gone to such a great deal of trouble to get the organisation right.

There were mixed feelings among Brummana Friends about the proposed luncheon with the Cultural Society (CS) in the School's dining rooms. However, it went ahead. On emerging from the reception room Friends found all the members of the Cultural Society, with their respective spouses, waiting outside on the terraces. The party was taken to the dining room and served with a traditional Lebanese meal. Patricia tried to talk to some of the wives, but she found she had little in common with them because of cultural differences, except for Najwa Cortas, Sami's wife. She worked at the AUB in the biochemistry department of the University's hospital and they found they had plenty to converse about. I found myself in the company of Dr. Joseph Semaan, the Dean of the Medical Faculty of the AUB, a Maronite by belief. I soon found I learned a lot from him about the University and its Medical Faculty and his department of Pharmacology. We discussed atmospheric pollution in Lebanon, and the increase of asthma among children.

Assembling outside the main entrance after lunch, we were taken on a conducted tour round the outside of the buildings and the grounds by the Chairman of the CS, Amine Daouk, a Sunni Moslem. He was an engineer, who trained at Loughbrough in England and, like other members of the all male CS, he was an Old Scholar of Brummana High School. To the credit of the CS, they kept the School running throughout the conflict, albeit with reduced numbers. The war damage to the buildings had been repaired, using local funding and without asking QPS for help. I was saddened to see the tennis courts in a state of disrepair, for in the 1950s the Lebanese equivalent of Wimbledon was played on them, and I remember watching Drobny and Stolle in 1955. Visiting Quakers were pleased with what they were shown and thanked their hosts for their kind hospitality.

Lebanon National Tennis Tournament held at Brummana High School 1955. Drobny playing the foreground.

81

In the final unofficial event, the company reassembled in the Reception Room to listen to Dr. Habib Badr, a Presbyterian minister and President of the Supreme Council of Lebanese Protestant Churches in Lebanon. Like the previous outside speaker, he gave a lucid and frank contribution, but this time on the current spiritual status of Lebanon. The Supreme Council's collective membership makes up 2% of the Christian population of Lebanon. Hence the Protestants are a small minority within a minority, as various expressions of the Islamic faith now dominate. Brummana Monthly Meeting is a full member of the Supreme Council, with two representatives on the Council. By Lebanese law, each religious group has to register with a recognised religious body, so that, in spite of the Council membership being of an evangelical persuasion, Friends belong to it. Apparently, according to Dr.Badr, other Protestant groups withdrew in a hurry from their Near East commitments, especially in Lebanon, often leaving their institutions vulnerable and not properly funded. Some had folded, thus weakening the Protestant open-minded contribution to Lebanese society. Dr.Badr asked Friends to make sure that Brummana High School continued, for he felt it still had a useful contribution to make. Much impressed by what he had to say, Friends thanked Dr.Badr for finding time to come and talk to them. The day ended with all the participants of the Yearly Meeting going to Renee Baz's flat for an evening meal, an occasion in which friendships were cemented. It was at this function, I learned that Hilary Baz, Sabah's wife, was the daughter of Father's radiographer in Tripoli and that Father, very likely, had been present at Hilary's birth. We watched the sun set over the Chouf and looked across the valley to Ras el Metn, where Daniel and Emily Oliver had their orphanage.

We, and others staying at the Manasseh home, remained for a few more days. After our usual hilarious breakfast, we all went our different ways. Patricia had hoped to go round a hospital to see what occupational therapy, if any, was being practised in Lebanon, but, instead, she was persuaded by Tony Manasseh to join a party of ladies on a shopping spree in Beirut. Women in her position, she was told, do not work! She found it a difficult and interesting exercise, accompanying Jean Zaru most of the time. She returned at the end of the morning having been round the fruit and vegetable markets, as well as looking at Lebanese silver and copper wares and embroidery.

I, meanwhile, meanwhile met Andrew Clark. We were driven down to Beirut by Joseph, the School's driver. For me, it was an exciting trip, one I had been looking forward to. Taking a back route, through some rich suburbs, I immediately noticed that there was continual development from Beirut up as far as Brummana. New properties were going up in an unplanned manner. Road surfaces were reasonable, but traffic was not well managed, especially nearer Beirut. We came across several Syrian army road blocks, but after a gentle word from Joseph we passed on our way. From time to time, we came across a tank or a burnt out piece of military equipment.

We entered Christian held East Beirut, and drove to the sea front. Soon we were in areas of massive destruction, with piles of rubble and badly damaged buildings. Often there were multi-storey buildings, with collapsed floors leaving open fronts and no signs of human occupation. We passed the American Embassy, left as it was after a suicide car bomber destroyed it in 1983, removing the whole frontage of the building. No attempt had been made to repair it, and, like other buildings in the 'down-town' part of Beirut, it would have to be pulled own, before a grand plan of reconstruction took place. Another building, the St. George's Club and Hotel was gutted. Mother and Father were members of the Club, which I was told still existed. At one time, its members consisted almost entirely of British expatriates, and when we came out to Lebanon in the 1950s, we used to swim there regularly. I tried to imagine what the burnt-out building looked like in former times, next to the clear blue Mediterranean Sea and the backdrop of the Lebanon mountain range, always clothed, even in summer, with snow.

Before going onto the AUB, Andrew asked Joseph to stop at the Canadian-run Mayflower Hotel in the Hambra area of Beirut. He booked in to the Hotel for two nights, so that he could make further contacts with non-governmental organisations interested in Quaker work abroad. Hambra seemed very relaxed. The Hotel was the one that Brian Keenan, the Irish hostage of the Hezbollah, spent some time at before he was kidnapped.

Andrew and I arrived early at the Medical Faculty's Department of Pharmacology. Not long afterwards Dr. Semaan appeared. Besides those members of the CS whom we had met on the previous day, we were introduced to Nadim Naimy, a Sunni Moslem and lecturer in Arabic studies at the University, and Raja Younis, a bank manager and a member of the Greek Orthodox Church. We quickly settled down to discussions about the future of Brummana High School, and it soon became apparent to me that there was a wide gulf between their aspirations and ours. Like anything else in Lebanon, it was difficult to get the truth of the situation. An American reporter once wrote, "There is no truth in Beirut, only versions". However, after lengthy discussions, some level of agreement was reached, with a timetable for implementing the decisions taken. The meeting was minuted by Sami Cortas.

After the meeting, Raja Younis asked Andrew and me if we would like to return to Brummana in his car. We accepted his invitation and he drove us to the commercial centre of Beirut where his bank was situated. We worked our way through Beirut's continuing traffic jams and, again, passing many damaged buildings, eventually reached his bank, which had somehow survived! From there we drove back to Brummana the way we had come, and en route Raja invited us to join him for lunch. Neither Andrew nor I had anticipated that he would take us to one of Brummana's most expensive restaurants. Situated up the road from the School, it overlooked the valley and the Chouf. We were served with a typical Lebanese meal, with several dishes which Raja pressed us into taking, not accepting 'no' for an answer. I was glad when it was all over, for I had eaten too much. As we were leaving the restaurant, a large flock of white storks *Ciconia ciconia* flew over, flying northwards on migration. I rushed out on to the verandah to see them passing directly over the building. The whole short-lived episode thrilled me and I learned afterwards that the Lebanese see the white stork as the harbinger of spring. Many were killed during the civil war, mown down with automatic rifles, often to supplement food supplies. Now, however, the Lebanese government was trying to protect them.

We thanked Raja for his kind hospitality and hurried back to the High School. By pre-arrangement, we met members of the

Monthly Meeting to report back on how our deliberations had gone with the Cultural Society. Andrew gave an outline of the agreements we had made with the CS, but he was also a little guarded in what he said. The next move was for a Friend, an expert in education, to come out and survey the scene. Andrew and I learned afterwards that Brummana Friends had been a little unhappy about us going to an expensive restaurant with Raja Younis, for fear that we would be offered a bribe over the School issue. This, of course, did not happen. The day ended on a happy note, with supper at the Manassehs' home and much laughter. The whole day had been of considerable interest.

For the remaining two days of our stay in Lebanon, Tony Manasseh took us out for the day. Travelling in his four-wheel drive vehicle, we went up into the Chouf mountains on the first of these days. The others all had front and back seats, but Patricia and I travelled in the boot looking backwards. Leaving Brummana by a back route, we plunged into the valley below, before making our way up the opposite side, negotiating several hairpin bends in the process. I noticed the small-holding terraces, which in former times were well kept, now were in a state of disrepair, the olive and fruit trees often neglected; due, no doubt, to the prolonged civil conflict.

The Chouf Mountains, the stronghold of the Druze, lies south-east of Beirut and the village of Ras el Metn is situated in the north of the range. On reaching the village, we made straight for the Quaker orphanage, or what was left of it. The orphanage at Ras el Metn, created by Daniel and Emily Oliver at the turn of this century, was a complete ruin following an earthquake in 1956. We reached the orphanage to find a guide, who was the local retired postmaster; he had known the Olivers in the past. He took the small party up the stone staircase into the main building, and so on through former classrooms and the sleeping accommodation for the orphans. A plaque over the front entrance read 'Friends' High School 1929'. Passing through the Olivers' house, we reached the upper floors and the flat roof. The views of the snow-capped mountains were breathtaking, especially Jabel Sannine, which is 8672 feet high. There was also evidence of recent bomb damage, the buildings having been bombarded by the Syrian army, who later occupied it. On the cream-coloured walls were scribbled Syrian army graffiti,

A portrait of Daniel Oliver now in the possession of a postmaster at Ras et Metn village. Painted in the 1920s.

according to Tony. There was much sadness about the place, which had seen better days of so much love and caring, especially for the local community. Following the earthquake, with so much damage to the buildings, it was decided to close the orphanage.

Our tour over, the postmaster invited us all back to his home, where we were served with coffee by the women of the household. It was the first time any of us, except Tony, had ventured into a Druze home. Unlike our visit to the Golan Heights in 1990, this seemed a very friendly occasion. The house was spotlessly clean and the living room formally laid out. Hanging on the wall above us was an oil painting of Daniel Oliver, painted when he was a younger man. The artist had captured in the portrait an Edwardian Scot of spiritual conviction, with sharp blue eyes and an impressive ginger walrus moustache, which, when I met him, in 1950, had turned grey.

Daniel and Emily, along with Emily's sister, Kathleen Wright, ran the orphanage for nearly half a century. Somewhat autocratic in their outlook, the Olivers, nevertheless, were not only devoted to one another, but also to the Quaker cause, which they saw as a beacon of peace and goodwill in a much-troubled part of the world. Daniel, aged 82, died after a short illness in 1952, and Emily two years later; both had spent most of their lives in the Near East. Our visit to the orphanage at Ras el Metn made me realise that it had been a privilege to meet Daniel in 1950, when I was seventeen years old. Our visit ended when we were taken to the small Friends' burial ground, below an old castle site in a grove among some pine trees. Several of the gravestones had been vandalised, including Kathleen's, but the joint one of Daniel and Emily was intact. The grove was overgrown in places. Their lives are described in Lettice Jowitt's short biography entitled, 'Daniel Oliver and Emily, his Wife', published by the Friends' Home Service Committee, but now out of print. For me, the visit had been a pilgrimage.

It was time to move on, the next place of interest being Kasr Mousa situated on the lower western slopes of Jabel el Barouk (6428 ft.). The names of some of the villages we passed through seemed familiar, for as a boy in the 1950s, along with Mother and Father and other members of the family, I used to explore these areas at weekends. Kasr Mousa was a Lebanese eccentric's dream castle; built brick by brick to no particular plan, it contained a dining hall and dungeons. The castle, which is not very old, now houses wax models of the indigenous peoples of Lebanon, dressed in traditional costume. The contents reminded Patricia and me of the Castle Museum at York, and in its way it had the same function of depicting the socio-economic life of Lebanon.

By the time we reached Beit-ed-Dine it was lunch time. Tony took us to the Amir Amin Place Hotel for lunch, an expensive affair in lush surroundings. Walking through the main arched entrance, the party found itself in a typical Arab courtyard. The meal in the main restaurant consisted of several dishes, mostly of a vegetarian content and very tasty. It was again a joyful occasion, with much laughter; the humour of Henry Selz was ever present. Having paid the bills, we moved on to the Amir Bechir Palace, one of Lebanon's show places.

Built in the nineteenth century by Amir Bechir, a local potentate of the Turkish empire, as his summer palace, Beit-ed-Dine eventually became one of the establishments of Kemal Jumblatt, the socialist leader of the Druze community in Lebanon. Now a museum, the palace exhibits showed how influential Kemal Jumblatt was in Lebanese affairs, particularly in the 1940s and 1950s. He was a deep thinker, and dabbled in various eastern religious philosophies, including Tibetan Buddhism. As a Druze, Kemal Jumblatt would have believed in reincarnation. On display, in some the glass cabinets, were some of his writings, including his thoughts on silence and its use in prayer. As I glanced through these exhibits, I thought how similar some of them were to Quaker writings, and how universal and similar are our thoughts about God.

Moving on from the museum, which had been badly looted of a number of historical objects by an invading Israeli army in the early 1980s, we went through a series of rooms and courtyards. The architecture is described as Damascus style, with elaborate patterned arches over doorways and tile patterns on the walls. The courtyards, sided by a set of graceful arcades, were paved, and there was a central fountain in the largest of them. We were shown the Emir's private suite of rooms, especially his reception room, where, in the past, local officials, sheikhs and heads of state would pay homage. It was extremely ornate, with purple covered wall seating, backed by carved wooden panels reaching to the ceiling, which was held up by a series of wooden beams. Eventually, some of us found the Turkish baths, all well laid out with coloured tiles and an elaborate plumbing system. The dome-shaped roofs over the baths let in light of different colours through stained glass. Patricia and I were to experience our first genuine Turkish bath in the small town of Elmali in south-west Turkey, a number of years later.

To return to the main entrance, the party walked through a series of small, box-hedged gardens, in which were set a number of Byzantine mosaics. According to William Dalrymple, author of *From the Holy Mountain* and an authority on Byzantium, they are the most magnificent collection outside the city of Byzantium itself. Walid Jumblatt, Kemal's son, rescued them from looting during the Mountain wars. As we finally crossed the first open courtyard, in which stands a bust of Kemal Jumblatt, I looked up and noticed some circling of birds of prey. They were golden eagles *Aquila chrysaetos* and griffon vultures *Gyps fulvus*; thrashing about in a nearby water tank were numerous amorous green toads *Bufo viridis*.

Tony had thought out an extensive itinerary for us, for he next took us to Mouhktara, the palatial home of Walid Jumblatt, who took over the leadership of the Lebanese Druze after the assassination of his father. After driving along twisting mountain roads, we reached the heavily armed gates of the palace. The overweight, macho guard, with his automatic rifle slung over his shoulder, was obviously expecting us, and after scrutinising the party, unlocked the gates and let us in. We drove up to the large terrace in front of the palace. Most decided to follow Tony into the building, but I decided to stay outside. Growing nearby, in the open-ended courtyard, was a mature cypress tree. I suddenly noticed a flock of small birds in the tree, flicking about and continually chattering. They were Syrian or Tristram's serins *Serinus syriacus*, a new species for me. We moved on to the terraced garden, typical of this area, designed for sitting outside. I could imagine all the political wrangling that must have gone on there, over cups of Turkish coffee and smoking hubble-bubbles. By now, we were all getting tired.

The journey back to Brummana took longer than any of us expected. Instead of retracing our steps, Tony drove due west to the coastal road south of Beirut. En route, we passed Sirjbal, a small plot of land donated to Lebanese Quakers by the British Council, following the sale of the British Victoria School in Cairo. It was dusk by the time we reached Beirut. We passed the Palestinian refugee camps at Sabra and Shatila, where those terrible massacres occurred in 1982. They were carried out by the Christian Phalangist militiamen, with the Israeli occupying forces standing by. Now, however, all was at peace, or at least on the surface. Everywhere in poverty-stricken West Beirut, the stronghold of the Shi'ite Moslems, were Palestinian flags and various portraits of Iranian leaders, including Ayatollah Khomeini, the founder of the Islamic fundamentalist group, the Hezbollah or the 'Party of God'. We drove on, silently taking in all there was to see. Flying over several bomb sites, which had become overgrown with invading vegetation, were small bats. They were Kulh's pipistrelle *Pipistrellus kuhli*, another new species for me.

What a day it had been, very exhausting and demanding, but very worth while. On reaching the Manasseh home, we discovered we had been asked out to a meal at Dr.Karam's house, a local G.P. and paediatrician, but, due to a misunderstanding, few of those invited turned up. We both went and eat too much, but found it an interesting occasion, in which we learned more about the internal conflicts between the CS, the Old Scholars and parents of present scholars.

Back on the road the following day, Tony drove the same party northwards towards Tripoli. We soon reached the coastal dual-carriage highway, full of cars racing at a hair-raising speed. Sitting in the back, Patricia and I marvelled at the driving skills of the Lebanese, for how we avoided an accident, I will never know. Ribbon development had spoiled the route, for no longer were there beautiful scenic views of the Mediterranean, with small beaches, orange groves and picturesque fishing villages, but, instead, numerous hotels, incomplete buildings and industrial complexes with no access to the sea. We had occasional glimpses of the old railway line, running parallel to the road and built by the British and Australian armies during the second World War, but now in a state of disrepair. Tony pulled up at the outlet to the sea of Nahr el Kelb or the Dog River. I had been there many times before, but, on this occasion, I found the whole place shabby, full of litter and uncared for. The Dog River site is important historically, for almost every invading army along this coastline gained access to the hinterland from here, including Alexander the Great and, in this century, British and French Expeditionary Forces. Commemorating these various invasions were plaques set into the steep-sided gorge. We did not stay long, but drove on through Jounieh, the Christian stronghold much ruined by high-rise building and laissez-faire development, and on to Byblos.

Having paid their entrance fees, Friends were taken into the metropolis at Byblos by a young English-speaking Lebanese guide. On passing through the main gate of the Crusader Castle, I immediately realised that little had changed since I last visited the site on that memorable Sunday in 1955 with Father. What had changed, however, was the massive development of the town Jbail or modern Byblos, on the landward side of the metropolis. It seemed to dwarf the site and somehow, for me, ancient Byblos had lost some of its charm. We wandered through the ruins, absorbing as much as we could of the history of the place, from the ramparts of the ancient Phoenician city, through to the British cannon balls lodged in the Castle's fabric following a bombardment in the nineteenth century. After about an hour Friends left the site and went to a neighbouring cafe for some shade and a long cool drink, before Tony took us down to the Crusader port, with its two chain towers at the harbour entrance.

Tripoli was very different. To reach it, we drove through Chekka, which even in the 1950s had its cement factory, which by now had become a large industrial complex dominating the coastline, with its chimneys belching out white smoke mixed with cement dust. Nearby buildings and foliage were coated white. The dual-carriage boulevard approaching Lebanon's northern city, passing through the orange groves, had not changed; what was a small town in the 1950s, had become a sprawling, thriving city, with high-rise flats and office blocks. The Iraq Petroleum Company (IPC) staff homes on Mont Michel, overlooking the boulevard, were still visible, but had become an army barracks. I hardly recognised Tripoli, which was little damaged in the civil war. Tony pulled up outside a patisserie in Rue Gemmayzet; the owner, Rafaat Hallab, was a friend of his. We all trooped in and were served with a cup of coffee and some very sweet pastries. The coffee break over, the company collected round Tony's vehicle, while I briefly walked a little way down the street. There, on the corner of one of the side streets was the building in which Mother and Father rented a flat when they first came to Tripoli in 1948. John, Jane and I had stayed there in the summer of 1949.

The others in the party were willing to help me find Father's old hospital, although we achieved nothing but frustration. We set off along what I thought was the El Mina road, on which there once stood the IPC Hospital and the adjacent senior medical staff accommodation. We reached El Mina, which in the 1950s was the fishing port for Tripoli, but we found no hospital. Tony made repeated enquiries from local residents, but no one seemed to know of it. He stopped at a run-down garage to make further enquiries. The garage turned out to be the old outpatients' department of the American Presbyterian Hospital in El Mina, run by Dr. Boyes and his wife in the 1950s. The Boyes were good friends of our parents, and when I was in Tripoli in 1955 as a medical student, I attended one or two of Dr. Boyes' operating sessions; in one which I fainted.

We turned round and made for the centre of Tripoli. By now, the company in the car was becoming restless. As one last effort, Tony drew up outside a school, or some such institution, run by nuns. One of the nuns introduced us to a young man, who, in a mixture of Arabic and English, was able to tell us what happened to the hospital. It seemed that it was turned over to the local medical community by the IPC in 1960, before it became an Italian school. Eventually, it fell into the hands of the Syrian army and was so badly knocked about, that in a road widening and building scheme, it was pulled own. So, according to Patricia, another ghost from my past was buried. The journey back to Brummana was uneventful. I felt uncomfortable because I had inflicted a wasted journey on my fellow travellers. The meal provided by Renee Baz and her family, on our return, was most welcome.

We were woken in the early hours of the morning, dressed rapidly and did our final packing for the beginning of our return journey to England. John and Marjorie Scott were staying a little longer, Henry Selz would be returning to Cyprus and Jean Zaru to Ramallah. We had said our farewells to them the previous evening, for it had been a wonderful two days with them, and, for me, never to be forgotten. Tony came down to see us off, obviously upset at our departure. Joining Patricia and me in the taxi was Jan Ramaker, who we collected from Edinburgh House in the School's grounds.

We left Brummana in heavy mist and light rain, travelling along empty roads. Quite soon we came across one of the many road blocks, which this time was manned by Lebanese soldiers. We were made to get out at gun point, frisked, and had our luggage examined. However, the young soldiers seemed friendly enough and we were soon driving on towards Beirut airport. Our driver told us that they had been searching for hashish - an opiate. The Lebanese government, so we were told, was desperately trying to stamp out the trade in this drug. On reaching the airport, we were joined by Andrew Clark. By mid-afternoon, we were all back in England and we reached York by the early evening. So ended an adventure, in which new friendships were forged, my past life looked at and then laid down and, finally, a time of responding to the Holy Spirit.

CHAPTER VI

Among Brummana Friends

Part of the 1994 Middle East Yearly Meeting Epistle reads -

'Whereas the guest Friends attending our Yearly Meeting have exclaimed the strength and resilience they have seen in our members, Brummana Friends in particular clearly see the need for loving assistance of an experienced Friend to help them rediscover of what it means to be a Lebanese Friend'.

IT WAS VERY APPARENT to some of us at the Middle East Yearly Meeting, held at Brummana in 1994, that Brummana Friends had had a difficult time during the many years of the civil war. Their numbers had dwindled to two or three members at the height of the conflict, as the families moved out to places of safety. They not only felt isolated, but the spiritual life of the Meeting had declined considerably. Those who remained, faithfully carried on worshipping in the Meeting House or the School, in spite of the conflict, around them. Friends were beginning to question their Quakerism and the relevance of it to their daily lives. It was for these various reasons that Brummana Friends requested that an experienced Friend should come and stay to help them rediscover their Quakerism.

The American Friend, Heather Moir, along with members of the Friends' World Committee for Consultation (FWCC) in the London Office, started to look for that 'experienced Friend or Friends' from the spring of 1994 onwards. It was thought then, that because of the stresses involved, a married couple would be suitable to carry out Brummana Friends' request for a six month period. However, no such persons or person, either from Britain or the United States, were available. I attended London Yearly

Meeting in May of 1994 and found that FWCC were still looking. I returned home and thought about the Brummana Friends' request. It was then that I thought that perhaps I should go to Brummana, even if for a shorter time than the original request. I discussed this with Patricia at length, and we agreed, that if I was accepted by Friends, I should go. I like to think that my proposed visit was Spirit driven and genuine, so I submitted my concern to York Monthly Meeting. Friends, being unfamiliar with the situation in Lebanon, had little advice to give me, but encouraged me to go with their loving support, and supplied a Travelling Minute. My mind made up, I contacted Thomas Taylor, the General Secretary of FWCC in London. A meeting with him, and Ena McGeorge, the then Clerk of the European and Middle East Section (EMES) of FWCC, was arranged at the London Office in Byng Place.

The three of us met in November. I had met neither Thomas nor Ena before, but they soon put me at ease. The meeting was an opportunity to discuss what I hoped to achieve by going to Brummana, and the problems that might arise from such a visit. I told them about my plans to have a weekly discussion group, and to make personal contacts with both Friends and, maybe, non-Friends, with the hope of telling them what my vision of Quakerism was all about. Having decided the trip would be a helpful exercise, and that I should go, we discussed practical details, such as funding and visas. Hans Weening, a Dutch Friend and Secretary of EMES, would be informed. Thus, with their blessing, I felt ready to go. I thanked Ena and Thomas for their support and returned to York.

Once I knew I was going, I contacted Jocelyn and Duncan Campbell and arranged to spend a day with them at their home in Arkengarthdale, North Yorkshire. I much appreciated seeing them, for they gave me a lot of the background to Brummana, which, I felt, would be helpful. A day or two before I departed, Erica Vere rang me up, not only to wish me well, but also to advise me not to get involved in the 'School issue' as it was at a critical stage of negotiations between QPS and the Cultural Society. This proved to be very helpful advice.

I flew out to Lebanon on Friday 3rd February 1995. I left home excited, but with a heavy heart, for I was leaving Patricia behind. She saw me off on the 6.am London-bound train from York station. She was unable to accompany me, because she was in full time employment as the occupational therapist on the Stroke Unit of York District Hospital. This was the first time we had been apart for any length of time. I was met at King's Cross by Elizabeth, an Ethiopian working at the QPS offices at Friends' House; she was carrying my passport, for there had been problems in obtaining appropriate visas for Syria and Jordan. I thanked her. The Olympic Airways flight to Athens from Heathrow was uneventful. There followed a five hour wait at Athens, in not the most comfortable of departure lounges, before boarding a flight to Beirut, reaching it by 9.00pm local time. On passing through Beirut airport's customs and security, I had anticipated seeing Tony Manasseh, but, instead, waiting for me were Albert Abu Kahlil and Joseph, the School's driver. I was pleased to see them. We made straight for Renee Baz's flat in Brummana, where I was made most welcome. She gave me a light meal, before insisting that I should ring Patricia. Patricia was surprised to hear my voice, but glad to know I had arrived safely. Renee then showed me the spacious room, which was to be mine for the next four weeks.

Almost from the start of my stay in the Baz household life developed some sort of routine. Renee's spacious flat was on the ground floor, and opposite that occupied by Sabah and Hilary Baz. The weather was cold, with heavy rain, which, at times, turned to snow. Some nights I was cold in bed, and, more often than not, I was woken in the mornings by cocks crowing, dogs barking, oil-fired generators starting up or, for a few days, the croaking of male Savignyi tree frogs *Hyla savignyi* in the concrete water tank next to the flat. Breakfast was to become a very special daily occasion for Renee and me. Starting with silence, the meal became one of fellowship between us, in which we came to know one another in those things which are eternal. I soon realised that Renee's Quakerism, or understanding the things of the Spirit, had real depth. Quite quickly our conversations centred on God and our understanding of the Christian message based on our individual experiences.

Usually, as on the first day, I was left to my own devices. Family members came and went daily, for Renee was the matriarch not only of the Baz family, but also of Brummana Meeting. Her advice was often sought and gladly accepted. Gradually, I came to know who was who, and who was related. My first full day was taken quietly, giving me time to recover from my journey. I sat in the morning on the balcony in the warming sun, taking in the surrounding scenery, especially snow-capped Knisse. Being a Saturday, traditionally the whole Baz family came together for lunch. Besides Sabah and Hilary Baz, I met Renee's other son, Rabi, and his German wife, Angelica, as well Renee's youngest daughter, Rema, and her husband, Jacky, and their respective children. There were ten adults and several children; the gathering made me realise that I was in the presence of an extended family, which is very much the norm in the Arab world. Soon after my arrival, news came through that Renee's teenaged grandaughter, who lived in the Wirral, had successfully undergone brain surgery for a tumour and was making gradual recovery. I was to meet her mother and Renee's oldest daughter, Niamid Little a few days later on one of her regular visits to Brummana from England. Renee naturally was very concerned about the outcome of her granddaughter's condition.

The second day of my sojourn was a Sunday, so, after a leisurely start, I accompanied Renee to the Reception Room of Brummana High School for Meeting for Worship. There was almost a full complement of Brummana Friends present. The silence was deep, the ministry plentiful, starting with Renee reading from the latest edition of the Advices and Queries that I had given to her on my arrival. Meeting over, the company moved over to Renee's flat for Monthly Meeting. This was a non-minuted informal affair, conducted by Tony Manasseh, the Clerk, in which the only item of business was my visit. Friends agreed that we should have a weekly discussion group, in which I would present some of my thoughts about Quakerism. I then told them about my environmental concerns and my work with the Yorkshire Wildlife Trust. It was then suggested that I should hold a public meeting in the School's Dobbing Hall on these issues and, possibly, take some of the scholars on a natural history walk. Sami was keen that I should meet his doctor brother, Nadim, who, as one of the Vice Deans of the Faculty of Medicine at the AUB, was interested in talking about the psychiatric service in Lebanon.

Everyone left after Monthly Meeting, leaving Renee and me to have lunch on our own. On other occasions we were joined for lunch by Renee's overweight, bachelor brother, Jamil. Jamil was a quiet individual, who spoke little English, and had been for many years the groundsman at the High School. Following this meal, Renee had a whole string of visitors, most of whom I could not communicate with as I did not speak Arabic. However, one person, Miriam Kalaan, a life-long friend of Renee's, arrived and I was introduced to her. Miriam, a graduate of the AUB, had been the maths mistress at the High School for many years. Now in her early 80s, she still had an active mind and spoke excellent English. She also spent some time giving Shareen Baz, Renee's granddaughter, lessons in Arabic. We had a long conversation, especially about the Greek Orthodox Church, of which she was a member. Miriam agreed to arrange a visit for me to her local Church. It seems that most Brummana Friends were converts from the Greek Orthodox Church, either in this generation or the previous ones.

As the days went by, I began to move around the community. Renee introduced me to numerous individuals. One afternoon we went to meet a Greek couple, Dr. and Mrs. Bragesti; the doctor, now in his 87th year, had advanced Parkinson's disease. In his day he had been the professor of medicine at the AUB. He knew Father, who had sent him his more complicated medical problems to deal with; they had first met in the 1950s at a reception at the British Embassy. He specialised in tropical medicine and, at one time, worked for the I.P.C. He described to me a patient he had seen with bubonic plague at the I.P.C.'s T3 pump station in the Syrian desert. We found we had much in common.

On another occasion Renee showed me the Friends' Burial Ground near her home. It was a beautiful oasis of peace and tranquility, surrounded by high-rise flats. There, before me, written on the gravestones was the history of Quakerism in Lebanon. Besides the Manasseh, Cortas and Baz family graves, there was the Theophillis Waldmeier grave. Renee showed me the grave of her husband, Najib, with its large white stone supporting the Quaker star. Like Najib before her, Renee cared for the burial ground with a great deal of pride.

She took me over to one of the surrounding walls of the burial ground, against which stood three memorial gravestones. On them were inscribed the names of three Friends' Ambulance Unit men, who lost their lives in the Second World War in the eastern Mediterranean sphere of operations. James Anderson was killed at Tobruk on 9.2.1942, aged 23, when the trench he was in received a direct hit from a German aircraft off-loading a single bomb. Michael Rowntree of Kirbymoorside Meeting in Yorkshire, serving in the same FAU unit, told me afterwards that he had witnessed the attack and would himself have been present in that trench had he not stopped to watch a mourning wheatear, a species of bird he had not seen before. Another person was William Wyon, a qualified doctor aged 24, who died in Beirut on 25.5.1945. His twin brother, Peter, also a doctor and a member of Thirsk Meeting in Yorkshire, who I subsequently contacted, told me that he had no idea that William's memorial gravestone was in Brummana. Finally, there was James Tonks, aged 24, killed near Jerusalem on 2.7.1941. He was collecting medical supplies from the coast on a misty morning with a colleague, when their FAU lorry plunged over the side of a bridge without parapets into the valley below.

Another member of the Baz family I was to meet soon after my arrival, was Karim. He, Renee's grandson, and the youngest of the Baz brothers, was a typical boisterous boy in his early teens. He liked to be out and about, and found school work was a bore. He spoke good English and we quickly struck up a friendship. He was keen to learn about some of the wildlife in the valley below the Baz apartments. So, whenever it was possible, the two of us would scramble down the steep slopes into the pine woods below. In spite of the inclement weather at times, spring was in the air. The Persian cyclamen *Cyclamen persicum* were out in clusters amongst the rocky terrain or the pine-needle covered woodland floor. Everywhere, were the brilliant yellow-flowered Bermuda buttercup *Oxalis pes-caprae*, an introduced species with culinary properties, that is now considered to be a troublesome weed. One day we watched several hummingbird hawkmoths *Macroglossum stellatarum* hovering over the yellow flowers, extracting nectar with their long tongues. Scurrying over the woodland floor were numerous Menetries' lizards *Ophisops elegans*. In among the rocks and a tumble-down building were green and brown lizards *Lacerta laevis*, starred agamas *Laudakia stellio*, bridle skinks *Maybuta vittatus* and a single gold skink *Eumeces schneiderii*. We discovered together several different sorts of amphibian. Upturning an old, rusty discarded car door, we found a large green toad *Bufo viridis*, a female obviously loaded with eggs! Emerging from a tunnel under the Baz building was a small spring-fed stream, in which several marsh frogs *Rana ridibundi*, along with the tadpoles of the banded newt *Triturus vittatus*, were present. Karim skilfully caught some of the tadpoles so that we could identify them. There were few birds about. I noted a passage movement of chiffchaffs *Phylloscopus collybita*, some of which were calling, along with several resident great tits *Parus major*. Those trips down the valley were precious moments, made so poignant by the recent news of Karim's death in September 1999, the result of an accident when out hunting .

Several times I was invited out for meals by Brummana Friends. Soon after my arrival, I went to Amal and Albert Abu Khalil's home for supper. There I met Juhaina, Samar and Sana, their daughters; Juhaina represented Brummana Friends at the meeting of the European and Middle East Section (EMES) of the FWCC, held in Prague in 1994. During a splendid meal, we found we had lots to talk about. Amal worked in the School's library and she suggested I should come and see what books it contained, especially those on Biology and wildlife. This I did, and found many books of interest, especially a copy of E.S.Bodenheimer's *Animal Life in Palestine*, published in 1935. Although dated, it proved to be very useful when it came to identifying some of the wildlife I was observing.

Within the first week, and true to his word, Sami Cortas rang me up one evening. He had arranged for me to meet his brother, along with several others, in Beirut. He collected me in the morning and drove me to the flat he shared in the Hamara district with his brother Nadim, who I had not met before. On arrival, I was introduced to Nadim first, and then one of their cousins, Namir Cortas, a managing director of a London-based financial firm. He was accompanied by a Lebanese lady architect, whose name I never gathered. To my delight, Phillippa Neave, the newly appointed QPS Middle East co-ordinator, was also present. I had been in contact with her over the telephone, but this was to be the first of several meetings. The aim of the meeting was to consider the post-war psychiatric services in Lebanon, especially around Beirut. Phillippa, Nadim and I travelled in one car and the others in another. Our first stop was at the main entrance of the AUB, there to collect Professor Antranig Manugian, an Armenian, and Emeritus Professor of Psychiatry at the University. British trained, and from the Maudsley, Professor Manugian was, at one time, the Chairman of the Friends' Mental Hospital at Asfuriyeh, founded by Theophilis Waldmeier. It was sold by Quakers in the early 1960s to a Lebanese building syndicate, with the proviso that land was found somewhere to build another psychiatric hospital. Such a hospital was built, but never used. We were going to see the reasons why it had not happened.

We drove through Shi'ite West Beirut, past the airport onto the main highway heading south. Suddenly, the driver left the main road and drove into the hills towards Aramoun. After a while, the leading car, with the Professor in it, stopped in front of a badly damaged, relatively modern, white stone-faced building. This was to have been the psychiatric hospital. Built in a 1970s style and designed by a British architect, it was severely damaged by the invading Israeli army in 1982. Presumably, the Israelis had taken it to be an important strategic building. Before it could be properly equipped, Israeli shells had completely destroyed the outpatients' department and the adolescent unit, and left the central block structurally unsound and uninhabitable. The 350 bedded unit was completely unoccupied, except for a unit of Syrian soldiers. The Professor and Nadim went over to meet the officer in charge of the soldiers to get permission for us to go round the ruins. Permission granted, we all entered the central building.

We wandered about the hospital, in the areas that would have been the main wards. There were no fitments, no windows or door frames; all looked in a state of complete neglect and destruction. The upper floors were regularly used as latrines by the soldiers. Photography was forbidden, but I did manage to take several pictures. I was saddened by what I saw. It seemed to me, that an act of madness had destroyed what was to be a place of refuge for those afflicted with 'madness'. The visit over, the party drove away in silence.

Destroyed Aramoun Mental Hospital. South Beirut, 1995.

Nadim asked his chauffeur to drive us up further into the mountains to Souq-el-Gharb and then on to Aley. Both places were very badly damaged, with hardly a house left untouched by the civil conflict between the Druze and the Christian militia, and most were uninhabitable. Adding to the destruction was the shelling of Souq-el-Gharb by the American Sixth Fleet in September 1983. I had never before seen such destruction, which had left areas of each as ghost towns. I saw no evidence of re-construction, but then it was only three years since hostilities had ceased. As we drove along, Nadim asked me about Quakerism, which seemed to me to be slightly odd in the circumstances. How much of what I had to say was meaningful to him, I will never know. Eventually, we left Aley behind and returned to Beirut, passing what remained of Asfuriyeh. Two of the original red-roofed buildings remained intact, but were currently occupied by Syrian troops. Subsequently, Renee told me that there had been a lot of upset among the Quaker community about the disposal of the hospital. Father had at one time sent some of his patients to Asfuriyeh.

Nadim took us back to his flat for a magnificent lunch of Arab food and a discussion about mental health in Lebanon. Unfortunately, Phillippa was unable to stay with us, so she left, along with the lady architect. The Professor told us that Lebanon, considering its current population, needed 3,500 psychiatric beds for both acute and long-stay patients. There was apparently an urgent need for short-stay beds, particularly around Beirut and that a 250 bedded unit would fill that need. He reckoned that the dominant psychotic condition was manic-depressive illness, with estimates of 1 in 1,000 of the population having the condition. Most of these, Professor Manugian thought, could be stabilised on Lithium in the community, but some would need hospitalisation. Also a lot of post-war neurotic conditions were now beginning to surface. Nadim then told us that there were plans afoot for a 48 bedded, acute unit near the American University Hospital. I was then asked to tell the company about The Retreat and its continuing history. Asfuriyeh, I felt sure, had been founded on the same guiding principles as The Retreat. Professor Manugian had visited The Retreat on several occasions and knew Sammy Bachour, a Lebanese patient I had looked after when I was on The Retreat's medical staff in the early 1960s. The meal and the discussions over, Nadim arranged for me to be driven back to Brummana, but before doing so he invited me to meet Lebanon's Minister of Health on the following day. This meeting never materialised because of the failure of Lebanon's telephone system. I had had a most interesting day, thanks to all concerned.

Within a week of my arrival, Brummana Friends had gathered one evening in Renee's sitting room for the first of the informal weekly discussion groups I had suggested. I had brought along some colour slides, and a projector and screen were made available. On the first occasion ten adults came, either Friends or their spouses, some of whom were not Friends. For most of my stay, the group numbers remained the same. After a period of worship, I would introduce a topic,and a wide ranging discussion followed. I felt, from the start, that these evenings should be partially structured, and that there should be a teaching element in them. I had prepared before leaving home, a set of small prompt cards, to guide me. The first evening was on the history of Quakerism, which, depending on how I put it across, was going to be a difficult topic. I tried to explain to Friends what brought George Fox to do what he did, and achieve what he did, using various readings from the Book of Discipline. Explaining the concept of the Inward Light of Christ is not easy, especially when your listener's first language is not English. I do not know how much they were able to follow, for I was basically talking about what happened in a northern European culture over 350 years ago. I hoped they had found it helpful.

During the coming weeks I covered such items as 'Why am I a Quaker?' - a personal statement, after which I asked others present to consider answering the question, if they could. This proved to be an interesting exercise, following which a number expressed their thanks. We dealt with silence and ministry in Quaker worship, the meaning of membership, the life of the Meeting and each person's commitment to the Meeting, the Books of Discipline, the Quaker business method and the responsibilities of clerks, the Quaker social responsibilities and the Quaker testimonies, including the Peace Testimony. On the afternoon of the day I was to present the Testimonies, I was sitting out on Renee's balcony in the sun doing my final preparations for the evening, when I became aware of a boom, boom. The moderate wind was blowing in from the south, carrying the noise with it. I learned from Renee that what I was hearing were the Israeli heavy guns firing in the south of Lebanon, some 75 kilometres away. This, I was told, was in response to some Hezbollah attack on the border between the two countries. For me, listening to the guns that afternoon, added a poignancy and a greater awareness of the importance of the Quaker Peace Testimony.

At the end of one of these sessions, arrangements were made for me to give a public talk on environmental issues The public address took place in the High School's main hall, named after the Dobbings, on the evening of 16th March. It was raining heavily at the time, so Tony took me down to Dobbing Hall in his car. The meeting did not start on time, but eventually, I was asked to speak, after a complimentary introduction by Tony. There were some sixty adults and almost as many children in the audience. The title of my address was 'The Care of our Planet', in which, after dealing with the general principles of conservation, I directed some of my thoughts from what I had observed ,or gleaned from others, about conservation issues in Lebanon. From some of the interesting questions at the end of my address, I assumed that most of what I had to say was understood and appreciated. I learned afterwards that quite a number of individuals in positions of responsibility in the community were present, including the local member of Parliament and the Lebanese chief of internal security. I was approached by a local reporter to write a short article in English based on my address. This I did and it was subsequently published in a Brummana newspaper.

Every family associated with the Meeting at Brummana, in one way or another, entertained me or took me out for trips. They also arranged for me to meet interesting Lebanese, some of whom were in influential positions. Sami Cortas and his wife, Najwa, were no exception. Quite early on in my stay Sami and Najwa took me out in their car into the mountainous villages above Brummana. We travelled through several villages or small towns, and eventually arrived at Bikfaiya, the home village Gemayal family. Bashir Gemayal, a Maronite, was Lebanon's President for a short while, until he was assassinated in September 1982. We were in the area known as the 'Mountain', the centre of the Maronite Catholicism, which is the largest of all the Christian sects and is dominated by a strong priestly hierarchy. En route, Sami pulled up outside an American Presbyterian School. We got out of the car and looked at the deserted campus, for, when the Americans left, the school was handed over to a local Lebanese committee, but due to mis-management it folded. So we returned to Brummana after an interesting journey, but not before going to their house for a cup of coffee and some sweet cakes. There we were able to relax in each other's company and talk about the School and its future.

Several times Sami took me into Beirut, either to meet some of the academics on the AUB staff, or, as on one occasion, to have a meal together in a small restaurant in Ras Beirut overlooking the sea and next to the tennis club where his daughter, Oussama, was having coaching from the Lebanese national coach - an American. Over the meal we talked and talked, covering many topics, such as his work and computers, but hardly mentioning the School. We touched on Quakerism, and I then began to realise how much it meant to him. The meal over, and with time on our hands, Sami walked me over to look at the Pigeon Rock, a limestone arch jutting out of the sea. The Mediterranean at this point was crystal clear, but with some pollution around the edges of the bay in which the Rock stands. We eventually collected Oussama from the club and drove back to Brummana through parts of west Beirut, which had been hardly touched by the conflict.

Before I left Yorkshire, Joyce Pickard of Friargate Meeting, had informed me that the August 1994 edition of the *New Internationalist* was entirely devoted to Lebanon. I got hold of the York Peace Centre's copy and photocopied most of the articles but especially one by Professor Mohammed Kwalie entitled, *The Land of Milk, Honey and Muck.* In this article Professor Khawlie, who was Professor of Geology at the AUB and Lebanon's leading conservationist, described the appalling conservation problems Lebanon faced, especially in its immediate post-war years. I told Sami about this article and said that I would be interested in meeting Professor Kwalie. He kindly said he would see what he could arrange. Eventually, after several attempts, I met the Professor in his office at the AUB on March 8th. He was obviously a very busy man, and was about to resign as the Head of Department to take up an advisory post on environmental issues to the Lebanese Government. His replacement was to be an expatriate Englishman, Dr. Christopher Walley, who I was going to meet again. The Professor and I soon settled into discussing several issues, such as soil erosion, forestry, hydro-electric schemes and water and air pollution, particularly as they related to Lebanon. He told me, for instance, that thousands upon thousands of tons of top soil were washed into the Mediterranean each year following heavy rains. This was due to deforestation and unplanned building and road construction. After three quarters of an hour I left his company, my head buzzing with facts and figures. I thanked him for giving me some of his precious time. I had arranged to meet Sami again for lunch, but, as I was early, I decided to sit on a park bench in the beautiful AUB campus grounds, and read a recent edition of the Independent that I had purchased that morning. Sitting there, I watched the giant jet aircraft coming in off the sea, passing very low overhead on their way to land at Beirut airport.

On another occasion, Sami took me down to the Department of Biology. Sami really did not know his way round the Department, so we started knocking on doors. Eventually, we came to Dr. Riyad Sadak's door, a lecturer in biology. After introductions all round, I discovered that Dr. Sadak had obtained his doctorate in Britain, his thesis being on the lizard *Lacerta leavis*, and that his external examiner had been Dr. Nicholas Arnold of the Natural History Museum, South Kensington. Dr. Arnold had succeeded Mr. Battersby in the post, and I had been in correspondence with him in 1994 over some of my lizard observations. Riyad, as I came to know him, immediately dropped everything he was doing and called Professor Eli Baydoun, Head of the Department, to his room to meet me. I met Eli Baydoun again soon afterwards, and he took me back to his flat on the campus for a meal. Like Riyad, he was trained in Britain, having done his research degree at Cambridge. Both academics were about give lectures, so Riyad took me to the Department's Museum and introduced me to its newly appointed curator.

The Museum, which had received a direct hit in the conflict, was still being reorganised by Dr. Khouzama Knio, a French graduate, with a doctorate in entomology. Amongst the accumulated dust, damage and neglect, I was shown their reptile collection, as well as drawers full of freeze-dried bat skins which belonged to the Robert Lewis collection. Robert Lewis was, in his day, a leading bat expert in the Levant. We had a long discussion about bats, an order of mammals she knew little about.

At midday I returned to Riyad's room. As Lebanon's expert in amphibians and reptiles, he had many live specimens in his laboratory, including a small finely patterned, grey-backed gecko *Cyrtodactylus kotschyi*, that he had found on an olive tree the previous day. I had not, as yet, seen one in the wild. He told me a great deal about his work, including his research work on black rats *Rattus rattus*, and the disease Leishmaniasis that human beings can contract from rats. He asked me if I would like to join him and his wife, Sana, on a trip to north Lebanon on the following day. He was going to examine some of his rat traps. I jumped at the opportunity.

Next morning Tony drove me down to Beirut and dropped me off at the entrance to the AUB. I walked across to Biology, and found Riyad and Sana loading up their four-wheel drive vehicle with scientific collecting equipment. Driving at a break-neck speed, we reached Tripoli in just over the hour. Above the noise of the engine, we were able to have some conversation about amphibians, reptiles, politics and religion. The Saddeks were Sunni Moslems, with a breadth of vision and outlook. Unlike my previous journey to Tripoli, I was sitting in the front passenger seat and was, therefore, able to take in the scenery. I was obviously getting used to the ribbon-development, for it was having less impact on me. We arrived in the centre of Tripoli at midday and parked outside a pizza take-away. Riyad ordered some food, and, while we were waiting for it, he took me over to the old central square of the town. It had changed little since 1955, when I was last there. Facing into the square was an old, traditionally designed Arab house, with its twin outside staircases, one on each side, leading up to a first floor balcony. I immediately recognised it as the old club house for the senior I.P.C. personnel; the place in which I used to play table tennis and drink soft drinks with my peer group in the 1950s. It was an extraordinary experience to see it all again after so many years, as well as the old Arab buildings, still intact, at the entrance to Tripoli's ancient souk.

Unable to stop for lunch, we drove north munching pizzas. The route took us west of Mount Turbol, which I was able to look at more closely. Its upper contours had been spoilt by a large mansion built on its summit, by some rich political tycoon, with no consideration for amenity or beauty. There was, also, an enormous quarry that cut across the path I used to take to the summit. My 'holy mountain', the place I used to go for the dawn, had been desecrated.

On our way we passed the old I.P.C. refinery, which seemed to me to be in a state of disrepair and rust. None of it seemed familiar to me, for many of the features I remembered from former times, were now screened by mature trees. About five miles south of the Lebanese-Syrian border, Riyad left the main coastal road and drove inland north-east towards Halba. Almost immediately, we came to a road junction and turned south-east up a narrow road to the villages of Begayel and Bzal. The scenery was becoming more and more dramatic. To the east was snow-capped Qornet es Saouda (10173 ft.), the highest mountain in the Lebanon range. This, I thought, was the Lebanon I knew in my youth, unspoilt by exploitation or human greed. On each side of the road there were well-kept terraces planted with olive trees, often associated with small settlements. We were now in the region of the Akkar Mountains.

The road became more and more bumpy the higher we got, so that Riyad put the vehicle into 4 wheel drive. Eventually, we came to a small, unnamed, Muslim village, clinging precariously to a bluff on a mountainside overlooking a deep gorge. Its minaret stood out among the single storey, flat-roofed houses. Passing through the village, we reached a narrow track that led to a small-holding. Here, we were welcomed by the owners, a local farming family. The farmer, dressed in his baggy black trousers, was helping Riyad collect black rats for his experimental work. We were all offered warm sweet Turkish coffee and sat outside their house on low, rush-covered seats. The conversation was entirely in Arabic; I sat, listened, and took in the surroundings. I noticed, as did Riyad, that the woman of the household had a large festering facial boil, which was not being treated.

Coffee over, we got back in the vehicle, taking the farmer with us. Plunging down into a gorge, along a single dirt track road built in Ottoman times, with plenty of hairpin bends, we came to a small, recently constructed narrow bridge that crossed Nahr Abou Maussa. The mountain stream, then in spate, flowed westwards towards the Mediterranean. The gorge got more and more narrow, with high, steep sided cliffs on each side. We travelled upstream, having crossed the bridge. Some of the scenery reminded me of the steep sided gorges we had seen in Jabel Sahro, Morocco in 1993, but here it was more wooded. Occasionally, we came across patches of cultivation, especially of almond trees, some of which were in blossom. Finally, Riyad pulled up at a ford, but because of the swollen stream, we were unable to cross it. On the other side of the ford were his live mammal traps. Disappointed, we turned round, but not before Riyad took several photographs of the stream, which was full of human garbage washed down from settlements upstream. Nearly every water course in Lebanon, according to Riyad, was polluted with either pathenogenic bacteria, industrial waste or garbage. He hoped to show his students the photographs during some of his lectures. We returned to the farmer's home and, after thanking him, left him there and made for the coastal road again.

Riyad had another collecting site in the village of Markabta, on the lower slopes of Turbol. He drove to a house in the middle of the village, hoping to find some captive live black rats. Again he was very disappointed, for although the lady of the house had caught 19 rats, they had all died from starvation. He needed live rats so that he could obtain blood samples from them. Leaving the village, with its more settled small farms, the three of us returned to Tripoli and then on to Beirut. The Sadaks had given me a wonderful day and kindly returned me to Brummana. The trip was not the last time I was to meet Riyad, for whenever I was on the AUB campus I made a point of going to his laboratory. He gave me a number of scientific papers, one on Lebanon's reptiles, written in French, and another, written by Robert Lewis, on Lebanon's bats.

My stay in Brummana was in two parts. The first four weeks I stayed with Renee, and the remainder of my time with Tony and Jocelyn Manasseh. My time with Renee, in the quiet atmosphere of her household, I will always remember. The comings and goings of family and friends, the meals, the discussions, her weekly Bible study group and many arranged visits. I went every day to the main Post Office in Brummana to see if there was any mail from Britain for me, for letters from home, especially from Patricia, were much sought after. Postal services were slow and letters often took some time to come through, but, besides those from Patricia, I also received letters from Robert, Claire, my brother John and Lorna Marsden and Joyce Pickard of Friargate Meeting.

In the evenings Renee regularly watched television, sometimes an American 'soap opera', but more often programmes in Arabic, especially discussion groups. She particularly liked the B.B.C. world news in English, but would always interpret Arab based programmes for me. There was plenty of choice on Lebanon's commercially-based television, much of it of poor quality. I learned a lot about Lebanese life and current affairs, especially those events surrounding the continuing conflict between Lebanon and Israel. Concern was being expressed by the Government about the amount of litter and garbage accumulating in the streets, so, every so often, Government sponsored advertisments would appear encouraging residents to use refuse bins and the new rubbish collecting lorries when they appeared.

Renee's Bible study group, held in her sitting room, consisted of members of the Greek Orthodox Church, the Church of God, a single Maronite, and Renee herself, a Quaker. The pastor of the Church of God was usually present, hence the discussions and study, according to Renee, consisted of orthodoxy. She would often tell me the contents of the meetings, which were conducted in Arabic, so I never attended. Her next door neighbour, Nadim Aswad, was a Greek Orthodox Christian. One day he took me, along with Miriam, up to the Greek Orthodox chapel in the centre of old Brummana. In the quiet forecourt of the chapel stands an ancient Turkish oak tree, reputed to be over 700 years old, and certainly the oldest tree in Brummana. The 1,300 year old chapel, which is dedicated to Elijah, gives a feeling of agelessness, with its wide walls, arrow slit windows and its thick old oak door and entrance. On the inside white-washed ˉwalls there were few embellishments, which gave the place an air of simplicity. The old oak screen, according to Nadim, was almost as old as the building. We lingered a while, taking in the spirituality of the church; I felt strongly I could worship there according the manner of Friends. I was also shown the the Roman Catholic orphanage of St.Vincent. Its 300 year old courtyard was badly damaged in the recent civil conflict, but had been completely restored by French sailors. Originally a Druze building, it was acquired by the Catholics when the Christians took over the Brummana area in the 1860s. The orphanage provided a home for over 100 boys of all religions.

Further expeditions were organised for me by the Baz family whilst I was staying with them. Sabah arranged for Joseph, the night watchman at the High School and a local taxi driver, to drive me round the Chouf. Sitting next to him in his 1970s B.M.W., we set off one morning into Beirut, but soon hit one of the proverbial traffic jams. Joseph then decided to take a short cut down a series side roads, most of which were in a poor state of repair. Again, I was able to observe a lot of war damage; particularly many industrial buildings that had been partially destroyed, but attempts had been made to repair some of the ground floors. We passed through the districts of Hadat, Ouadibaa and Chouaifete in the south-east part of the city, and drove south to Damour. Around Damour, a massive building programme was going on, much of it unplanned, with many buildings, as yet unoccupied. Soon after Damour, Joseph turned inland.

The road to the mountains, I noted, was smooth and well kept. Joseph, in his broken English, told me it was because we were in Druze country. Apparently, of all the sects, the Druzes, under the leadership of Walid Jumblatt, showed a greater sense of civic pride than other Lebanese. Suddenly, Joseph pulled up at a sharp bend next to a parapet. Getting out of the car, we looked over the valley below at rough scrub land and a few derelict farm buildings. This was Sirjbal, which Tony had shown us in 1994. Topped by a small plateau, the area was being partially cultivated by some squatting farming family. With a river running below the site, it seemed to me to be an ideal place to develop into an environmental educational centre, which is much needed in Lebanon. Subsequently, when I came to talk to Phillippa Neave about Sirjbal, I found she already had similar ideas. However, Sirjbal is in the hands of a Lebanese committee, who, because of its high monetary value, probably have other ideas.

Our next stop was Deir el Qamar, a small historic town, the home of the Chamoun family. It was Chamille Chamoun who, as President of Lebanon in the late 1950s, signed Father's Lebanese Order of Merit document. The town was very photogenic, many of the buildings being in a good state of repair. Overlooking the whole scene was Jabel el Barouk which is part of the Lebanon range. On its western slopes are some of the remaining sites where the Cedars of Lebanon still grow; and the Lebanese parliament has passed laws to create a national nature reserve. The scenery became more and more impressive the higher we went. Driving past Beit el Dine, which we visited last year, Joseph took me up on to the road running along the Lebanon ridge, through the settlements of Ain Zalta and Ain Dura. Finally, through Ras-el- Metn and so back to Brummana, via the Donkey Bridge in the valley below the Baz house, in time for lunch. It had been a splendid opportunity for me to see some of Lebanon and I was grateful to Joseph for taking me. He, according to Tony, had taken an active part in the conflict in one of the militia, but I would never have known. Subsequently, every time I saw him in the streets of Brummana, he would give me a cheerful wave.

Another trip was with Hilary Baz and three of her four children, Murhaf, Karim and Sherine in their four by four Range Rover. Like many other well-to-do Lebanese families, the four-wheel drive vehicle was in common use, especially by the women folk, who felt more safe in such a vehicle. We decided, initially, to return to Tripoli to see which of our old haunts we could still find. Hilary took back a route via Roumie to reach the dual carriageway going north. While she was driving she told me, in vivid language, about the frightening escape she and the children had in 1987. During some heavy shelling, they had driven along the same route we were taking that morning, to get to Christian held Jouniehh to board a boat going to Cyprus. Once on the boat, they had to take shelter until the firing had ceased. Sabah had to stay on throughout the whole of the civil war. It was after such conversations, I began to realise what hardships Brummana Friends had to endūre during the civil war and what courage they had shown, especially during the last phases of the conflict.

On arriving in Tripoli, we drove straight for the refinery, which I had seen on my previous trip. We made for what we thought was the I.P.C. sports club and leisure complex, but could not gain access to it as it was in the control of the Syrian army, who were using it as a training centre. The soldiers guarding the site looked at us suspiciously, so we moved on, having only identified the old club house.

El Mina sea front was different. Many buildings had been flattened. Gone were the Arab dhow boat building yards and horse drawn gharries of former times. The gharries, no doubt, had been phased out by competition with motor transport, but at one time they had been very much part of the Tripoli scene. The port facilities had been expanded to take larger ocean going vessels. We walked along the newly paved promenade, having parked our vehicle. Looking back over Tripoli, I realised that the view had not changed, with its backdrop of the snow-capped mountains. We managed to find a boat to take us out to some of the islands off El Mina, but were only able to go round some of the inner ones, hardly venturing beyond the harbour. I was keen to get to Palm Island, three miles off the mainland, but because of choppy sea conditions, and because we could land only by special permit, we did not get there. Palm Island, like Jabel el Barouk, has been declared a National Nature Reserve by the Lebanese parliament, but, at that time, was under the control of the Syrian army. In the inner harbour there were plenty of sea birds, especially Mediterranean gulls *Larus melanocephalus*, several cormorant *Phalacrocorax carbo* and a solitary migratory black-necked grebe *Podiceps nigricollis*. They were all swimming among a number of abandoned medium-sized merchant ships, in whose rusty hulks dispossessed people were living. The children enjoyed the trip, whilst Hilary and I recalled the yachting and boat trips we used to take in former times.

The day did not end with the sea trip, but a further journey into the hinterland. Before driving on, we lunched at the pizza restaurant where Sadeks had bought some take-away pizzas on my previous visit to Tripoli. To begin with the roads up into the mountains were straight and well surfaced, passing through miles upon miles of olive groves and well-kept terraces. We passed through Zgharta and eventually reached Sabaal, from where the road twisted and turned in a steep climb on to the ridges overlooking a deep-sided valley. Small red-roofed villages were clinging precariously to the cliff edges. We entered Ehden, the object of our journey; we had come at my request to visit Horsh Ehden, the National Forest Nature Reserve, which had been declared in March 1992. On reaching the entrance gate and information centre, we found it was closed. However, access was possible, so we wandered along one of the main forest tracks. The Reserve's superb position and unique forest ecosystem was very apparent to me, but, because of the time of the year and the cold climatic conditions, there was little to see other than the variety of mature mountain trees clothing the mountainous terrain. Some spring flowers were emerging on the forest floor, and I saw my first white-throated robin *Irania gutturalis*. Judging by the number of spent shotgun cartridges lying about, illegal shooting was still going on. After a while, we all returned to the Land Rover, to make a start on the long journey back to Brummana. Hilary decided that, rather than retrace our route, we would cross over the valley, and go via Bcharre. In the distance I could see the Cedars of Lebanon and the ski-lift going up to the snow covered Dahr el Oadib Ridge, which overlooks the ski resort. I suspected it was the same one that John and I used in 1955, when we went for a walk along the Ridge. After three hours' driving, we reached home. Hilary was obviously very tired and was glad to be there. For me, I had again seen much of northern Lebanon after a gap of forty years. I thanked Hilary and the children for taking me on such a wonderful trip.

On many occasions Tony arranged for me to come down to Beirut with him, on his way to his offices in the Achrafieh district. More often than not, we were driven by his chauffeur, Elie, whilst Tony made contact with his business colleagues using his mobile telephone. Mobile 'phones, according to Tony, would eventually replace conventional telephone wires, which were in a state of complete chaos. The telephone authorities were making no attempt rearrange the wires piling up on telegraph poles, or anywhere else on which the wires could be supported. One morning, at the end of February, he collected me from the Baz household and, after he stopped off at his office, asked Elie to drive me over to the Mayflower Hotel. There I met Phillippa Neave, who had just returned from one of her regular visits to Friends' House in London. We planned to have most of the day together and she would take me through some of the worst war damaged areas of Beirut, especially what was left of the old souks. Other than Hilary, Phillippa was the first British person I had seen since my arrival in Lebanon; we had a lot to talk about. The day was warming up and my chest was beginning to feel tight from all the car fumes, after sitting in a traffic jam for over an hour to get to the Hamra district in the first place.

We left the Hotel and walked past the AUB towards the St. George Hotel on the sea front. I was glad I was with Phillippa as she spoke fluent Arabic, and, in her company, I felt quite safe. I asked if I could photograph the St. George's Hotel, but a Syrian army soldier was reluctant to let me do so. We moved on to the entrance of what was the St. George Club, and Phillippa explained to three men, standing just inside the entrance, about Mother's and

114

Father's previous membership of the Club. We were invited in. It was an interesting experience to see what was left of the expatriates' Club. There, on the sea wall, was the remnants of a diving board. 'Could it be the same diving board I dived from in my youth?' I asked myself. Certainly, the sea water below was polluted with human sewage, just as it was in former times.

Leaving the sea front, we walked up to what remained of the Phoenician Hotel and the Holiday Inn. At one time both Hotels had been some of the most expensive in the Levant, but now they were skeletal, shrapnel-ridden buildings, that were still recognisable and structurally sound. In time, Phillippa told me, they would be fully restored, but, meanwhile, as elsewhere in Lebanon, they were housing a contingent of Syrian soldiers. Obviously some of the most ferocious fighting had occurred in the area, for close by, in what had been Beirut's fashionable shopping centre, there were many war damaged streets. Living amongst the rubble, and in grossly overcrowded, slum conditions, were Shi'ite families eking out an existence. These people were refugees from the south of Lebanon, where the conflict between Lebanon and Israel still existed. However, with improving security in the south, many were gradually returning to their homes. In the narrow streets, ill-clothed children played, women, their heads covered, were hanging out washing from the badly damaged flats, whilst their men folk were either hanging around or carrying on some trade, such as car repairs. Everywhere were posters of the mullahs, especially Ayatollah Khomeini, the spiritual founder of the Hezbollah. They were stuck up on every available space, along with the emblems representing the Amal militias. We walked cautiously through the area; I took photographs, whenever it was possible.

I vaguely remembered Martyrs' Square, which must have been an important shopping centre for Mother and Father the 1950s. Now the Square was completely flattened, with red painted, metal public benches laid out neatly around the original Martyrs' Statue It had originally been erected to commemorate rebels who had been executed by the Turks in 1915. Riddled with bullet holes, the Statue had become a symbol of all that was destroyed in the civil conflict. Nearby was an old Maronite Church, the interior of which had been completely destroyed, and opposite the church stood what remained of the old gold and silver souks of Beirut. I looked, and absorbed all that was around me, wondering, as did Phillippa, what all the destruction had achieved. Below some of the destruction, archaeologists were unearthing much of Phoenician Beirut. We stopped to look at some of the work in progress, but, by now, it was lunch time.

We crossed what was the green line between the warring factions into Christian East Beirut. There was plenty of evidence of shrapnel damage, but, on the whole, the buildings were in a better state of repair than those in the west. Following a conversation in French with a friend that we met, Phillippa took me to small cafe, called the Beirut Barrel, for a light lunch. We had an excellent meal, in pleasant surroundings with air conditioning, during which we talked at length about the Lebanese scene. We touched on the present situation between the Cultural Society and Q.P.S. and the negotiations between them. According to Phillippa, some members of the Cultural Society thought I had been sent out to Lebanon to spy on them. The meal over, we caught a service taxi back to Hamra and the Mayflower Hotel. While there, I was introduced to Admed El Hussani, an educated Shi'ite Moslem, whose firm installs domestic water purifying units all over Beirut, a much needed activity. In conversation with the owner of the Hotel, I learned that he, Mr. Samaha, once worked for Airworks, the I.P.C. subsidiary based on Tripoli airport. He knew Father and recognised him from the photograph I carried with me. He remembered the old B.O.A.C. Argonaut aircraft which used to land at Tripoli. Again, I had been on a steep learning curve, for Phillippa had shown me so much of Beirut, for which I was very grateful. On parting, we arranged to met again. Returning to Tony's office to join him, it then took us a long time, because of the traffic jams, to get back to Brummana. Meanwhile, he had arranged for me to meet the Greek Orthodox Archbishop of Beirut at his palace the following day.

After a time consuming journey, we arrived at the Archbishop's palace at our appointed time. Elie, Tony's driver, skilfully manoeuvred Tony's American car through the traffic. I was accompanied by Tony, and we had a short wait before I was introduced to the Archbishop Elias Aoude, a medium-sized man in a long black cassock, with a large crucifix hanging round his neck. With him was the Archbishop of Tripoli, who, after making a few comments, left. Tony knew Elias Aoude through various contacts, and his in-laws, Jocelyn's mother, lived a few blocks away in the same street. Dr. Aoude ushered us into his study, a large book-lined room. When we were comfortably seated and Turkish coffee was being served, I looked round the room at my surroundings. Besides a comprehensive set of religious books, there were several icons hanging on the walls between the bookcases, as well as a large sentimental painting of the crucifixion. According to Tony, the Archbishop had put aside an hour of his precious time to see me, so I felt I had to make the most of my time. I asked him two prepared questions.

My first question was about environmental issues and what were his Church's responses to such issues, and, secondly, how was the Greek Orthodox Church trying to heal the religious and secular divisions within Lebanon's society. His reply, in excellent English, was delivered in a thoughtful manner and at length, although, at times, rambling in content. The Archbishop had obviously thought a great deal about both questions. Basically, he thought the pressing need of the Lebanese was survival in a situation of post-conflict, and by that, he meant, material and spiritual survival was paramount, over and above environmental issues. I told him about my visit to Brummana Friends and was able to explain to him the Quaker Peace Testimony. Tony was a great help in the discussions, intervening from time to time. When the hour was up, I felt pleased with the way the discussions had gone. I thanked Dr. Aoude for seeing us, shook hands with him and departed down the palace steps to Tony's waiting car. In the car, Tony expressed disquiet about some of my questioning, especially my analytical approach to my faith. However, we drove off to the American University Hospital, there to see Sabah Baz who had been admitted with acute abdominal pain, from which he made a complete recovery.

Tony had to attend to his business, so he made arrangements for me to meet with Phillippa again. We met at the Mayflower Hotel, and from there walked over to the Pigeon Rocks promenade. We selected a restaurant called the Grotte aux Pigeons and ventured in. We were shown to two seats at a table overlooking the bay and were served with an entirely Arab meal that Phillippa ordered. It proved to be very expensive, considering its contents! Possibly, we were paying for the view. There was much to talk about, especially on Quaker faith and practice, which, I hoped, Phillippa found helpful. Although she came from a family with a Quaker background, she had little, if any, contact with Friends until her appointment to her present post with Q.P.S. It was then that she told me how she came to apply for her job, having come to it from free-lance journalism and a degree in Arabic studies. I found her story fascinating. By mid-afternoon it was time for me to return to the hospital, where Hilary was to collect me and drive me back to Brummana.

It was about this time that I took up residence in the Manasseh household and I was to remain with them for the rest of my stay in Lebanon. I was sorry to be leaving the company of Renee, but looked forward to my time with Tony and Jocelyn. The contrast between the two households was immediately apparent, to begin with the sleeping accommodation was very different. My bedroom was downstairs, at the bottom of the building, away from the rest of the family. It was the same one that John and Marjorie Scott had had the previous year, with its high-arched, traditional Arab ceiling of rough cut local stone and bars on the windows. It was 'cellar-like' in appearance, and at night, especially during some of the overhead thunderstorms, or when an Israeli airforce jet went through the sound barrier, the sounds reverberated around the ceiling. It took some getting used to, but, curled up in my sleeping bag and covered with blankets, I felt cosy.

Breakfast was a more formal affair, in which I was served at table. More often than not, I had the meal on my own. On my first Sunday there I accompanied Tony to Meeting for Worship, which was well attended. It was followed by Monthly Meeting, which on this occasion was more structured, and a number of items were considered. However, Tony read out a letter he received from Andrew Clark that triggered a heated debate. The whole issue of the future of the School came up. I felt, at that time, that a lot of anger and frustration felt by Brummana Friends was directed at me, as I represented British Quakers. I listened and tried, often in vain, to redirect their thoughts to the more positive aspects of

Andrew's letter. In the end a Minute was drawn up to be sent on to Q.P.S., with a covering letter.

That afternoon, instead of taking another trip to Tripoli, the Manasseh family took me to Tony's recreational Club at Kaslik, south of Jouniehh. This was not my first visit to Kaslik, for I came with Patricia and the Scotts in 1994, and, briefly, soon after I arrived in Lebanon this time. Tony liked to come to his Club, where he was able to relax completely. Being Sunday afternoon, there were many families about and the restaurant was full. Eventually, we found somewhere to sit and have a meal. In this holiday atmosphere I perked up after having had something to eat. Kaslik was certainly not my scene, for it was for the rich and well-to-do. There were many expensive motor boats and yachts in the marina. Tony's brother-in-law, Ron, was there with his wife and child. They owned a speed boat and mostly used it for water skiing. After taking the children out for a spin in Jouniehh Bay, Ron took Tony and me for a more extensive tour. As an architect, Ron was able to point out the planning and design faults of buildings erected round Jouniehh Bay following the cessation of hostilities. Most were far too tall and out of keeping with their surroundings, with little heed being taken to use traditional Lebanese and Arab designs and materials, such as red roofing tiles. The sandy beaches and coves of earlier days were now infilled with massive rock harbours, designed for speed boats and leisure craft. The whole coast line was one of ribbon development.

In a wide sweeping arc, and at full throttle, we headed out to sea. What an exhilarating experience, with the spray and wind in my face. We came close to the oil tanker mooring terminal, where tankers offload their crude oil to supply the Ras et Tair power station, one of Lebanon's three such stations. Its tall chimneys, which normally belch out black smoke, caused by burning crude oil, were inactive. There were no tankers present, but a few seagulls and sandwich terns *Sterna sandvicensis* resting on the moorings. We returned to the marina and joined the rest of family, before returning to Brummana after I had thanked Ron and the others.

The first time I met Charles Ayoub was on the third Sunday of my stay with Brummana Friends. However, I was very much aware of how important he had been to the families I had been staying with from the way they talked about him, especially amongst the womenfolk. Charles was their family paediatrician. Tony had taken me, after Meeting for Worship, to Jocelyn's mother's flat, near the AUB. There I was introduced to her mother, who was a widow in her mid 70s, and I met again Jocelyn's sister and brother-in-law, Ron. After a large and very tasty Lebanese lunch, Tony rang up Charles Ayoub, who lived in the same district. Within 15 minutes he walked in the door and I immediately recognised a similarity between him and his older brother, Ibrahim, who had been Father's surgical deputy at the I.P.C. Hospital in Tripoli for ten years. Charles, like Ibrahim, was a quiet-spoken doctor of the old school of British and Australian medicine, in which he had been nurtured. He told me the story of how Father had seen him off from Haifa's railway station in 1947 to start his medical training in Australia. Father, at that time, apparently said to Charles, 'Do not come back to Palestine after you qualify'. How right Father's advice had been; Charles never returned to Palestine, but eventually established himself as consultant paediatrician at the AUB. He remained in his post in Beirut for most of the civil conflict, leaving in 1986 to settle in the Gulf, when his life became threatened. Prior to his departure, he dealt with injured and orphaned children and gained an international reputation. He returned to Beirut as soon as the conflict ceased. Charles was an anglophile, but, like Tony, felt that the British had let down the Arab peoples. We had, Charles thought, 'pulled the rug from under their feet'. It was a great experience to meet him and he spoke of Father in glowing terms, saying of him that he was the best surgeon, in his day, on the Levant coastline. 'Why is it,' he asked, as he disappeared down the lift at the end of his visit, 'that the British no longer produce occidentals as they used to?'

I was to meet Charles again, along with his wife, Monica, who was recovering from a minor stroke. On this occasion Hilary and Sabah Baz, the Manassehs and I were invited to the Ayoubs' flat in Ashrafiah for supper. No sooner had we settled down to the meal, than we became aware of low flying Israeli airforce jets over Beirut. Knowing that the Lebanese had no jets, we all rushed onto the balcony to see tracer bullets from the Lebanese army anti-aircraft guns firing into the night sky. The firing had come from the south of the city. We returned to the dinner table, everyone feeling tense, but quite philosophical about the meaning and outcome of the event. Charles put on the television, which reported the raid. My friends wished that the Israelis would leave weak Lebanon alone. For me, the whole episode was a new and frightening encounter. The drama of the evening ended on a quiet note, as Charles and I chatted about life during the Palestine British Mandate days.

In Haifa, although Father was very much the driving force in the medical services, he was responsible to Dr. Hamze, the Director. Colonial policy, especially in Mandated territories, was to place, where possible, a local person at the head of a department. The Hamze family were Lebanese Druze, and Leila Abu Ezzeddine, Dr. Hamze's daughter, lived in Beirut. Leila's brother, who worked at Beirut airport for British Airways in the 1970s, married Isobel Sugden, who was an air hostess with B.A. Isobel originally lived in Shipton-by-Beningborough, near York, with her parents. I was, for many years, the Sugden family doctor. Through a series of coincidences, Phillippa Neave met Isobel at a supper party arranged by Amine Douk, the Chairman of the Cultural Society, and his English wife. As a result of these contacts, Tony drove me one afternoon to the Abu Ezzeddine flat so that I could meet Leila and her husband, Joseph. We were ushered into an over-furnished sitting room, typical of middle-class Lebanese society. I did not recognise Leila, but she thought she saw similarities between Father and me. Over Turkish coffee, we soon got into conversation about the Palestine days, which they remembered with affection. They showed me some of their photographs. Even Tony found that the Abu Ezzeddines had links with his past. We stayed until the early evening, after a most enjoyable meeting.

During my stay in Lebanon I visited the British Embassy at Rabieh twice. To get to the Embassy, a house set in a leafy suburb of Beirut, I was driven by Eli, Tony's chauffeur. Phillippa, who was accompanying me, was already there when I arrived. Gaining access to the building was quite an exercise, with all the security checks involved. The car, having passed an angled blockade, came to a standstill, after which its undercarriage was inspected with a large mirror on an angle pole. On reaching the front door, we were let in after identifying ourselves on an intercom. Passing through a series of locked doors, we reached the interior of the building. It was not long before Innes Rae, Deputy Head of Mission, introduced himself to us. He was a chain-smoking Scot, who had a sense of humour and a healthy amount of cynicism. Phillippa had met him before. We sat in a medium-sized room, opposite a portrait of Queen Elizabeth. The whole atmosphere of the place was so different from anything I had experienced since arriving in Lebanon.

The object of the exercise, for me, was to let the Embassy know of my visit and find out a little bit about Britain's involvement in the country. I found it difficult to get the conversation going, possibly because I had not been fully prepared. His replies were short and to the point, leaving me floundering round for the next question. Phillippa had her own agenda and dealt with these items accordingly, often filling an awkward silence. Some of our questions related to the future of Brummana High School and any involvement the Embassy might have in its future, should it ever be returned to overall British Quaker control. After half an hour, the meeting came to a close and we left the Embassy, passing through the locked doors, to find a taxi to take into central Beirut.

Ten days later I was back at the British Embassy, the Villa Tohmeh, but this time it was for an Embassy reception, to which I had been kindly invited. Again Eli drove me there, and again we had to go through the same checks. I was ushered into a smoke-filled room crowded with Brits, all talking to each other. I gathered that they were mostly business men, and that, at that moment, the main thrust of the Embassy's work was to encourage business contacts in Lebanon. From time to time, a Lebanese waiter would squeeze his way through the throng and offer guests drinks and small eats. I was welcomed by Innes Rae, but, until Phillippa arrived, accompanied by Dr. Lloyd Precious, a British lecturer at the AUB, I knew no-one. Further introductions followed, including Miss Thomas, a Scottish lady in charge of the British Council offices in Beirut, and Dr. Christopher Walley, the British geologist now in charge of the Department of Geology at the AUB. He, like Dr. Lloyd, was evidence that expatriate academic staff were again being appointed at the University. Finally, I was introduced to the Ambassador, Caroline Fort. We had a brief conversation. I thanked her for her invitation to the reception and told her of how Mother and Father, in the 1950s, used to come to similar receptions at the British Embassy, but not in the same building. Eventually, I made my way to an outside terrace , where there was a small swimming pool. The warm night air was full of sounds of crickets and croaking tree frogs. 'Had the life of the British expatriate changed much since the 1950s?', I asked myself. I could have stayed longer, for I was enjoying the reception, but, instead, left after an hour and was driven back to Brummana by Eli, who had patiently waited for me.

Life with Tony and Jocelyn was never without interest. Their children, Philip and Joya, played together contentedly, often in my presence, but I never really got to know them. Tony loved talking, and most evenings, instead of watching television, he and I would talk for two to three hours, covering such subjects as medicine, family affairs and Middle East politics. He rarely went to the cinema, or, at least, he had not been for many years. So, one weekend at the end of March, he decided that we should all go to Beirut and stay there overnight at his mother-in-law's flat. That evening, after a meal, the three of us went to the cinema. Showing at the local cinema was 'The House of Spirits', with Meryl Streep and Jeremy Irons. The place was crowded with chattering Lebanese, but eventually we found some seats. The film started at 10.00 pm, and did not finish until well after midnight. Once it had started, the audience settled down and all became absorbed in an excellent plot, based on South America. Tony agreed, on this occasion, that he enjoyed the experience, which we were to repeat later.

Next morning, Tony contacted the Rev. Habib Badr, the Presbyterian Minister, who I had met on two previous occasions. The second of these visits was with Phillippa at his office, after our morning interview at the British Embassy. Habib Badr was a personal friend of Tony's and he, the Minister, was very keen that we should go to his Sunday morning service. On entering the Chapel, I found it crowded with worshippers, and the entire service was in Arabic. Being Mothering Sunday, there were many children present and they made their own contributions, which, for some parents, was very emotional. Half way through the service, when I thought there was going to be a sermon, Habib Badr beckoned me up to the rostrum and asked me to speak to the congregation about my visit to Brummana Friends. Standing in front of a large wooden cross, I felt very nervous and unprepared. Still, words flowed, as I explained my reasons for being there, including my concerns about Lebanese environmental issues. The service over, I was approached by a number of people in the Chapel's foyer and made very welcome. Some knew Father through his work at the I.P.C. Hospital, including one lady, who showed me her thumb, which he had apparently operated on successfully many years ago. I was glad I had been to the service, and thanked Tony for the suggestion. I felt sure that Tony had enjoyed the service, and he told me that, at times, in his frustration with Friends, he felt he could join this Christian community.

Of the many books Tony encouraged me to read, while I was with them, was the autobiography of Theophilus Waldmeier, the founder of Brummana High School. I was particularly interested to read that, after his contact with the Allen family and at the time of his convincement, he used to worship at Stoke Newington Meeting when he was visiting London. It was at Stoke Newington Meeting that I was registered as a birthright Friend by my parents in the 1930s, and used to worship there regularly in my medical student days. Besides the bust of Theophilus Waldmeier erected next to the School's reception building, there is, still standing in the old part of the town, the house that he and his wife moved into when they first came to Brummana; it is now occupied by squatters. Among Tony's many friends was Jolie Tebut, the great grandson of Theophilus. A businessman of repute, Jolie lived with his family in a grand house, with extensive grounds Like many others, he left Lebanon during the war and returned two years ago. Now he was restoring his home in the grand manner and at great expense; money seemed no object. At Tony's suggestion, we went to visit him. I was shown various heirlooms, including a portrait of Theophilus painted at the end of his life. This painting gave me some idea of the old Swiss missionary's facial appearance. He died in 1916. I was also shown the Waldmeier family tree and their connections with the Ethiopian Royal Family, into which Theophilus married in 1859; his wife, Susan Bell, being the granddaughter of the Ethiopian king. Jolie, over soft drinks, talked to us about Lebanon's plight and the lack of civic planning, especially over housing. Our visit over, we returned to Brummana via Beit Mari.

On passing through Beit Mari, which, like Brummana, has become part of the extended development up the mountain slopes from Beirut, we noticed people going into the house of a local notable, who had recently died. Tony knew the individual concerned and felt he would like to go and offer his condolences. I was invited in. It was to be an interesting experience. In two large rooms, lined with chairs, were men and women, all dressed in black, talking quietly to each other. Occasionally, a waiter would move along the rows of mourners offering black coffee and cigarettes. I followed the mourners towards the bereaved family, a local doctor, his solicitor brother and their respective wives, along with their mother, the widow of the deceased. I was asked to sit next to the doctor, having shaken hands all round and offered my condolences. The doctor and I talked quietly about medical topics, but, from time to time, he would get up to receive more visitors and go through the same ritual of shaking hands, kissing three times on alternating cheeks and receiving more condolences. We had remained in the room for half an hour, when Tony indicated to me that it was time to move on. I was pleased to do so, thinking that was the end, but it was not to be. We went next door to see the deceased's eldest brother, who was a retired doctor. We had to go through the whole procedure again! It seems, over a few days, the whole community mourns in this way.

Prior to the civil conflict, Lebanon was both the financial and cultural centre of the Arab world. Gradually, with the cessation of hostilities, its cultural life was recovering, and indicative of this was the Al Bustan Hotel International Festival of the Performing Arts. With Tony and Jocelyn, I went to a preview of modern art at the Hotel, which is in Beit Mari. There were about sixty persons present, mostly rich and expensively dressed women, who, according to Tony, were there as 'socialites'. Neither the Manassehs nor I understood the paintings, which were done by Michael Biberstein from Switzerland and an Englishman, Ian McKeever, a post-graduate lecturer at the Slade School, who lived and worked in Dorset.

Tony also took me to an art gallery opposite his mother-in-law's flat to look at Lebanese paintings, mostly in a modern style, but not very much to our liking. When it comes to art, I have a minimal understanding, which, with an artistic family background, is a little surprising. We found it an interesting exercise to work out the confessional of each artist. On emerging from the gallery, in the fading evening light, Tony took me across the road to the residence of Lady Cochrane, so see if she was at home. Unfortunately, this English eccentric, who had lived in Lebanon for many years, was not at home.

I was able to attend two musical events at the International Festival of Performing Arts, and on both occasions I was taken by Sabah and Hilary. Each event was very different, but most enjoyable. On the first occasion, and in the presence of the First Lady, the wife of the Lebanese President, we sat in a crowded concert hall; the audience being mainly politicians, industrialists and academics. We had come to hear a piano recital performed by Abdel Rahman El Bacha, Lebanon's leading classical pianist. In front of us, but with the keyboard not visible, was a grand piano, beside which was a large display of artificial flowers. Starting with Bach's Partita in C minor, Rahman El Bacha went on to perform Beethoven's Waldstein sonata. I was carried away by the music, especially the Beethoven, which I had heard many times before, but never as a live performance. It made me long to get home and back to Patricia. The artistry seemed to me to be perfect, but then I am no musician. Others were of a like mind, for the performer got an enthusiastic standing ovation in the interval. In the second half he played pieces by Schumann, Chopin, De Falla, and Balakirev.

On the second occasion we went to hear Edvard Antousen, a young Norwegian trumpet player, and Wayne Marshall, a London-based, British black piano player, perform duets of classical jazz. Most of the pieces I was able to recognise and much enjoyed what I heard. It was all very relaxing. At the end of the programme, they invited requests from the audience, but none was forthcoming. So after much hesitation, I shouted out for 'When the Saints Come Marching Home'. They performed my request, which reminded me so much of my student days at King's College Hospital and the May balls. The concert over, the Baz family moved over to the

Italian restaurant, within the Al Bustan Hotel, for an excellent meal. Opposite us, at another table, was Mrs. Bustani, the Hotel owner, along with Wayne Marshall. When the meal was almost over, I went over to Mrs. Bustani and introduced myself. Sitting with her was her mother-in-law, who, when I showed her a photograph of Father, immediately recognised him. Mr. Bustani, her son, who died many years ago, worked for the I.P.C. in the 1950s, before setting up his own Middle East construction firm known as C.A.T. It was interesting recollecting our respective pasts, for the Bustanis knew Mother and Father quite well. The meal over, we all got back to Brummana well after midnight. For both occasions, I was profoundly thankful to Sabah and Hilary for taking me.

The task of describing all I experienced in 1995, while in Lebanon, is almost impossible. I met so many people and visited so many places, that to do justice to both people and places, within the limited space of this chapter, has proved to be difficult. All I have been able to do is to touch on some of those experiences, and thus, I hope, to give a flavour of life among Brummana Friends and middle class Lebanese society. With the poor, I had no contact, but was fully aware of their plight. On many occasions, who I met and what I did, had a high recall element, and I found myself remembering events of over 40 years ago and making comparisons between then and now. If there are readers of this travel journal who I met and have not mentioned, it was not with the intent of causing offence. However, before closing this chapter, I will recollect some of those persons and occasions. There was the occasion when Najwa Cortas, took me round the pathology laboratories, the X-ray department and some of the wards at the American University Hospital, where she worked as the Director of Biochemistry. Then there was my visit to Naasib Sohl's establishment in Brummana for mentally and physically handicapped children, followed by a visit to the home of Renee's friends, Devina and Philip Mallouh, who were originally from Jaffa and remembered the Mandate days with affection. I met one of Lebanon's leading psychiatrists, Dr. Eli Karam and his wife, a clinical psychotherapist, over supper at the Manassehs', as well as their local G.P., Dr. 'Gabby' El Khouri, who listened to my chest after a mild asthma attack. Renee introduced me to Khalil Mufarg and his widowed mother. Her doctor husband worked for the I.P.C. in the 1940s, and from what she said, I felt sure, he would have known Father. Khalil, who has multiple sclerosis, gave me booklets describing two of Lebanon's newly created National Nature Reserves at Ehden and Palm Island, as well as an English edition of Professor Kamal Salibi's book entitled, A House of Many Mansions - the History of Lebanon Reconsidered; a book, written by a Brummana Old Scholar, and well worth reading. The visit was not without its sadness, for I received a letter from Patricia telling me that Rosemary Sykes, a general practitioner in York with whom I worked for four years on an out-of-hours rota, had taken her life with an overdose. Life among Brummana Friends went on, with its ups and downs, joys and sorrows, but always with love and friendship.

The final phase of my stay in 1995 is related in the next chapter.

Crusader Castle at Athlit. Drawn by JOHN THOMPSON

CHAPTER VII

Amman

IT WAS LATE ONE evening at the end of March that Tony and I went to Beirut Airport to meet Philip Manesseh, Tony's father's first cousin. I had heard a lot about Philip, mostly from Tony, so I was pleased to meet him at last Although his grandfather was Lebanese, this was the first time that Philip had been to Lebanon, so, for him, this was a great occasion. Philip was British, a life-long Friend and a member of Oxford Meeting. He was here to visit the Lebanese side of his family, and as representative of London Yearly Meeting at the Middle East Yearly Meeting to be held in Amman later in the week. His plane arrived late, so that by the time we got back to Brummana it was well after midnight. Introductions were made all round, before Philip and I retired for the night, he sleeping in one of the guest rooms opposite to mine.

Next morning Tony was busy, but, as Philip wanted to maximise his stay in Lebanon, Tony left us at the medical school entrance of the AUB, so that I could show him round the campus, or at least the parts that I knew. We made our way to the Department of Biology, only to find that both Riyad and Eli Baydoun were giving lectures. However, we returned later, after a walk round the grounds. Eli invited us to his apartment for lunch, but, before doing so, he introduced Philip to Professor Barbour, who worked in the Department of Agriculture. They had a lot in common, for Philip was a retired lecturer in agriculture, and they talked at length about poultry farming. Lunch, hurriedly put together by Eli, was a new experience for Philip; new foods, in a new setting. The AUB visit ended with our going to the Computer Department to meet Sami, who had been disappointed not to have joined us at lunch. It was not long before Tony joined us and took Philip and me to meet his sister, Rosa, and her husband Freddie, who spoke very good English. Freddie, who had a degenerative muscular condition, walked with an unsteady gait.

On the third day of Philip's visit, Tony took us to Byblos, my third visit to the metropolis. On this occasion, instead of taking a guided tour, I took the Manesseh cousins round, trying my best to remember the history behind the main archaeological features. This time I was able to find what I thought were the Tyrian dye vats; the purple dye that made the Phoenicians so famous. We did not stay long at Byblos, but returned south to Kaslik for a late lunch. As usual, Tony was generous with his hospitality, for sitting in the shade, with a cool onshore breeze, we ate a large lunch. Facing us, and dominating the skyline overlooking Jounieh, was a large statue of the Virgin Mary. At Tony's suggestion, we left his Club and drove up to the Church of Our Lady of Lebanon, a large modern Maronite cathedral. After looking round the cathedral, we climbed the spiral staircase to the base of the 13 tonne statue of the Virgin Mary, erected at the end of the 19th century. The views were the best in the area, according to Tony. The Cathedral shop was full of various sized statues of the Virgin Mary; it seemed to me that the Maronites were worshipping idols. There were, however, a few crucifixes on sale.

It was still dark at 5.00 am when Tony woke us on his intercom. Both Philip and I dressed quickly, packed a few items in an overnight bag and went upstairs to join Tony for breakfast. An hour later we were being driven, along with Amal Abu Khalil, in a model 1970s Chevrolet. It was a monster light blue limousine with shining chromium-plated, grilled bumpers, and a large 'gas guzzling' engine. In south-east Beirut, we met up with Najwa and Sami Cortas, who were travelling in a large yellow Dodge. Amal transferred to the Cortas' taxi, before the small convoy set off eastwards towards Damascus. We were all going to Amman for Middle East Yearly Meeting.

Initially, the journey was in low cloud, but once we got over the pass and were plunging down into the Bekaa Valley, the weather improved considerably. The journey was not without its incidents, for one of the taxi drivers was driving through Lebanon with Syrian number plates, and at Chtaura, where we had a refreshment stop, the issue was sorted out with the police, Tony using his 'diplomatic' pass. We were stopped again by the police, and it was discovered that our driver had no passport or visa to enter Jordan. Eventually, after passing through the Lebanese-Syrian border without incident, we reached the outskirts of Damascus. We stopped at a house, and, after much haranguing, our driver handed over his taxi to another driver. We continued along better, smooth roads. I expected the countryside of southern Syria to be arid, but parts of it were well cultivated and green. The border post at Der'a, the site of Lawrence of Arabia's exploits, was not inspiring; after having our passports stamped, we drove across no-man's land to the Jordanian border post.

Immediately we entered Jordan, I, at least, sensed a new atmosphere. To begin with, the passport checks were dealt with more rapidly by smartly dressed officials in blue uniforms. One of them commented on my birth place being Haifa, and, after some further questioning, decided I was a genuine British citizen. The passport office, like others we had been through, was thronging with Arabs of all nationalities, some of them wearing traditional dress. The men were often dressed in ankle-length, white flowing robes, their heads covered with red and black chequered keffiyehs and a set of black rope aqals. We were soon on the road again, heading the 50 miles south towards Amman.

The roads were in excellent condition, well marked and maintained. The predominantly green countryside, adjacent to the road, was intensively cultivated and I soon realised that Jordan, of all the Arab states, could probably feed itself. Before entering Amman, we passed through some well wooded hills. Amman was very different from anything I had experienced in my travels in Al Mashrek. It was obvious that other influences were at work. 'Could it have been the British?', I asked myself. But, maybe, that was a patronising thought.

The majority of houses were only two storeys high, well built of local limestone. There were some tall buildings nearer the centre, but they were the exception. The streets were wide, and, on the whole, clean. The traffic was orderly, responding to traffic lights, with few traffic police to be seen. I had a feeling that town planning was more acceptable and that there was none of the laissez-faire of Lebanon. We were eventually driven up to one of the tall buildings, the Philadelphia Hotel, a large and expensive hotel in the centre of the city, where 1995 Middle East Yearly meeting was to be held.

Tony, through his Brummana connections, had made arrangements for Yearly Meeting to be held here, at much reduced rates. The owners of the hotel had been at one of the two Friends' Schools, and were, therefore, very pleased to have a Quaker gathering on their premises. We were soon surrounded by other participants, including Henry Selz from Cyprus and Renee and Phillippa, who had flown in to Amman that day from Beirut. I was pleased that I was asked to share a room with Henry, for I knew I would enjoy his conversation and humour. After a long tiring journey, I retired to our room for a prolonged nap, which greatly refreshed me.

The first session of Yearly Meeting was arranged for early that evening, so, before attending it, I accompanied a number of Friends to an excellent restaurant for an evening meal. It was at that meal that I met, for the first time, Hans Weening, the Dutch Friend, who was the secretary of E.M.E.S. of the Friends' World Committee of Consultation. I had been in correspondence with Hans before I came out to Lebanon, so I was pleased to meet him. I was immediately struck by his charming and easy manner.

The conference room on the tenth floor was ample in size, with comfortable seating. Compared with the previous year, representation of the two Monthly Meetings of Ramallah and Brummana was more even. Jane Tod, who once worked with her husband, Stephen, for Q.P.S. in Amman, was there representing London Yearly Meeting. I was very pleased to see her as I had known her for a number of years; we were both members of York Monthly Meeting. She brought with her a letter from Patricia. I had to wait to the end of the session before I could read it. Following a partially programmed Meeting for Worship, for Ramallah Friends were organising the gathering on this occasion, Friends sang two hymns. Jean Zaru of Ramallah was appointed Clerk, and Tony assistant Clerk. I was asked to be one of the three Recording Clerks, and Renee, Violet Zaru, Henry Selz and I were nominated to the Epistle Committee. Some Travelling Minutes and Letters of Introduction were read, after which the programme for the coming few days was discussed and agreed. Three young Quaker American couples, working for various charitable agencies in Israel or the West Bank were with us, along with their young children. At the end of two hours of deliberations the session came to an end, but the Americans decided to stay on for a further period of fellowship. Most of the older Friends, including me, turned in for an early night.

Before the start of the second day of Yearly Meeting, I went to the top floor of the Philadelphia Hotel so that I could look out over Amman. The few tall buildings blended well into their surroundings, and I could see that the city, which stretched away from me, was built on several hills. Below me I could see the smooth flowing traffic; the whole effect was one of lightness. I was reliably told that Amman was a pleasant place to work and live in.

More Letters of Introduction were read out, followed by reports from Ramallah and Brummana. The two American Recording Clerks were using a laptop computer, but one with silent keys! The reports from the Friends' Schools were similar in content, indicating that they had similar aims and ethos, but also similar problems. Sami, as a member of the Cultural Society, gave a most informative contribution about Brummana High School. It was non-controversial and just what some of his audience wanted to hear, for it seemed that the situation at the School was improving. Life at the Ramallah High Schools, according to Jean Zaru's architect brother, Selim, was going through a quiet phase under new leadership.

In the afternoon Friends had reports from the various Quaker Service Agencies, with contributions from Phillippa Neave, Paul Lalor, Rethe McCuthen and Hans Weening. The contribution that really captivated the gathering was given by Paul, who analysed the current situation following the Israeli-Palestinian peace accord. He gave a very pessimistic picture of its outcome. There then followed a very 'heated' open discussion, in which it became apparent that communications between the various Agencies and the Monthly Meetings had been wanting. Some of these failures were not of Friends' making, but were related to the recent civil war or occupation, through which they had lived.

Dinner was held at the Hotel, at the expense of Ramallah Monthly Meeting. It was a great occasion and after it was over most of those present went upstairs to the lounge. However, Henry and I decided to retire early, for we still had to write the Epistle. Violet Zaru and Renee had asked us to complete an early draft before the next morning. Thus, sitting up in our respective beds, we set about our task. It was not easy, for we were aware of the underlying tensions and frustrations of Middle East Yearly Meeting Friends, some of it related to Brummana High School. These we tried to reflect in the Epistle, but adding that there was considerable trust and a fundamental unity. We found a quotation from William Penn (1693), in Quaker Faith and Practice, which we thought was most appropriate for this Epistle. It read; *'Love is the hardest lesson in Christianity, but, for that reason, it should be most our care to learn it'*.

The third and final day of Yearly Meeting started again by considering the relationship between the Friends' Schools, their respective Monthly Meetings and the Quaker Agencies. The contributions became quite acrimonious at times, especially from Tony, who walked out at one point. I, like Henry, became quite uncomfortable and tried to calm things down. How the Recording Clerks managed to get a Minute out of the Session, no one knows. In the lunch hour Henry and I put the finishing touches to the Epistle, with the blessing of the other two Friends and in readiness for the final Session.

In the final Session, Violet Zaru, speaking with feeling and hope, described the work that Quakers started, and are maintaining, in a number of infant schools in the Palestinian refugee camps in the West Bank. It was just the sort of contribution that Friends needed. Finally, the Epistle was presented, and, after some alterations, was eventually accepted. After a Meeting for Worship, Jean Zaru ended the 1995 Middle East Yearly Meeting, which, in my opinion, had not been the happiest of occasions. She suggested that next year it should be held at Brummana.

Being Sunday, Friends gathered in the upper conference room for a Meeting for Worship, in which there was lots of appropriate Ministry, including a first contribution from Phillippa. Meeting over, we all assembled downstairs in the hotel's foyer to pay our dues and say our farewells, before departing. Travelling northwards out of Amman in a taxi, we passed the modern King Abdullah Mosque, with its beautiful magnificent blue mosaic dome. My visit to Amman had been brief and limited, for I was only able to explore in the immediate area of the Hotel.

Philip and I requested that we should stop off at Jerash, but by the time we got there, according to Tony, we were running out of time. I would have to wait for another visit, before I saw its ancient ruins, I thought. We reached Damascus around mid afternoon and booked in at the Sheraton Hotel at reduced rates, three of us sleeping in a twin bedded room, with the extra bed provided. The Hotel was far too expensive for my tastes. By now all of us were very hungry, so Tony took us to a small restaurant in the embassy area of Damascus, where we were served with a full meaty Arab meal. By the time we emerged it was dark.

Back at the Hotel, the lounges were busy with tourists, businessmen, local dignitaries and visitors. Most were men, often traditionally dressed, carrying their hand beads. The whole oriental atmosphere reminded me of an Agatha Christie 'who done it?' People were sitting round in comfortable, well upholstered leather settees, placed on ornate Persian carpets on marbled floors, and surrounded by Byzantine-patterned marble-faced walls. Smartly dressed waiters hustled here and there serving Turkish coffee or other drinks. Some individuals were smoking hookahs. As an exercise in 'man-watching', it was all very absorbing, but was not for us that evening. We retired to our room to watch some Syrian television, before going to bed.

Next morning, after a light continental breakfast, we took a taxi to the entrance to Damascus's ancient souk or the 'Long Market'. In my time, I have visited many souks in Mashrek, but this one was different. It consisted of a long, high-arched covered way, stretching in a straight line for over a quarter of a mile towards Damascus's famous Mosque. In places shafts of light penetrated to the cobbled street below. Side roads entered the concourse. When we entered the souk it was relatively empty, with few shoppers or tourists about and many of the shops still had their shutters down. Tony, it seemed to me, had an insatiable desire to buy things, almost as if it was a game of monopoly. In one small shop, full of oriental wares, I bought a small lacquer covered inlaid box for Patricia, while the other two looked at table cloths. On emerging from this shop, we found a youth hovering about touting for business for his shopkeeper boss. He said a few words in Arabic to Tony, who then told us to follow him.

We dived into a narrow alleyway and up some stairs to the first floor room of a house behind the main throughway. There before us was every conceivable souvenir that any right-minded tourist might want to purchase. Metal wares, coins, inlaid boxes, jewellery, table cloths, you name it, and it was on display. It was like entering Aladdin's cave. The owner ordered some Turkish coffee and we settled down to bargaining. Tony was in his element and seemed to me to be an expert bargainer. The sky seemed the limit. Having little money left at the end of my visit, I sat back, watched and marvelled. Eventually, having made a few purchases, we returned to the main street, which, by then, was bustling with people. This was the Arab world I had experienced and remembered from my youth in Tripoli. We walked on towards the Mosque.

The Long Market ended abruptly just before the Great Mosque, with a Roman arcade of Corinthian pillars. The side stalls were now selling Islamic religious books and tracts, along with cassette tapes of the Koran. There was a constant movement of people, with some small huddles of heavily veiled women, all in black, sitting in the side walks. People were entering a heavy, wooden, arched door, which was part of the main gate to the Mosque. We did likewise. On entering, we were momentarily overpowered by the glare from the sun reflecting off the predominantly white stone work of the walls and paved courtyard opposite the Mosque.

The Great Mosque of Damascus is considered to be the fourth most holy site in the Moslem world. Originally the Christian basilica of St. John, it was taken over by the Moslems in the eighth century and converted into a mosque. The extensive and beautiful mosaics over the main entrance showed Byzantine influences, with no human or animal figures depicted. Around mid-day we took off our shoes and entered the Mosque.

The whole floor area of the Mosque was covered with Persian carpets, on which small groups of people, some worshipping, others, mostly women and children, having picnics. Two central columns of Romanesque pillars supported the roof. There was no focal point, for the central shrine of St.John the Baptist had long since been removed, and much of the original splendour of the interior had been destroyed by fires started by the Mongols. The plain wall contrasted with the carpets and the stained glass windows. We lingered a while and listened to the chanting of the Koran, and watched some male chanters rocking themselves into an emotional frenzy, with tears in their eyes. I decided that they were members of some Islamic sect. The whole atmosphere of the place captivated me. It had been memorable visit.

Out again into the bright sunlight, we walked back through the souk to take a taxi back to the Hotel. After a light lunch, we set off by taxi to Brummana. Our taxi driver this time spoke reasonable English; he was an Armenian, who guided us through the border check points without difficulty. Soon after entering Lebanon, we passed the road to the Arab Umayyad settlement ruins at Aanjar, where Tony and Jocelyn had taken me early on in my visit and I had spent a happy afternoon exploring with them. Our driver drove fast, too fast for Tony's liking, but it did mean that we were back at Brummana by early evening for a much welcome meal.

By now, I felt that my mission was completed and all that remained to do was to say thank you to all who had cared for me. I was aware of the tremendous support I had received from Patricia, members of the family, Friargate Friends, along with those involved in QPS. I had been swamped with love and kindness by Brummana Friends, for which I will always be grateful. At a highly emotional farewell party, I was presented with an engraved silver plate and a large ornate, deep blue tablecloth, which had been given to us both. On April 6th, very early in the morning, I flew out of Beirut and returned to Britain. My beloved Patricia was waiting for me on York station. I was really pleased to see her.

A young starred agama. Drawn by MICHAEL THOMPSON

CHAPTER VIII

The Quaker Natural History Tour 1996

A SEED SOWN TAKES TIME to germinate, and so it is with ideas. At the end of the 1990 Woodbrooke Holy Land Tour, David Gray asked me if I would like to lead a future journey with him, adding a natural history dimension. Years went by and nothing happened; I had lost contact with David. However, we met again in 1995 soon after I had returned from Lebanon. Quite quickly we realised that another Quaker tour to Al Mashrek was possible, and we started planning for one in 1996. We exchanged letters and I went up to Richmond for two planning meetings at the Grays' home. We decided that we would call it a Quaker Near East Natural History Tour, and soon we were booking places to stay in Israel and Jordan. Because of the Peace Treaty between Jordan and Israel, it was now possible for us to take a party of Friends to Jordan for the first time. We placed the final arrangements for the tour with Mr. Rezik Petro of Atic Tours, a Palestine based company in East Jerusalem. In October 1995, we placed an advertisement in The Friend, which brought a positive response from 26 Quakers, but at the final count there were 16 in the party. We all met at Friargate Meeting in January 1996, so that introductions could be made, plans shared and information given. David and I knew most of the participants, but some Friends were new to us. One such person was Stan Murrell of Welwyn Garden City Meeting. Stan was a retired Professor of Geology from University College London, and he proved to be a tremendous asset on account of his geological knowledge. Eventually, the 14th. of March, the day of departure arrived. Saying goodbye to Patricia on York Station, I boarded a mid-afternoon London-bound train with Joyce Pickard, and there we met David.

We reached London in the middle of the rush hour, and boarding the Piccadilly line to Heathrow with all our luggage was quite an exercise. Once at the airport, the three of us made our way to the El Al reception desk, where we found the rest of the party. As we were going to Israel, passport, customs and security checks were particularly rigorous. David and I, as leaders, were subjected to a more intensive interrogation, and as my passport contained a number of Arab visas, the Israeli officials wanted to know about my background and why I had visited these countries. On emptying my luggage, I had to show a young female Israeli my bat detector, which she found very interesting. It turned out that she had a degree in zoology and was aware of such an instrument, but had never seen one before. We sailed through security after that!

There were delays in taking off, so some of us had a meal. Once on board, I found myself sitting next to Moira Thomson, of Berkhampstead Meeting; the booking staff had probably assumed that we were related. One small incident before take-off attracted our attention. An ultra-orthodox Jew, with his curly sideboards and skull cap, refused to stow away his luggage, for, according to him, it contained some important papers. He almost came to blows with the senior cabin steward, a secular Jew, who took it from him forcibly and stowed it away in a locker. It seemed to me to be an element of obsessional obstinacy in the Orthodox Jew's behaviour. The cabin was stuffy, and the aircraft full. Two members of the party fainted soon after take-off, and I was particularly concerned about Hugh Maw. By dawn, after some of us had grabbed some sleep, we found we were flying over the Israeli coastline and soon afterwards landed smoothly at Ben Gurion airport. It took the group over an hour to get through the security formalities, with some more in-depth questioning. Eventually, on reaching the airport restaurant for a light breakfast, we were met by Romano, a representative from Atic Tours, who made us most welcome. David and I sat with him for a while to discuss the day's activities. Waiting on the departure lounge forecourt was a minibus, ready to take the party north towards Haifa.

In spite of overnight fatigue, everyone was very cheerful and raring to go. Our driver, an Arab with Israeli citizenship, drove us north along the main highway, passing through densely populated areas. We asked him to take us to Me'agan Michel, a fish-farming kibbutz on the coastline renowned for its wildlife. I had last visited the kibbutz in 1982 with Mother and Father, but that was only a fleeting visit. This time, however, was different, for we were able to stay longer, and also to explore more widely, in spite of there being some restrictions because it was Friday, the Jewish Sabbath. Some of the workers were out collecting fish from one of the lagoons, but most of the area was deserted.

The minibus was parked and the group walked down a well marked path along the edge of a small river, on which there was an old Ottoman mill. We were soon in a reed bed, and, suddenly, we were surrounded by birds. I saw my first penduline tits *Remiz pendulinus*, flitting around in the upper reed bed canopy. From nowhere, three Indian mongooses *Herpestes ichneumon* appeared; a common species, I later learned, in Israel. Next to the bus park were some hewn-out rock burial caves, over which several mature starred agama lizards *Laudakia stellio* were scrambling. We asked the driver to take us down to the beach, for David and I had promised Friends that we would show them the Med, the Dead, the Red and the Sea of Galilee. There before us, was a stretch of untouched sand dunes and a wide expanse of the beautiful blue Mediterranean. The sea was gently undulating, its surface occasionally broken by a white plume whipped up by an onshore breeze. Inland was a mixture of used and unused fish ponds, some of which were covered with wire netting to keep out the grey herons *Ardea cinerea* and the little egrets *Egretta garzetta*. Among the dunes were several coastal flower species, including the honeywort *Cerinthe major*. Hugh Maw, along with Brenda and Pat Alexander, were already beginning to put together a flower list. There were rafts of ducks on the lagoons, mainly mallard *Anas platyrhynchos*, wigeon *Anas penelope* and teal *Anas crecca*. Before the party departed, a pair of marsh harriers *Circus aeruginosus* was sighted feeding on a dead seagull.

Lunch was taken at a picnic site in the Carmel National Park. Sitting on park benches, below some Aleppo pines *Pinus halepensis*, and surrounded by bunches of of wild cyclamen *Cyclamen persicum* emerging through pine needle ground cover, Friends had a much needed rest and a meal. Nearby, the botanists identified several species of orchid, including the greater butterfly orchid *Plananthera chorantha* and yellow bee orchid *Ophrys lutea*. In the middle distance, two mature Judas trees *Cercis silquastrum* were in full bloom. The meal over, it was decided to make for the Church of Scotland Hostel at Tiberias without delay. Dropping down from Mount Carmel, we saw the northern end of the Yizrael Valley and Acre in the distance. Immediately before us was the extensive oil refinery, established initially by the Iraq Petroleum Company in the inter war years. I had not seen the refinery since the 1940s, when, as a boy, I had watched from Mount Carmel as it was bombed by Axis Power aircraft.

For me, it was a great pleasure to be back at the Hostel, but for most of the party it was their first visit. Quite quickly we found our rooms and were soon absorbing the friendliness and spiritual atmosphere of the place. David and I were allocated a room overlooking the Sea of Galilee. Here, at last, we were able to relax and take in the fact that we had reached our first objective, Tiberias, without a hitch. Supper over, Friends collected in an upper room and settled into a deep and very meaningful Meeting for Worship. This was followed by a discussion on the day's events and plans for the following day. David asked John Harvey if he would manage the Tour's incidental expenses. Botanical and bird lists were started. along with comments about other animals. The meeting over, we retired to our rooms; on the way back I noticed a number of small Turkish geckos *Hemidactylus turcicus* crawling over the upper walls of the communal balcony feeding on small insects.

Next day we awoke at dawn to experience, yet again, the rising sun coming up from behind the Golan Heights, casting a brilliant yellow shaft of light across the water. Silhouetted against the light were mature eucalyptus trees, planted in the Hostel grounds. The birds were beginning to sing; there was the cooing of palm doves *Streptopelia senegalensis*, the loud penetrating call of the pied kingfisher *Ceryle rudis* and the rasping chat of the hooded crows *Corvus corone cornix*. Friends were refreshed from a good night's sleep and, after breakfast, they piled into a bus provided by the Nazareth Bus Company. David, on a previous visit, had acquired some old military maps, which gave more details of the surrounding countryside and its topography. We decided to walk the whole length of Nahr Amud, starting at the village of Amrin, high up in the Galilean hills. After negotiating several hairpin bends, the driver

141

dropped the party in the village, leaving us at its war memorial. Below us and to the south we could see the Nahr Amud gorge, but finding the right path down proved to be difficult. Eventually, in ideal weather conditions, we found a farm track going south, having lost an hour of our valuable walking time.

Initially, walking on the track was easy, surrounded by a great variety of spring wild flowers, low shrubs and a rocky terrain. The track petered out to become a footpath, surrounded by thorny bushes; progress was slow, but ahead we could see the main road between Acre and Galilee. By now the sun was high in the sky, and conditions were becoming very warm. Finding what shade they could, Friends settled down to a picnic lunch and, with Alison Bush's help, treated their developing blisters. There was still a long way to go, and it became obvious that David and I had not read the scale of the maps correctly. David, concerned that we might miss the bus waiting for us on the main road next to the bat caves, decided to press ahead, leaving me to guide the party down to the rendezvous.

To begin with, all went well. We crossed the main road, and then plunged down into the main Nahr Amud gorge, following a stream. The high cliffs of the gorge came into sight. Geologically they were very interesting and Stan Murrell explained to us how they came about. We had to cross and re-cross the stream, which slowed us up. However, there were times to look up and admire the scenery, the wildflowers and the numerous birds nesting in the cliffs; these included colony-nesting lesser kestrels *Falco naumanni*, alpine swifts *Apus melba tuneti*, along with several long-legged buzzards *Buteo rufinus* circling on rising thermals. At some stage we missed the path, and, instead of continuing down the gorge, the party walked up on to the western edge, towards a well-established kibbutz. The pace quickened, and from there we could see our parked bus. I raced ahead, waving my arms to attract the attention of the driver, for I had no idea if David had reached him. These were some anxious moments for me. Within 200 yards of our reaching the bus, David appeared, much to my relief. I knew the party was getting tired and I did not want them to have to walk the remaining miles back to Tiberias. David, as far as I was concerned, had shown real leadership. Friends had walked too far on their first full day in Galilee, but none seemed to complain for they had experienced walking in the beautiful Galilean hills. That evening, after supper and Meeting for Worship, some Friends joined me in the Hostel's garden to look for bats, using my bat detector. I identified several pipistrelle bats *Pipistrellus kuhlii*, along with a larger unidentified species, flying among the trees.

There was no 'Jesus boat' available for Friends. When we arrived at the quayside at Ginnosar, David discovered there had been a booking failure and our party was not expected. He had asked for a boat to take the group across the Sea of Galilee to Ein Gev, but somehow our tour operators had failed to book one. This meant delays, while alternative arrangements were made. Friends sat around enjoying the sun, whereas I explored the quay itself which was made up boulders and a tarmac path to the boat staging posts. It was an ideal habitat for reptiles. Sunning themselves and preying on ants, were several species of lizard, including a fan-tailed gecko *Ptyodactylus puiseuxi*. Among the rocks a small snake appeared, which I eventually identified as Dahl's whip snake *Coluber rubriceps*. It was similar to the one I had caught in Tripoli in 1955. Eventually, a boat arrived and Friends stepped aboard.

These Jesus boats are meant to be replicas of those found on the Sea of Galilee two thousand years ago, but how authentic the design was is difficult to say. Unlike the 1990 Woodbrooke Holy Land Tour, this time we had the boat to ourselves. The Sea was completely calm and the engines were cut once we were in the middle of the lake; Friends settled into a Meeting for Worship. The deep silence and the lapping of the water on the boat's sides was broken only by ministry from David. The skipper and his mate, I suspect, were taken aback by our form of worship, but duly issued each one of us with a small certificate stating that we had worshipped on the Sea of Galilee.

Owing to the misunderstanding, we did not go to Ein Gev, but landed at Capernaum instead. Cruising close to the shoreline, David and Hugh Maw pointed out various landmarks, including the Arbel Valley, where Jesus would have walked on his way to Jerusalem, and the basilica on the Sermon on the Mount site. There were large rafts of tufted duck *Authya fuligula* to be seen, a regular passage migrant at this time of the year on the Sea, along with a small colony of pygmy cormorants *Phalacrocrax pygmeus*. Friends

143

did not linger at Capernaum, but boarded the bus, which had been brought round from Ein Gev.

The route to Gamla, on the Golan Heights, went past the reed beds at the north end of the Sea of Galilee, where the River Jordan enters the Sea. It seemed to me to be an ideal place for wildlife, but there was no time to linger. Once on the Heights, the road climbed steeply to a vantage point overlooking northern Galilee. It was from this point, we were told, that the Syrian army shelled the Israeli settlements in the valley below, before it was captured by the Israelis in the Seven Days War. We were now in Israeli occupied Syria. Gamla, a National Nature Reserve, situated on the Rift Valley escarpment, was a popular place for visitors, especially school children. Visitors came to see the raptors and the archaeology, for on a small wedge-shaped hillside spur, jutting out from the main escarpment, the Zealots had a fortified settlement, which eventually fell to the Roman legionnaires in CE 67. Leaving the visitors' centre, Friends walked the short distance to the cliffs and marvelled at what they saw. Small stone plaques at the viewing point, explained in several languages a brief history of the site. It was not long before the first of the breeding griffon vultures *Gyps fulvus* appeared, sailing past on an up-current of air coming off the cliffs. I wondered at the effortless flight of such a large bird, which was joined later by an Egyptian vulture *Neophron pernopterus* and a pair of long-legged buzzards *Buteo rufinus*. The hour came and went, leaving no time to explore the rest of the site. At the visitors' centre, Friends noticed parties of mainly Ethiopian-Jewish, teenaged school girls being collected together by their armed guards. Joyce went up to one of the guards and asked him why it was necessary to carry arms, to which he replied, 'All Arabs are terrorists and the girls need to be protected from terrorists'. His opinions seemed fixed and he could not see that there were two sides to the conflict.

There was still time to return to the Sea, so climbing back on the bus David asked the driver to take us to the St. Peter Primacy site on the foreshore. As was usual with such Jesus sites, it was crowded with visitors and pilgrims, so it was difficult to get the atmosphere of the place. After several photographs were taken of the bronze statue showing Peter kneeling before Jesus, in which Jesus asks Peter to feed his sheep (John 21), Friends moved on.

There now seemed an opportunity to visit the bat caves in Nahr Amud, which the party had failed to reach on the previous day. On stopping at a lay-by near the site, the party split into two, with several Friends coming with David and me. At the cave entrance there was a Nature Reserve Authority (NRA) notice board prohibiting entry, in order not to disturb the bats. Having come so far, I decided that we should have a fleeting visit, just to see what had happened in the intervening years since 1990. From my estimation the number of Egyptian fruit bats *Rousettus aegyptiacus* had trebled. It was obvious that the NRA was doing all it could to protect Israel's bats, especially the fruit bat.

It was six years earlier that David and I had visited the Hula National Nature Reserve, but on that occasion we arrived too late! This time we made sure that a visit to Hula was part of the group's itinerary. After following the main road along the western shore of the Sea of Galilee, the route turned up into the Galilean hills passing east of the Arab hill town of Safad, where Rifka Ghantous, who had helped in our household, originally came from. On reaching the crest of the hill we looked back, and I had a wonderful panoramic view of the Sea, its foreshore and the surrounding countryside.

> *In simple trust like theirs who heard,*
> *Beside the Syrian Sea,*
> *The gracious calling of the Lord,*
> *Let us, like them, without a word,*
> *Rise up and follow thee.*

> *O Sabbath rest by Galilee*
> *O calm of hills above,*
> *Where Jesus knelt to share with thee*
> *The silence of eternity,*
> *Interpreted by love.*

I am reliably told that John Whittier, the Quaker journalist and anti-slave campaigner, never visited Galilee, but in his famous poem he captures, for me, the whole prevailing atmosphere of the place particularly in the middle two verses.

It seems to me, that the only authentic 'Jesus scenes' are in the Galilean hills, and that his philosophy and teachings were rurally based, not urban, as they later became.

145

Eventually, the bus plunged down into the northern end of the great Syrian-African rift valley. Now travelling along a modern road, we could see a number of small settlements, and Qiryat Shemona, the Israeli frontier town, which is subjected to frequent rocket attacks from south Lebanon, though on that day all was quiet. Parking under a stand of eucalyptus trees outside the entrance to the Hula Reserve, Friends paid their fees and entered. Hula, in Mandate days, was a huge swamp, but the Israelis, after conquest of the area, drained most of it for farming. The swamp, according to Father, was a source of malaria, and that was another reason for draining it. Conservationists had fought hard to save about 10% of the original area, and it was this remnant that the party was visiting. Walking along a well-maintained gravel footpath, Friends soon reached a north-facing, viewing platform. There were birds everywhere, producing a cacophony of various calls. Immediately in front of the platform there was a mixed adult and juvenile night heron *Nycticorax nycticorax* roost, along with a small party of marbled teal *Marmaronetta angustirostris* swimming on one of the many small canals that criss-cross the Reserve. I was particularly pleased to see the ducks, which are indigenous to the area. A loudly-spoken American guide, who knew his birds, was showing a party round, so some of us attached ourselves to his party and learned a great deal about Hula's birds. Situated in the middle of the Reserve there is a large observation tower, and from it we had a magnificent view of the whole area. It was from there that the group saw a large eagle get up and flap across the top of the extensive papyrus reed beds. It was one of several white-tailed eagles *Haliaeetus albicilla* to be found round Hula, part of a successful captive-release programme. Moving on, there were swamp turtles *Mauremys caspica rivulata* sunning themselves on swamp debris, and, in the areas of open water, white pelicans *Pelecanus onocrotalus*, that breed successfully on the Reserve. By over-draining the Hula swamp, the Israelis have interfered with the region's hydrology, thus leading to a down-turn in agricultural production. Therefore, there has been a marginal increase of the swamp area, but, in spite of that increase, Hula is subjected to other pressures, such as increased urbanisation and tourism. In the N.R.A. leaflet on Hula, I found the following quotation -

'Everything I created, I created for you. Take care not to damage or destroy my world, because the damage you do, no one can repair' (Midrash).

There were heavy clouds over Mount Hermon, so it was not visible, and by the time Friends had climbed down from the bus at Nimrod Castle's car park, having passed through Qiryat Shemona to get there, it was beginning to rain. This was my second visit to the Crusader castle that dominated the countryside, with magnificent views from its upper ramparts. It was built in the late eleventh century and captured by Moslem forces in CE 1156. A recent earthquake, which made some of the masonry unsafe, caused access to the upper ramparts to be prohibited. Heavy rain was now driving Friends to take shelter before returning to the bus. Disappointed with the visit to Nimrod, we decided, with the passing of the rain, that there was time to walk down to the now swollen river, one of the sources of the Jordan. Situated below Nimrod, the small river plunged over a waterfall into a small gorge. It was then that some of the party noticed a singing lark sitting on a fence. It proved to be a male calandra lark *Melanocorypha calandra*. For the ornithologists, this was an exciting find. By now, it was time to return to Tiberias, for a rest and an opportunity to explore the town's water front and shops.

David and I were full of anticipation on the day we ventured into Jordan, for, in a sense, we were moving into unknown territory. I, of course, had been to Amman in the previous year when I attended Middle East Yearly Meeting, but that was only a fleeting visit. Before we set off from the Hostel, along with other Friends, we watched a pair of Palestine sunbirds *Nectarina osea* building a nest near the door to the refectory. The oval-shaped nest of closely woven fibres, lined with small feathers, was suspended from a drooping branch of a flowering shrub. The highly coloured male and drab female seemed unaffected by human beings moving about; and many of us were able to get photographs of the birds. However, on that morning, much to the distress of the sunbirds, a yellow-vented bulbul *Pycnonotus xanthopygos* was observed robbing the nest of its materials. Leaving behind the sunbirds and the kind hospitality of the staff of the Church of Scotland Hostel, the party joined the bus to go to the King Hussein Bridge border crossing into Jordan. The plan was to reach the crossing by midday.

147

David, having obtained the R.S.P.B. video *Gosney in Israel* and looked at it at home, suggested that Friends would like to visit kibbutz Kapar Ruppin, for it was apparently a good place to see birds. The kibbutz, situated in the northern lower Jordan valley, was next to the Israeli-Jordan border. Founded in the early days of the state of Israel, Kapar Rippin consisted of a well-established farm complex, containing extensive fish ponds and a large dairy herd. It was the fish pond that attracted the birds. The settlement consisted of predominantly single storey, flat roofed dwellings, surrounded by administrative and community buildings, mature shrubs and eucalyptus trees. In spite of feeling uncomfortable, we asked our Arab driver to take us to the reception centre, where we arrived unannounced. We were made very welcome, paid our dues, and were provided with a guide, Chuck.

Chuck, who originally came from Czechoslovakia, was a short, stocky man in his late seventies, who spoke English with a mid-European accent. He had come to Palestine at the end of the Second World War as an illegal immigrant, and once there helped to smuggle in more Jewish immigrants into the Mandate from Europe, in spite of the British Navy's blockade. In telling his story, he expressed a lot of anti-British sentiments, some of which I found difficult to accept. Knowing, through my parents, the difficulties Britain had after the War in keeping the peace between the conflicting parties, I nearly walked out on Chuck. However, once Chuck had got his version of history 'off his chest', I found him, like the others, a likeable personality, with a wonderful sense of humour. He then told us about the kibbutz and suggested where we should go to see the birds, touring the area in our bus.

Accompanied by Chuck and travelling along dusty, unmade farm tracks, past numerous cows at feeding troughs, we reached the fish ponds. Immediately, we realised that Kaper Ruppin, as stated in the ornithological guides, was an excellent place to watch birds. The kibbutz was literally right up against the Israeli-Jordanian border wire, which was on the Israeli side of the River Jordan. Beyond we could see Jordanian watch towers, manned by Jordanian soldiers. Having completed a circular tour, the party returned to the reception area and said good-bye to Chuck, whom we thanked. It seemed from what Friends said to me afterwards that they were

148

pleased to have had the Israeli side of the conflict told to them. On Chuck's advice, the party walked back to the fish ponds. It was an ornithological feast. Not only were there numerous birds, but also a great variety of species. Dominating the scene were migrating white storks *Ciconia ciconia*, taking off or landing on one of the disused, partially drained, fish ponds. Mixed with them were a few of the rarer black storks *Ciconia nigra*, many little egrets, a few grey herons and the first spoonbills *Platalea leucorodia* recorded on the tour. Waders were represented by red shank *Tringa totanus*, green sandpiper *Tringa ochropus* and common sandpiper *Actitis hypoleucos*. Again, as was observed at Ma'agan Michel, there were black-winged stilts *Himanitopus himanitopus* and spur-winged plovers *Hoplopterus spinosus* present. To the party's delight, three ospreys *Pandion haliatus* were seen, one carrying a fish in its talons. Finally, a black francolin *Francolinus francolinus* crossed the road in front of the bus, just as Friends were leaving Kaper Ruppin.

Waiting for us on the Jordanian side of the King Hussein Bridge border crossing was Gus. Gus, whose full name was Ghussan Oweis, was to be our Jordanian guide for the tour in Jordan. Of medium height, with dark hair and moustache, and wearing a light grey suit, some of us wondered if he was going to take us round the wilder parts Jordan in that attire. But no, he soon changed into the appropriate clothing once the tour got underway,and he spoke excellent English; we all warmed to Gus. He conducted us quickly through the custom formalities, and almost immediately Friends began to relax; the tensions of Israel were lifting. It was at this border post that the first major failure in the organisation of the tour occurred. The bus to take us to Amman did not arrive. Gus hurriedly made alternative arrangements; five taxis were hired. Travelling three or four to a taxi, the party headed south and then east towards Amman. I travelled with Jane and John Harvey.

Travelling at speed along poor quality roads, with quiet Arab music coming from the car radio, we passed a lot of poverty-striken, ribbon development, and inadequately constructed houses belonging, I assumed, to Palestinian refugees. The largest number of Palestinian refugees living outside Palestine, we were told, is to be found in Jordan, with the largest concentrations along the Jordan- Israel border. By the time the small convoy reached the eastern Rift Valley escarpment, the roads had improved. We stopped there briefly for a leg stretch and a panoramic view of the Rift. It was not long before the taxis were driving through the outskirts of Amman, passing areas of affluence before reaching the Manar Hotel, located in the Shmeisani district. Some would say that the city was becoming more and more westernised. We certainly did not see the poor areas in Amman, centred round the Palestinian refugee camps.

The release of tension that David and I experienced on booking in and retiring to our hotel room, was palpable. We had achieved another objective. We rested awhile, before joining Gus and Mr. Yousef Atieyh of Atic Tours in the hotel foyer, to discuss the Jordanian itinerary, and plans for the next day.

There was still time before the evening meal for David and me to explore the older parts of Amman. We hired a taxi, but somehow the taxi driver, thought we wanted to go to the Philadelphia Hotel, where Middle East Yearly Meeting was held in 1995. Having arrived at the Hotel entrance, we eventually persuaded him that it was the Graeco-Roman theatre that we wanted to see. Built originally as part of the Graeco-Roman city of Philadelphia, the near-perfect theatre could seat up to six thousand people. The stone work glowed yellow in the light of the setting sun. We scrambled up one of the aisles to the upper seating to get a better view of old Amman. Mixed in with some recent buildings were many from an earlier time, especially the Ottoman period. On the opposite slope was a mosque. We lingered a while, taking in the scene, before returning to our Hotel for supper and the end our first day in Jordan.

Jerash is a colossal Graeco-Roman site, one that has to be seen to be believed. This visit was to be more thorough than the previous occasion in 1995. Friends were driven north from Amman, crossing the River Zarga. Gus asked the Jordanian driver to stop the luxury air-conditioned coach next to the bridge crossing the river. The river looked polluted, and, according to Gus, river pollution was a major problem in Jordan as the country became industrialised. Water shortages were always present, especially as several of Jordan's underground aquifers were drying up or becoming salinated. The Zarga valley, Gus told us, played an important part in the military exploits of Lawrence of Arabia in the final phases of the Arab revolt.

To gain entrance to the metropolis at Jerash, the party passed through the South Gate, but not before seeing Hadrian's Arch and one of the best examples of a Roman hippodrome in the ancient world. Jerash, its name derived from the Roman word Gerasa, is a fine example of a Roman provincial city, with its colonades, streets, theatres and buildings well preserved. Gus first took Friends to the Temple of Zeus, built on a small hillock overlooking the site, which was founded by the Romans in 1st. century BCE. One of the most remarkable features of this Decapolis city is its elliptical forum, surrounded by Corinthian columns, some of which had been re-erected and restored. The columns indicated the Hellenistic influences in Jerash. The Temple, like other structures on the site, was partially destroyed by earthquakes, so that, in places, it was a jumble of fallen columns and masonry. We then walked over to the South Theatre, and Gus showed the party three ruined Byzantine churches built in the sixth century CE. Of these, I found the Church of St. John the Baptist the most interesting, particularly its mosaic frieze showing the images of the local fauna and flora present at that time, such as lions and elephant, which, of course, are now extinct in Jordan. The ornithologist amongst us noted crested larks *Gelerida cristata* and desert wheatears *Oenanthe deserti* in among the ruins, along with house martins *Delichon urbica* flying overhead. I watched a fan-toed gecko *Ptyodactylus puiseuxi* on some fallen masonry; it was more blue and darker than the one I saw a Ginnosar in Galilee.

The Temple of Artemis was, in its time, one of the most important on the site. Artemis, a many breasted goddess of love, was in Roman mythology the daughter of Zeus and her influence spread wide in the Roman world, with Ephesus being the centre of her worship. The ruined Temple at Jerash is known for its standing Corinthian columns, which formed part of the portico. We explored its inner sanctum and marvelled at what we saw. Then on to the North Theatre where Gus sat us down on one of the upper tiers and explained about life in Roman Jerash. On the opposite hill we could see modern Jerash. Sharing the theatre with Friends was a party of singing, clapping school children, mostly dressed in their blue uniforms. Gus told us that they were singing the praises of

151

King Hussein, their much loved monarch. Before leaving Jerash, we looked at the Nymphaeum and its elaborate fountain systems, the chariot wheel markings on the paved main street, the Roman equivalent of a zebra crossing, and a building called the Cathedral, which in Roman times was a temple; after Constantine's conversion to Christianity in the fourth century CE, it had become the Byzantine Church of St. Theodore.

The ornithological guide books suggested that Dibbin National Park was worth a visit, as it was the last remaining natural forest in Jordan, mostly of the pine *Pinus halepensis*, evergreen oaks and Arbutus or strawberry trees. Our driver, Traseen, knew exactly where to take Friends, but, unfortunately, it was not what we had imagined it to be. Driving through hilly countryside, predominantly of fruit trees and olive groves, we landed up at a picnic site just off one of the roads in the National Park. It was obviously well used by picnickers, judging by the amount of litter. Friends decided to stay, have their lunch and then explore the forest, which was surprisingly deserted, with few birds about and the occasional unidentified lizard. Walking through the silent trees, with a light, cool breeze blowing, I explored the immediate area with Anne Strauss We identified a scrub warbler *Scotocera inquieta* and found some squirrel-nibbled cones, probably chewed by the Persian squirrel *Sciurus anomalus,* the only squirrel species to be found in this part of Jordan.

Disappointed, the party re-boarded the coach and returned to Amman. Back at the hotel, after a rest, David and I went to visit the local Bird Garden. There were few birds on display and some of them , such as a long-legged buzzard, were in cages that were far too small. We were amused when we came across some caged domestic hens labelled as 'local chickens'. The gardens were used by local residents, including courting couples. It surprised us, knowing the Islamic traditions about seeing women in public, that such an activity was going on.

The journey to D'ana was a long one. I had always wanted to go to D'ana, especially after reading about it in Guy Montford's book *A Portrait of a Desert,* published in 1965. Thus, when planning the Jordan itinerary with David, a visit to D'ana became a high priority. The party set off from the Manar Hotel early, having been welcomed aboard the Jett coach by Gus and Traseen. Traseen, who had few words of English, was to be our bus driver for the rest of our stay in Jordan; he was a cheerful character with a broad smile. We learned that his son had been ill and had to be admitted to hospital. Traseen, in spite of his anxiety, dutifully stayed with the party. Driving through some of the richer suburbs of Amman, we soon reached the King's Highway so called because, over the centuries, kings and rulers had used the route to go south. As we drove along, Gus expounded at length on various Old Testament tribes, such as the Ammonites, Moabites and Edomites; modern Amman derives its name from the Ammonites who settled the area. He wanted to stop off at Madaba to show us its ancient map, but that would have to wait for another visit for we wanted to get to D'ana. By the time we reached Wadi Heidan, the country was becoming more arid, with a few isolated settlements. The next wadi en route could be described as Jordan's equivalent to the Grand Canyon; Wadi Majib was vast. The party stopped at the top of the northern escarpment to see a multi-hairpinned, snake-like road plunging down into the wadi bottom. By now, there was little vegetation to see, only the occasional oasis associated with a mountain spring. From the parapet of the viewing point, a single male blackstart *Cercomela melanura* could be seen flitting among some boulders, along with a brown-necked raven *Corvus ruficolis* sitting on a large rock. Traseen pulled the coach up at Karak for our next stop for a leg stretch, photo call, drinks and conveniences. On the opposite side of the valley, Friends could see Crusader castle, built at the beginning of the twelfth century CE by King Baldwin the First of Jerusalem, but taken by Saladin by the end of that century. The party did not stay long, but long enough for Joyce to try smoking a hookah!

Somehow we missed the road to D'ana Nature Reserve, but, instead, arrived at a car park overlooking the village of D'ana. Looking down on the village from our vantage point, we could see that its mud and wattle houses, with their flat, sand-covered roofs, were all huddled together on a cliff edge overlooking Wadi D'ana. The settlement looked like a large, multi-cracked mudflat. Friends walked down the slope to the village, passing a villager going up the hill on his baying donkey. In the distance, a beautiful male blue rock thrush *Monticola solitarius* was heard singing its repetitive fluty call from a high rock. On reaching the village, we were welcomed by the cheerful, often ill-clad children, while the adults stood by, often in doorways, wondering who we were. The central village well gushed forth its drinkable cold water, and several Friends satisfied their thirst. We reached the village edge and peered into the wadi below. The scenery was stunning. Unfortunately, there was no time to linger.

With fresh instructions, Traseen soon located the Nature Reserve. Gus had not been there before and did not know of its existence. Parking at the upper car park next to the visitors' centre, we all waited for the shuttle to arrive. From the parapet, Friends could see it approaching in the distance, kicking up dust from the sandy track that climbed up to the car park. The shuttle was a multi-coloured pickup truck, which seated twelve people, but somehow managed to take aboard the whole party, including Traseen and Gus. In the distance, we could see the encampment of white tents which was our destination. To our delight we were greeted by Michael Appleton, a young English ecologist, who had been seconded to the Jordanian Royal Society of Nature by the British-based Fauna and Flora International. He was helping on the Reserve, and when he heard that a British party was coming, he made a special effort to be there to greet us. The Reserve was officially opened by the Jordanian Government in 1990, although the Guy Mountford expedition had recommended that it should become a reserve as far back as 1963. Funded by the World Wide Fund for Nature, the Reserve, according to Michael Appleton, was being run according to best practice, thus avoiding, it was hoped, the mistakes made by other major reserves in the area. There were simple camping facilities available, but conditions were spartan, with limited visitor access being enforced. D'ana Reserve covered over 300 sq. kilometres, and stretched from the Rift escarpment to Wadi Araba in the west. The mountainous terrain was rugged, at least in the areas that Friends walked through. At one time, the vegetation was over grazed by domestic goats and the local Bedouins had to be compensated for loss of livelihood when the goats were removed.

Michael, who accompanied us, introduced us to one of the Jordanian guides, who took us on a short guided tour, limited by time. Many features were pointed out to us, including a purple flowering shrub *Globulavia alypum* which is indigenous to the area. Besides seeing kestrels *Falco tinnunculus*, short-toed eagles *Circaetus gallicus* and rock martins *Pytonoprogne fuligula* flying among the crags, we were all surprised to hear a European cuckoo *Cuculus canorus* calling. According to Michael, a few turn up every year. Both footprints and discarded quills of the Indian crested porcupine *Hystrix indica* were seen. The guide told us that there was a pack of wolves *Canis lupus* on the Reserve. Everyone wanted to stay longer, but by now the setting sun was casting our long shadows across some of the large, smooth-faced boulders. We returned to our coach in the shuttle, having thanked Michael Appleton and the Jordanian guide for showing us round. The journey in the dark to Petra was uneventful; the party reached Petra Hotel late, but were given a warm welcome.

From soon after dawn in Wadi Mousa, people were stirring. What started as a slow trickle became quite a flow of men and boys on their Arab horses, making their way towards the hotel complexes. They dismounted on some rough, uncultivated ground opposite the Petra Hotel. As the area filled up, I was struck by the similarity to the annual Appleby horse market in Cumbria. The horses and their owners were collecting for the daily tourist rides down the gorge to the historical site at Petra.

The Arab horses collecting opposite the Petra Hotel, Petra, Jordan, 1996.

On Gus's advice, Friends walked the one and half miles to the site. According to Gus, visitors who travelled on horseback missed many interesting features when approaching the gorge. Although historical Petra covers a large area, the number of tourists allowed in at any one time is limited to 1500, thus avoiding the pressures of high numbers. We queued at the entrance gate and, after showing our pre-paid tickets, walked down the slope towards the Siq, the slit-like entrance to the gorge. Before reaching the entrance, Gus pointed out the Nebataean tomb of the Obelisks, its surface stone work much eroded by sand, wind and water. It was the first of many we were to see that day. The party stopped briefly at the souvenir stall at the entrance, and watched the horse drawn, two-wheeled carts going down the gorge. Nearby was the storm barrier created in 1963 to prevent flash floods going down the Siq; it was built after 23 tourists died after such a flood in that year.

Describing the Siq is difficult, for no words do it justice. Its vertical walls, often over 300 feet high, were almost touching in places, so that the gorge became cavernous. Suddenly, it would open up and let the warming sun pour in. The deep red sandstone, often with Nabataean inscriptions, dominated. Water conservation was important for the Nabataeans, and along the sides of the Siq were shallow water channels cut into the rock's surface, along with sections of clay piping. Halfway down the Siq, we came across the nest of a Sinai rose finch *Carpodacus synoicus*, where both birds were busy. At the lower end the gorge narrowed, but through the gap we could see a yellow sandstone structure beyond. The gorge opened up and there before us was the El Knazneh or Treasury, a magnificent, almost complete tomb, carved entirely out of the rock. Except for damage done by vandals, its outer facade showed little sign of erosion. The pillars, the portico, the statues and urns showed strong Graeco-Roman influences. By the time we were looking at its edifice, the area in front of the Treasury was milling with visitors of all nationalities, guides, souvenir stall holders and horses. As I wandered about, I wished I had seen it in its 'undiscovered state' in 1812, as did the Swiss explorer, John Burckhardt, disguised as an Arab, who announced its presence to the Western world. Gertrude Bell, the British orientalist, in 1900 camped alone among the tombs, accompanied by her Arab retainers.

Leaving the Treasury, we walked into an open space, known as the Outer Siq, which was surrounded by tombs of various ages, sizes and designs; the richer the deceased, the more elaborate the tomb. We stopped for a cup of Turkish coffee, served within a natural multi-coloured rock tomb, by a Bedouin woman. We sat cross-legged on mats in the cool chamber, while outside the colourfully dressed Bedouin children played. The rock colours varied according to their mineral content of iron, magnesium and other base metals. Stan explained the geology of Petra, which added another dimension to our visit.

Before reaching the Colonnaded Street, erected in Roman times, the party passed the Nebataean theatre that had been carved out of solid rock. It had been modified by the Romans around 106 CE, when they took control of Petra. Much of the seating had become eroded, but, in its day, the theatre could hold 3,000 people. Higher up and to our right were several of the royal tombs, one of which was converted into a Christian place of worship in the fifth century CE. The Monastery or El Deir was beyond our reach on that day. By now the midday sun was beginning to make conditions uncomfortable, so it was decided to have lunch at a small cafe, sitting under large sunshades near the Triumphal Arch. Nearby, hopping around on the ground was a small party of Creztscmar's buntings *Emberiza caesia*, while scampering among the masonry were several Bosc's lizards *Acanthodactylus boskianus*. There was so much more to see, but it was becoming unbearably hot, so, after a short visit to the museum, Friends returned to the Hotel. Gus continued to tell us all about the site as we made our way back up the shaded Siq. For me, a visit to Petra was a dream come true.

We drove south on our way to Aqaba, but, once out of Wadi Mousa, Gus stopped the coach at a viewing point We looked back to where we had come from; it was almost impossible to work out the entrance to the Petra gorge. No wonder Petra remained undiscovered by European explorers for so long. We were soon on the Desert Highway, a modern road between Amman and Aqaba, which at its southern end ran parallel with the railway line carrying potash to Jordan's only seaport.

The Miramar Hotel was situated on palm-lined King Hussein Street and over looked the port and the Red Sea. From our balcony facing the sea front, David and I could see the port with empty cargo vessels anchored offshore, and old Aqaba with its backdrop of arid mountains. Nearby was a modern mosque, with its tall minaret from which we would hear the daily call to prayer. The whole place had an atmosphere of the Arab orient. With time on our hands, we slipped out of the hotel and made our way to the old Turkish fort, which fell to the Arab tribesmen in CE 1917. It was smaller than I had imagined from Lawrence's description. By now, Friends were becoming seasoned travellers. The sunset that evening was spectacular, silhouetting the ships against the mountains of Egyptian Sinai.

Entering Wadi Rum for the first time was for me a wonderful experience. I had read so much about it over the years, that it was difficult to believe that I was at last there. To get there from Aqaba, Traseen drove us north along the Desert Highway, in a valley with steep rugged mountains on either side, before turning east along a secondary road. The arid terrain had scattered clumps of scrub. Stan asked for a 'geology' halt, so that he could explain to us the rock structure of the mountain range to the north-east. I noticed on a small acacia bush a masked shrike *Lanius nubicus*, on its way, no doubt, to its breeding grounds in the north. Quite quickly, after the stop, we were at the northern end of Wadi Rum.

This was true desert, but desert with a difference. The sand was light red in colour, and from flat bottomed valleys rose massive mountains, with some of their vertical cliffs over two thousand feet in height. Gus stopped the coach again, and there in front of us, in the midday sun, was a small range of mountains called the Seven Pillars of Wisdom, the title of Lawrence's classical description of his desert exploits in the first World War. We counted the Pillars. Rum village was a tourist 'honey pot', as well as being the local headquarters of the Jordanian desert police. To refresh our parched tongues, Friends were ushered into a Bedouin tent, erected on a cement base covered with carpets! There we were offered drinks. Beyond we could see a group of untethered camels of various ages. Above us towered Jabel Rum, reaching almost 6,000 feet. The vertical cliffs and lack of vegetation told me how inhospitable Wadi Rum could be under certain climatic conditions.

Gus thought it was a good idea for the party to visit the local police station. We walked over and stopped at the sentry box. Some of us spoke to the sentry, who was dressed in a dark olive-green ankle length robe uniform, and a white and red chequered kaffiyeh. We returned his greeting in Arabic *'Ahlan wa sahlan'* with our reply *'Ahlan bekum'*. The Arabic inscription over the sentry box, below the black, white and green national flag, was *To God, Country and King*; Gus explained to us that the order of these was important. We passed the box and walked into the camel enclosure. The camels, all belonging to the Royal Jordanian police force, were branded with a royal crown. To travel south further into Wadi Rum, three small four-wheel drive trucks were hired. Friends clambered aboard and set off at high speed, throwing up a considerable cloud of dust behind each vehicle.

The Arabs know Wadi Rum as the Valley of the Moon, for its scenery is what they imagine a moonscape to be like. The flat bottomed valley was covered with a stunted, and sparsely distributed, species of tamarix *Tamarix sp*. After travelling for 15 minutes, the vehicles pulled up next to an isolated Bedouin tent, belonging to a shepherd. There Gus walked over to a large boulder on which were some Nebataean hieroglyphics. He explained that the Nebataeans were originally a nomadic people, who came to control the important trade routes from the east, and thus became powerful and rich. As I listened to Gus, I noticed several lizards scurrying across the sand; they were more Bosc's lizards, like the ones we had seen at Petra, but slightly larger. The extended scales on their feet helped them to travel at speed over soft sand. Our mode of transport left tyre tracks in the sand. Again, I felt I would like to have experienced it in its pristine state, as did Lawrence. He writes in the Seven Pillars of Wisdom on reaching Wadi Rum, *'Our little caravan grew self-conscious, and fell dead quiet, afraid and ashamed to flaunt its smallness in the presence of the stupendous hills'*. We stopped again at a cleft in a massive cliff, from which, in former times, gushed a small spring, now completely dried up. On the lower rocks were more Nebataean drawings and letterings. To quote Lawrence again, *'Lewis explored the cliff, and had reported the spring good to wash in; so to get rid of the dust and strain after my long rides, I went straight up the gully into the face of the hill, along the ruined wall of the conduit by which a spout of water had once run down the ledges to a Nebataean well-house on the valley floor … On the rock bulge above were clear-cut Nebataean inscriptions'.* The view and scenery all round was remote and unspoilt. Nearby, I found a fox scat *Vulpes vulpes*, the same species that we have in Britain. I was much moved by what I saw.

Once back at Rum village, our desert experience was not over. There was still time to visit the village of Disi, which is further east of Rum and at the foot of the Rum mountain range. This visit was not part of our planned itinerary, but proved to be very interesting. Travelling along unmade roads which were not usually marked on tourist maps, we got some idea of what desert life was like. On reaching the village, we were welcomed by the headman, who ushered us into a Bedouin tent and offered Arabic coffee. It was obvious that other tourists had found Disi, for we were not only entertained but also shown numerous souvenirs, including mammalian skulls collected from the surrounding hills. David, and Brenda and Patrick Alexander were particularly delighted by the fact that the local sheikh was a bee-keeper.

Disi, like other oases, depended on spring water, issuing out of the mountain side, though it had more recently been dammed. We walked among the olive trees, and found that there were birds everywhere, among them a single female blue throat *Lusinia svecica* and a pair of blue-cheeked bee-eaters *Merops supercilious*. Friends were shown the portraits of Prince Faisal, who was later to become King Faisal of Iraq, and of Lawrence of Arabia, that had been carved on the surface of a large smooth boulder. I was pleased that this diversion had been suggested, for it showed how human and wildlife could co-exist in such a barren place. By late afternoon, it was time to return to Aqaba, but there was time enough to be able to walk along the sea front before supper. We noted a small flock of house buntings *Emberiza striolata* hopping about on some waste ground, and a single exhausted quail *Coturnix coturnix* that had flown in off the Red Sea on its migratory route north.

Why do people seek out desert places? Having visited Wadi Rum, I think now I have a clearer idea. Until now I had a romantic view of deserts, but now, I know, they are harsh and inhospitable places that sometimes make ultimate demands on human existence. Human beings seek out deserts because it gives them a freedom from everyday living in our overcrowded cities; deserts have space and a timelessness. Patricia and I felt we got a flavour of such an experience when we went trekking with Berber muleteers and mules in Jabel Sahro in Morocco. Jesus sought out such places to renew his relationship with God, as did the early Christian desert fathers.

The Royal Diving School at Aqaba is well worth visiting. Being a free day for the party, some of us chose to visit the School, while others explored the old town, the castle and the Marine Science Station. To get to the School, we had to catch the regular minibus from opposite a neighbouring hotel. Driving south past the docks, where several ocean going cargo boats were being loaded with potash, we soon reached the Diving School that is on the Jordanian side of the border with Saudi Arabia. It was wardened by two helpful British expatriates. The fenced compound was well laid out, with swimming bath, showers, changing rooms, cafe and circular thatched sunshades sheltering groups of chairs. The whole place reminded me of the 1950s beach facilities of the Iraq Petroleum Company beach at Tripoli, Lebanon. Everyone, except me, decided to snorkle on the reef just beyond the foreshore. For some, this was an entirely new experience. Friends had been told not to damage the reef, which was razor sharp in places and could cut their feet. I watched Friends enjoying themselves and decided I had seen a new variety of Quaker; the 'snorkling Friend'. From the same jetty I could see a variety of small colourful fish, as well as several jelly fish *Aurelia aurita*. I then wandered round the compound and watched the Caspian terns *Sterna caspia* and the white-eyed gulls *Larus leucophthalmus* winging their way backwards and forwards just offshore; on some waste ground a single Isabeline wheatear *Oenanthe isabellina* was hopping about. By midday it had become very hot, so after a short snack, we returned to our hotel to meet up with the others, some of whom had been to the Marine Museum.

I had another opportunity to look at some of the tropical fish. While David, John and Patrick decided to try their hand at some windsurfing, others of us hired a small glass-bottomed boat and headed out into the bay. Dodging between some large cargo boats, one of which was noisily hauling up its anchor to tie up at a loading quayside, our dwarfed boat reached some of the coral reefs.

161

Through the glass bottom we could see that many of the reefs had been permanently damaged, and showed little sign of marine life, but others, such as a coral-encrusted sunken barge, were swarming with small, highly coloured tropical fish. Unfortunately, none of us had any means of identifying the fish that we were observing; there was a variety of sponges, large sea cucumbers, and large, black needle-spined sea urchins *Diadema setosum*. These creatures, present in infestation numbers, crawled slowly over the sea bed. I later learned from my friend, Dr. Rupert Ormond of the Department of Biology at York University, that *Diadema setosum* had become a pest species and was, through its boring activities, damaging the reefs, especially at the Egyptian end of the Red Sea. The infestation, according to Rupert, was due to over fishing of the urchins' natural predator. For all of us in the boat, it had been a brief encounter with an underwater paradise. Time passed and we had to return to our moorings, but not before we admired Aqaba, with its back drop of mountains, in the golden light of a late afternoon's setting sun.

By the time our party was ashore, David and the others had finished windsurfing. David and I went into old Aqaba to a book shop, which we found closed, but would open in an hour. We decided, therefore, to have some Turkish coffee at a wayside cafe. Sitting out on the pavement, we watched the Arab world go by, some dressed in traditional Arab dress and others in western clothing. Eventually, the book shop opened and I was able to purchase a copy of *The Birds of the Hashemite Kingdom of Jordan*, by Ian Andrews. It was a book that had been recommended to me and would prove to be a useful addition to my Maskrek natural history library. It was a quiet end to our last evening in Jordan.

We had to make a dawn start for our crossing into Israel. Gus joined us for an early breakfast, and, while it was still dark, we were driven to the southern Jordanian-Israeli border posts by Traseen. Gus quickly got Friends through the Jordanian border formalities, before we had to say good bye to him and Traseen. Gus had been a wonderful guide and companion, for which we had all been very grateful. With the changing colours of Jordan's mountains and the rising sun behind us, we carried our luggage across to the Israel border post, and, in the dawn light, we became aware of hundreds of swallows *Hirundo rustica* sitting on the telegraph wires chattering and resting, before moving off north on their migratory journeys.

The International Bird Ringing Station at Eilat was reached with difficulty; we asked our new Arab driver to go there, but he was not certain where it was. Eventually we found it. I was one of the first persons off the bus, and, to my surprise and delight, I realised that the person getting into the car parked next to our coach was none other than my friend Tom Lawson from York. He was accompanied by his wife, Julie, and Heather Reynolds, who, at one time, was in charge of physical education at The Mount, York, when Joyce was headmistress. Tom, who is a well-known British ornithologist and a medical colleague, was able to tell us about some of the birds we could expect to see in the immediate area, before they went on their way. David and I had read and heard a great deal about the Ringing Centre, which had been founded by Israeli ornithologists, but staffed by people of many nations. In charge that morning was a Welshman, John Morgan, who had been there for a number of years. Eilat was an important stopping off point for migratory birds.

For a number of Friends, bird ringing was a new experience. From time to time, one of the young ornithologists would disappear into the nearby thick shrubs to collect birds trapped in the mist nets suspended between the bushes, and bring them back, one bird per soft bag In the ringing station they were analysed and measured before release. The information so gleaned was recorded, and while Friends watched several different species of bird passed through the ringer's hands. A ring was slipped round a leg before the bird, completely unharmed, was released. We were shown sand martins *Riperia riperia eilat*, a newly identified sub-species thought to be travelling to its breeding grounds in Iran and Afganistan, red-rumped swallows *Hirundo daurica*, a water pipit *Anthus spinoletta*, a sedge warbler *Acrocephalous schoenobaenus* and an orphean warbler *Sylvia hortensis*. In the adjacent shrubbery, there was a male Arabian babbler *Turdoides squamiceps* in full song, along with both a woodchat shrike *Lanius senator* and a masked shrike *Lanius nubicus*. I could have stayed there all day, but it was time to move on. Before reaching the main road going north, David, based on information provided at the Centre, asked the driver to stop next to a large heap of maturing manure! It contained a wealth of birds, including a European wheatear *Oenanthe oenanthe*, a pair of bluethroats *Lusinia svecica*, a red-throated pipit *Anthus cervinus* and both sub-species of yellow wagtail, the black-headed *Motacilla flava fledegg* and the blue-headed *M.f.flava*.

At Kilometre 33 going north, according to the ornithological guides, it was worth stopping to see some of the desert birds. We arrived to find we were at the entrance to the N.R.A. Alemonim Nature Reserve. Driving east, along an unmade road, between well marked mine fields, we eventually stopped. Ahead was the border wire with Jordan; the terrain was empty of birds, except for crested larks *Galerida cristata*. Hugh Maw started turning over small boulders, and under one of them he found a sluggish agama lizard, still cold from the overnight temperatures. It was the pale agama *Trapelus pallidus*, a new species for me. Disappointed with this site, we drove on north, hoping to stop off at Ne'ot Hakikar Nature Reserve, which we failed to find. By now it was beginning to rain heavily and Friends wanted a meal and a convenience stop. In the neighbouring kibbutz, we found what appeared to be a cafe. Sitting under large plastic sheets, we were served with a simple meal. Our driver, an Arab, felt distinctly uncomfortable in this setting and was pleased when Friends decided it was time to drive north again towards Jerusalem.

En Boqeq was swarming with tourists; it is one of the Dead Sea resorts to which thousands of visitors flock every year to swim in the highly concentrated salt Sea, and plaster themselves with mud, often for medicinal reasons. The smell of sulphur filled the air. Friends wandered down to the waterfront to observe the swimmers. Tristram's grackles *Onychognathus tristramii* were everywhere; more numerous than in former times, no doubt, due to people feeding them. These predominantly black birds have a characteristic call and beautiful orange-brown primary wing feathers that are only apparent in flight. We did not stay long, passing the road to Masada, which we planned to visit later in the week. Suddenly, from my front seat in the coach, I became aware of thousands upon thousands of white storks circling high above the western escarpment of the Rift valley. We stopped the coach and alighted. Grabbing my camera and using my 500 mm. mirror telephoto lens, I pointed up into the air and took a photograph. Later, in the frame, I counted over a thousand storks, only a fraction of those passing through. Some had landed on the rocky terrain, their white and black plumage standing out in contrast to the yellow ochre of the limestone rocks. According to Tom Lawson, numbers were increasing again since the cessation of the Lebanese civil war, during which thousands were killed at random, but often for food. Watching the storks was, for me, the most exhilarating wildlife experience of the whole trip.

Friends continued on their journey north, stopping again to explore one of the numerous reed beds found along the western shore of the the Dead Sea. On approaching east Jerusalem, our driver had to take us to the Arab part of the city via a back route; there were restrictions on movements imposed upon the Arab population by the Israeli authorities, because of a recent series of suicide bus bombings. Both David and I were pleased to be back at the Holy Land East Hotel again, where, as usual, we got a very warm welcome from the staff, and a little later by Mr Rizek Petro of Atic Tours. We were allocated a room overlooking the Dome of the Rock and the old Ottoman city walls. The Hotel was full of noisy European visitors; it seemed that the current disturbances in Israel were not having any effect on the tourist trade. During the evening I was able to ring home and talk to Patricia direct. It was wonderful to hear her voice again. After a tiring journey, most Friends retired to bed early.

The atmosphere in Ramallah was quite different from the experiences in 1990. No longer was it being patrolled by young Israeli army recruits, but by Palestinian policeman in their blue uniforms. Many were out shopping and going about their daily tasks in a more relaxed manner. Friends were taken there from the hotel in two minibuses; each had a special number plate which indicated to the Israeli authorities that the drivers were reliable. The minibuses were stopped at a road block, passports inspected and our party waved on. In the cold damp conditions, we drove through the almost continuous urban development between north Jerusalem and Ramallah, much of it of a poor quality. The minibuses eventually pulled up at the gates of the Friends' Girls' School. The party had arrived earlier than anticipated and had to wait in the cold for a member of the staff, who was still teaching. Eventually, Anna Kennedy appeared. I had met her twice before, firstly at Brummana and then Amman. She was now working under the auspices of Q.P.S. at the Girls' School. I remembered being present, with Andrew Clark, at her interview at Brummana in 1994 for her present post. She took us up to the flat, which she shared with Nancy Evans, a Friend teaching music at the school, who came from Scarborough. David, who knew the school well from previous occasions, had made arrangements for us to visit. Over a cup of Turkish coffee in the reception area, the headmistress, Diana Abdul-Nasser gave Friends a very frank and vivid description of life in the Friends' Schools, for the Girls' School had become a mixed junior school and the Boys' School the senior equivalent. The restrictions and deprivations under the current political situation imposed by the Israelis showed in the stressful expressions in her face and in what she had to say. Diana and her staff much appreciated our visit, and the Quaker ethos that it brought with it, for she, a Sunni Moslem, thought it was important. Most of the questioning came from the teachers in the group, of which there were several. We were then shown round the School and were introduced to members of the staff and pupils. In spite of the difficulties, the place seemed to me to be functioning well, with a happy atmosphere; but then ours was only a short visit.

Anna walked with the party over to the Boys' School to meet Peter Kapenga, an American Lutheran, who was the Acting Headmaster. He talked to the group before taking them into the school hall and the main buildings. Outwardly, the buildings of local stone, some of which were over a hundred years old, looked in a good state of repair. I was most impressed with the library, which had a wide range of books, some of which were about environmental and wildlife issues. It was in the library that Friends were introduced to Suad Jarawi and Sahar Othman, two pupils who had spent some time at Sidcot School during the previous year. As Hugh Maw, Anne Strauss and I were Sidcot Old Scholars, we had something in common with them, which we were able to share. The party climbed the stairs to the attic to see an art class in progress. Here, we saw what classroom conditions were really like. The room was shabby and cold, with no heating and a leaky roof.

Yet, the American art master was coping cheerfully in the best way he could, with keen students milling round him. On the walls of the art school were paintings and drawings of some of the pupils, some depicting the strife within their lives. Before departing from Ramallah, Friends handed over several gifts they had brought with them, including some musical instruments. In doing so, we thanked the staff and pupils for having us for the morning.

It was well after midday when Anna guided us to a restaurant in the middle of Ramallah. It proved to be a good choice and after an excellent meal, laughter and fellowship, the party returned to the main gate at the Girls' School, to wait in heavy rain for transport back to east Jerusalem. The raucous call of a jay attracted my attention; it was the Syrian jay *Garralus glandarius atricapillus*, a subspecies of our British jay, which has a black crown and white forehead.

After our exciting and successful trip to En Gedi in 1990, David and I decided that on this expedition we must go again. As far as I was concerned, En Gedi was a very special place. My hope was that Friends would have the same indescribable spiritual experience, but it was not to be.

To get there, of course, we had to retrace our steps south along the Rift Valley west of the Dead Sea. Our driver, who seemed to know what he was doing, took the party to the En David Gorge, which, he said, was where most visitors wanted to go. In 1990 David, Hugh Maw and I, along with Patricia and Anne Fletcher, had visited the En Argut gorge, which is longer and more dramatic. However, En David was not without its interest, although recent dry conditions meant that the amount of water coming over the Window Falls, which visitors were encouraged to climb to, was minimal. Draped on each side of the Falls were large clusters of the maidenhair fern *Adiantum sp*. Rosemary Day and Moira Thomson reported seeing sand partridge *Ammoperdix heyi*, along with rock hyrax *Procavia capensis* and ibex *Capra ibex*. I was aware of several lesser whitethroats *Sylvia curruca* and a clamorous reed warbler *Acrocephalus stentoreus*. To my delight, I found a recently published, beautifully coloured illustrated book on the amphibia and reptiles of Israel, by Professor Yehudah Werner, who I had met with Mother and Father in 1982. In spite of its being written in

Hebrew, I bought a copy as each animal illustrated was labelled with its scientific name.

Included in this journey round Israel was my second visit to Masada. Some 18 kilometres south of En Gedi, in arid, desert-like country, it was comparatively easy to reach. On arrival, we realised that the place was full of visitors, judging by the number of empty, parked tourist coaches. Friends joined the hustling queues to get on to the cable car, and, packed in like sardines, they were soon on the flat-topped mountain on the western Rift escarpment. Having been there before, I joined David and walked over to the Herodean Palace, leaving the rest of the party to explore the site on their own. The Palace, which I had not seen previously, was built on the northern, almost vertical edge of the mountain. Facing north over the Rift; we had to descend a number of steep steps to reach it. The view, like all views from Masada, was stupendous, but there was a midday heat haze. We stood and took in the timeless scene before us. An Egyptian vulture *Neophron percnopterus* sailed silently past us on an up-current of air. For a moment, I thought of those unfortunate Zealots who committed mass suicide in C.E.73, rather than submit to Roman rule. Friends had more to do that day, so the party moved on.

Again, on the advice of our driver, instead of going to En Boqeg for a swim in the Dead Sea, we landed up at the En Gedi foreshore. I was the only one who did not venture in for a dip. Apparently, according to some of the swimmers, the water was particularly refreshing at this site, as there was an influx of fresh water from a local stream following recent rains. Hopping around on the pebbly foreshore were several blackstarts *Cercomela melanura*, along with a single raven *Corvus corax* looking for carrion. Back on the road, we headed towards Jerusalem, stopping briefly at what we thought was Qane We-Samar Nature Reserve, but it turned out not to be so. We asked our driver to take us to the viewing point overlooking Wadi Qilt, so that Friends could see the Greek Orthodox Monastery of St. George, but, somehow, he took us to the wrong site, beyond which were the hills of the Judean wilderness. Disappointed, I set off down a rough track to see if I could get a view of the Byzantine Monastery, but without success. On returning to the main party, I turned over some medium-sized rocks, and to my delight found a pair of leopards lizards *Acanthodactylus pardalis*; another reptilian species to add to my ever increasing life list. With the help of John Harvey, I was able to photograph them. In the failing light of the setting sun, all were able to take in the atmosphere of the wilderness, which Jesus wandered through in his time. The final effort of a very full day, was walking past the Church of Peter Noster to the ancient city walls, and entering Jerusalem at St. Stephen's Gate, and so on to the Hotel.

The last day of the 1996 Quaker natural history tour was billed as a 'free' day, but, by popular request, Friends asked for a guided tour round old Jerusalem. The Hotel staff quickly found a guide named Raymond, who was a stateless Palestinian Arab. He was a Roman Catholic and he spoke excellent English. Like Gus, he proved to be an excellent choice. As on previous tours, we set off to the Damascus Gate on foot. The Gate, which is often a flash point in the current conflict, was crowded with crouching or sitting Arab tradesman and veiled woman selling fruit and vegetables, along with Israeli soldiers and armed policeman. Passing through the Gate, Raymond turned right leading the group down an alley way into the Christian Quarter of the Old City. Treading our way along unmade, often litter-strewn, snickleways, we reached the Armenian Quarter. He took us to the Syrian Monastery of St. Mark. There, on one of the walls behind the church portal, was an ancient Aramaic inscription; the native tongue of Jesus of Nazareth. I found this most interesting, for here was an authentic historical inscription that I could relate to Jesus. Guided through some more back streets, we again reached the City walls, but this time at the Zion Gate. Having viewed some recent Roman excavations en route, Friends passed through this Gate to get a view across the Kidron Valley to the Garden of Gethsemane and the Church of All Nations. From there, following the walls round to the Dung Gate, David and I noticed a colony of lesser kestrels *Falco naumanni* nesting in the walls of the Temple Mount, as they had for generations. Their nests were in the cracks and crevices in the south facing wall built by Herod the Great. The party walked through the Dung Gate, to find themselves in the Jewish Quarter of the Old City, which was very evident from the amount of activity around the Wailing Wall. As on the 1990 Woodbrooke Holy Land Tour visit, Friends had to

169

pass through a weapons search, before gaining access to the precincts of the El Aqsa Mosque and the Dome of the Rock. Nothing had changed since that last visit. Again, I was immediately aware of the sheer beauty of the Dome of the Rock. Much careful restoration work, both inside and out, had been done on this great Mosque. Monies from Jordan, Egypt and Saudi Arabia helped in the restoration work, including the gilding of the Dome. As on my previous visit, I stayed inside for some while, only to emerge again into bright sunlight. While waiting for the party to re-assemble, I saw a Syrian woodpecker *Dendrocopos syriacus* fly across the concourse. Friends then moved on to visit St. Anne's Church, which, on this occasion, was full of pilgrims of various persuasions all trying to sing some of their favourite hymns. The peace and tranquillity that I had come to accept at St. Anne's was not there on that day! So on to the Pool at Bethsaida, tucked away below layers of previous civilisations, with its brackish water and supposed healing properties. Scurrying over bits of recently excavated antique masonry were several green lizards *Lacerta laevis laevis*.

Raymond then took us to the Holy Sepulchre. To get there we passed along Lion Gate Street, with the Chapel of the Flagellation on our right and the Islamic El Omariye School on our left. The narrow street of the Via Dolorosa was packed, as usual, with pilgrims, tourists and visitors. Again, I looked at the stone-carved Stations of the Cross, but most were meaningless to me. Of all the Christian churches I have visited, the Holy Sepulchre is the most unattractive and least spiritual; what it has to do with Christianity I cannot say. It is far too ornate and subjected to all sorts of inter-faith squabbles. I found myself reminding Friends, as they entered the building, of George Fox's preaching on Firbank Fell in CE 1652. Christ was not to be found in a building, but in the individual hearts of men and women. Reluctantly, I followed the others in, only to find it crowded with pilgrims. I was pleased to emerge into the daylight again. Raymond then guided the party back to the Damascus Gate, before going on his way. We thanked him for his guided tour. A light lunch was taken at a small Arab cafe just inside the Gate, where we all were able to sit back and relax.

David and I decided to visit the headquarters of the Society for the Protection of Nature in Israel, which was within easy walking distance of the Damascus Gate. Others joined us, and we found the place in Queen Helena Street very busy. However, the bookstall was less busy and had some interesting natural history books in English. No one seemed to respond to our presence or our enquiries about Israel's nature reserves. I began to wonder if I had joined the right organisation before coming out to Israel this time, for the S.P.N.I. seemed more concerned about general environmental issues. However, a young lady told us about the National Reserves Authority (NRA) and kindly gave us the address of this Government Agency. David and I hailed a taxi to Yirmeyahu Street.

We soon located the offices and on entering through a glass door found ourselves at the reception desk. We explained to the young man the reasons for our visit; he immediately took us up two flights of stairs to meet Dr. Eyal Shy, the director of the NRA's wildlife and nature protection wing. From the start, we found it easy to talk to him, for he spoke perfect English. He had done his pre-graduate studies under Professor Yehudah Werner at the Hebrew University of Jerusalem, before coming to Oxford University to study at the Edward Gray Institution and complete his doctorate in ecology. Dr. Sly told us a great deal about Israel's wildlife and its conservation, and we soon realised that we should have come to him in the first place. He gave us half an hour of his valuable time, before we were taken elsewhere in the building for leaflets and a very useful map in English showing the NRA reserves.

At David's suggestion, we decided to catch a bus back into the centre of Jerusalem. We found the appropriate bus and settled in for our journey. It was then that a young Ethiopian Jewish soldier came aboard, with his Kalashnacov rifle slung over his shoulder. He took a careful look at all the passengers, including us, and eventually took away, at rifle point, a young male Arab who was sitting innocently opposite to us. It seemed that the Israeli authorities were highly sensitive about who should ride on their buses, especially after a recent spate of bus bombs. The bus moved off, and the soldier and his charge disappeared into the crowd; no one seemed to notice or care. However, as the bus neared the centre of Jerusalem, the predominantly Jewish passengers became mostly Arabs, but without any feelings of tension. After about twenty minutes, we disembarked and walked towards the garden Tomb.

I had been to the Garden Tomb in 1990 with David and was pleased to go again, but, on this occasion, we found a quiet corner of the beautiful gardens for a time of quiet reflection. We were both thankful that so far the tour, into which we had put so much effort, had gone without a major hitch. Sitting in the silence, we became aware of a nightingale *Luscinia megarhynchos* in full song. For both of us, the experience of the Garden Tomb was a fitting end to a most exciting and rewarding journey.

From an early start next day, we departed from Ben Gurion airport on our return journey to Britain. After an uneventful flight, we reached Heathrow in the early afternoon. By the end of the day I was home again for a tremendous welcome from Patricia and our dog, Jess.

The reservoirs north of Eilat. Drawn by BEN BARMAN

CHAPTER IX

The Second Quaker Study Tour 1998

TWENTY FOUR QUAKERS landed at Beirut airport in the middle of the evening on 19th March 1998, after a comfortable flight on a British Mediterranean Boeing aircraft. Waiting at the airport was Phillippa Neave, the Quaker Peace and Service Middle East co-ordinator. Customs and passport checks completed, everyone boarded a bus to be driven the ten miles up to Brummana. It was cold on arrival, with light drizzle on the coast and snow in the mountains. So began the second Quaker Natural History or Study Tour of the Near East. I was delighted to be back in Lebanon after three years, and it was not long before I was greeting old friends. The majority of the party, along with David, were booked into the Kanaan Hotel, which is opposite to the entrance to Brummana High School. At the request of Renee, three of us were to stay with her. I showed Candia and Ben Barman, who were from near Bristol, the way to Renee's flat and there we were made very welcome. We stayed up late talking to Renee and catching up with news. I was to sleep in the same room I had in 1995, so it was quite like home.

David and I, when planning this second tour, decided that we should try out an entirely new route. He had never been to Lebanon or Syria, and it seemed an ideal opportunity for us to take a party of Quakers to Brummana, for it had been many years since a party of any size had visted Lebanese Friends. So, we had spent some time poring over maps and looking in natural history guide books to see what was available in these two Arab countries. I was able to tell David some of the places that I had visited in the past. With some idea of what we wanted, we had approached Phillippa and asked her if she could help to put together a programme for the four days we would be in Lebanon. With permission from Q.P.S. in London, she set about her task with her usual vigour. Thus, on arrival, she presented us with an itinerary, full of interest and excitement. The programme and itinerary for Syria and eventually Jordan, we had left in the capable hands of the Jordanian office of Atic Tours.

Next morning, from Renee's balcony, I looked out at Knisse, which this time covered entirely with snow and drifting cloud. While at breakfast, I was delighted that Karim and Shareen Baz came to see me, looking quite grown-up. I introduced them to the Barmans, and Ben was soon entertaining Shareen with one or two simple conjuring tricks! Breakfast over, we three joined the main party at the Hotel, there to board a bus to take us to the Chouf. Friends were introduced to Katia Hayek by Phillippa. Katia, a young professional guide, was to be with the party for the rest of the week. The bus, a little the worse for wear, and unlike the luxury coaches we had used in 1996, struggled a little on the hairpin-bends. We were soon passing through Ras-el Metn, on the opposite ridge south of Brummana. I told Friends about the Olivers' orphanage, but we did not have time to stop and look over it. Our objective was the Moukhtara Nature Reserve in Jabel Barouk, but it soon became obvious we were not going to get there, for the higher we got, the thicker the snow. There were at least 3 feet in places, which not only made driving hazardous, but also slowed us up considerably. At one place, getting the bus through a snow-bound village was difficult, because of on-coming vehicles. Eventually, after three hours in the bus, we reached the mountain village of Moukhtara at 3500 feet. There we were met by Faisal Abu Ezzedine, the Director of the Nature Reserves project of the Lebanese Ministry of the Environment. Faisal, who was a practising Druze, told us that it would be impossible to see the Moukhtara Nature Reserve, because of the wintry conditions. Taking Friends into one of the rooms within the Jumblatt palace at Mukhtara, Faisal told us, in well spoken English, about the Reserve and its cedar trees. Its cedar grove was one of the few remaining in the Lebanon mountains, and every effort was being made to conserve it. He was well versed in many conservation issues. From small beginnings, it seemed that the conservation movement in Lebanon was gradually having some impact. His excellent contribution was very encouraging and positive, especially in view of some of the environmental damage that I was aware of in 1995. With some time available, after he had finished talking to the group, Faisal took Friends round some of the visitors' rooms within the palace. An audience had been arranged with Walid Jumblatt, the political leader of the Druze community, but, unfortunately, due to road conditions, he was unable to come. After thanking Faisal Abu Ezzedine, Friends moved onto Beit-ed-Dine.

I had been to Beit-ed-Dine palace before, but this time it was different in that I was seeing it under winter conditions. Katia took Friends through the various exhibits and the museum, before moving through to the formalised gardens. On this visit I looked particularly at the Byzantine mosaics that William Dalrymple wrote so highly about, which I found fascinating. Once outside, it was too cold to hang about, so a rapidly prepared light, take-away lunch was obtained from a local restaurant and Friends boarded the bus. The drive down towards the coast south of Beirut went without a hitch. On Phillippa's instructions, the driver stopped on the main road opposite Sirjbal, the site owned by Lebanese Friends, but whose future had not yet been worked out. Friends were able to look down on the site, which, for some of us, seemed to have great environmental possibilities. Driving through south Beirut, past the Shi'it communities, the party arrived in what is known as 'down town' Beirut. In the failing afternoon light, we were guided by Phillippa through some of the damaged parts of Beirut to the offices of Solidere, the company formed to carry out the reconstruction of central Beirut. There, spread out on a large table, was a three-dimensional model of the proposed reconstruction. One of the architects responsible for the project explained to Friends what was hoped to be achieved. It was all very impressive and our only hope was that it would succeed.

Unfortunately, on leaving the Solidere offices, we hit the rush hour. To travel in the rush hour in Beirut, especially in a bus, is something to be experienced. A journey that normally would take

175

half an hour, took over one and a half hours; Friends' patience was sorely tested. The party arrived at Brummana just in time to go into the first of three lectures arranged by Q.P.S. and Brummana Friends on wildlife and its conservation in Lebanon. The evening meal had to wait. I introduced the first speaker, Dr. Christopher Walley, to a reasonable sized audience of Friends and local residents in the Dobbing Hall at Brummana High School. Dr.Walley, a British geologist, who was the Principle of the Department of Geology at the A.U.B., gave a lecture entitled, "200 Million Years of Lebanese History". I found it a most interesting lecture, which gave me a lot of facts and new insights about Lebanon. With the lecture over and the speaker thanked, I met up with Tony Manasseh, who I had not seen since my last visit. He appeared to have made a complete recovery from his recent surgery. We made arrangements for some of us to have supper with him and Jocelyn, his wife, on the following evening. Meanwhile, I joined David and Christopher Walley and his wife for a meal at the Kanaan Hotel, along with the rest of the party. So ended an extraordinary day, with little, if any, bird watching. I think most of the party were exhausted, and retired to their rooms as soon as it was possible.

Phillippa had gone to a great deal of trouble in arranging the Lebanese part of the Quaker Near East Tour. She not only arranged places for Friends to visit, but also for the party to meet various Lebanese who were experts in their disciplines. The plan on the second day of the Tour was to go to Tripoli and meet Dr. Ghassan Jardini, Lebanon's leading ornithologist and Reserve Manager of Palm Island Parks. I had visited El Mina, Tripoli's port, three years earlier in the hope of visiting Palm Island, but had been prevented by weather. Now, once again, by the time the bus reached the parking place next to the port, strong, cold, onshore winds made sea conditions too dangerous for a crossing by open boat. Instead, Friends had to make do with a walk along the coastal promenade at El Mina and look at the few birds that were about, which included cormorants *Phalacrocorax carbo*. I enjoyed pointing out to some members of the party Jabel Turbol, the two thousand foot, coastal mountain that I used to climb in my youth.

Again, frustrated by unusual weather conditions, the party, lead by Dr.Jardini, went to the Tripoli Offices of the Environmental

Department, to meet members of Tripoli's Environmental Protection Committee. They were obviously expecting us, for we were given Turkish coffee and "nibbles". Dr. Jardini addressed the group on their local wildlife conservation measures, including that of Palm Island. In spite of all the pressures on the Island, such as illegal dynamite fishing and unauthorised visitors, the bio-diversity, with the help of a wardening system, was improving. He told us that the green turtle *Chelonia mydas mydas* had returned to nest again, after many years of absence. Following, his contribution, the manager of the Horsh Ehden Forest Nature Reserve talked to Friends about the Reserve, which I visited in 1995 with Hilary Baz and her children. Protective measures in such a remote area were difficult to enforce; illegal shooting still occurs, as does over grazing by sheep and goats. Having thanked all concerned for their kind hospitality, I had the opportunity to talk to the Chairman of the organisation, who was a long time resident of Tripoli. He told me that the old I.P.C. hospital still existed. This came as a great surprise to me, for on my previous trips I had looked for the hospital, only to be told that it had been pulled down for other development.

Under the forceful supervision of the Tour guide, Katia, Friends walked up the ramp at Byblos Castle to look at the metropolis. I tried my best to listen to what she had to say, but found my attention drifting away, as this was my fourth guided tour of Byblos. Instead, I looked to see what birds were in the area. In the party were two American Friends, Bill and Judy Matchett; Bill was a keen bird watcher and very knowledgeable. We spotted a black-eared wheatear *Oenanthe hispanica* in among the ruins, along with some red-rumped swallows *Hirundo rustica*; this was the second time we had seen these swallows on that day, for we had stopped briefly on our journey north at the small 16th century castle at Moussalayha, where some of them were flying about. We were shown the neolithic site, indicating the length of human activity at Byblos. After a short visit to Byblos's Crusader port and purchasing some light refreshments, it was time drive back to Brummana. The journey time, as usual, took longer than it should, leaving Friends tired by the end of the day. On return to Brummana, I went to Sabah and Hilary's flat to find that Renee's granddaughters were putting on a Mother's day show.

Again, it fell to my lot to introduce and thank the speaker, who was Professor Ricardus Habar, a consultant in ecology, biodiversity and environmental sciences, who is very much involved in conservation issues in Lebanon. He gave the second of the Nature Lectures in Dobbing Hall, entitled 'The Fauna and Flora of Lebanon'. He was obviously a skilled photographer, for his slides were magnificent. Friends were particularly pleased to see many of the beautiful photographs of the Horsh Ehden Forest Reserve, which the party was unable to visit. Along with his wife, Myrna Semaan-Haber, he had helped in the production the Reserve's booklet. Unfortunately, his lecture went on far too long.

It was very late in the evening when David, Hugh and Elizabeth Roberts and I sat down for an evening meal with Jocelyn and Tony Manasseh at their home. The conversation was wide ranging and not too controversial, in spite of Tony's difficulties over the School and its future. There was more than enough to eat of traditional Lebanese food, and we all enjoyed it. We thanked them both for their kind hospitality. It was well after midnight before I turned in for the night, feeling slightly feverish.

In spite of feeling unwell, but having had a reasonable night's sleep, I decided to join in all the day's activities. Brummana Friends opened the old Meeting House for morning worship. With a number of visitors, local Friends and our party, the numbers attending were considerably more than usual. The Meeting was well gathered, with some beautifully moving ministry, including some by Tony Manasseh. Meeting over, Friends gathered outside the Meeting House for a group photograph, before being shown round the school. Then it was time to go to Renee's for a buffet lunch, which we all enjoyed. There we were able to meet all the Baz family.

For an afternoon's outing, Phillippa arranged for the party to visit the Jeita Grotto, north of Beirut. We entered an extensive cave system, with its beautiful stalactites and stalagmites, most of which were floodlit, and vaulted like a cathedral. Now commercialised, the caves were so different from the 1950s, when we entered down stream on rubber dinghies and with head lamps. Access to the lower cave system was prohibited, because the Nahr-al-Kalb, which flows through the caves, contained too much water. I found the dry still air aggravated the cough which I was developing, so I did not stay long. Waiting for the rest of the Friends to emerge, I sat outside and watched a few birds. From Jeita, we were bussed to Phillippa's flat in the Hamra area of Beirut, but got there too early for the buffet supper she was preparing, so I took Friends for a walk round the A.U.B.'s extensive grounds. With dusk approaching, all seemed deserted and peaceful. Flying in among the trees were greenfinches *Carduelis chloris* and yellow-vented bulbuls *Pycnonotus xanthopygos*, along with swift *Apus apus* above. Suddenly, at least two species of bat appeared on the wing, probably Kuhl's pipistrelle and the greater horseshoe; unfortunately, I had not brought my bat detector, so no definite identification was made. We all returned to the flat, to find a wonderful buffet meal prepared for us. The meal over, Friends decided to go to the ballet, a French production. However, by then I was feeling feverish, so, along with Brenda Bailey, I returned to Brummana by taxi.

Still feeling unwell, I decided again to accompany the party to Saida (Sidon) and Tyre. I was glad I did so, for the day proved the highlight of the Lebanese part of the Tour. We collected Phillippa, along with Hind Sharaawi and Nick Waterman, in Beirut. Hind and Nick were the Q.P.S. field workers in Lebanon, helping to organise what was proving to be a successful training programme. Again accompanied by Katia, the plan was to see some of the work carried out in Saida at the 'Solidarity and Development' centre. This we reached without incident, but not before stopping at the quayside in old Saida fishing port to look across the water at its Crusader sea castle. The castle, which is one of the most photographed buildings in Lebanon, is reached by a causeway that encloses one side of the harbour. At the centre, Friends were introduced to the Director, Reina Zoazoa, who, with her enthusiastic staff, showed us round the establishment. With limited facilities, they were doing a remarkable job with mentally and physically handicapped children and young adults, some of whom were orphaned. In many cases they had been denied a vocational training, because of the civil conflict, and the team were trying to teach them a trade. The Q.P.S. input to the scheme was to train the vocational trainers as a non-sectarian exercise, and thus, it was hoped, to bring together people of differing religious backgrounds.

After a welcome coffee, final speeches, and a word of thanks to our hosts, Friends boarded the bus again and headed for the hills above Tyre. The party passed through two Lebanese checkpoints, and finally a U.N. post, before reaching the small town of Qana, one of the supposed places where Jesus converted water into wine at a wedding. It was at Qana that the Israeli army bombarded the community, killing 105 Lebanese civilians in April 1996 in the Grapes of Wrath Operation against the Hezbollah. Most were killed while taking shelter in the U.N hospital outpost and the outcome was an immediate international outrage against Israel, which brought the hostilities to an end. In the centre of Qana, next to the hospital, the surviving residents have erected a shrine to those who died. Black and white marble-clad coffins, laid out in rows, told their own story. Spontaneously, Friends gathered together some nearby chairs and placed them in a circle. The ministry in the ensuing Meeting for Worship was powerful, as Friends came to terms with the evidence of violence around them, made all the more poignant by the constant, booming Israeli artillery gun fire up the valley to the north. The Hezbollah had that morning entered the buffer zone. Nearby, wearing their light-blue helmets, were some Fijian soldiers of the U.N. forces, unable to prevent what was happening.

The Friends' Garden at Zibqeen is not really a garden, but a children's playground. To reach the Garden, we were driven furthur up into the hills on the demarcation line between Lebanon and the buffer zone of Israeli occupied south Lebanon. In the distance to the south, we could see the Israeli military look-out posts. The Garden, which consists of playground equipment surrounded by a medium-sized wall, was built on land cleared of mines and donated by the village. It was funded by British and American Friends, along with the American Save the Children Fund, after the Grapes of Wrath episode. In the centre is the Quaker Star. Zibqeen suffered heavily in the 1996 conflicts, with the deaths and injury of several children, especially from land mines.

On arriving in the village, Friends were initially taken to be welcomed by the Mayor and Kamel Chaya, the leader of the Save the Children Federation. Over a cup of coffee, we were able to meet others involved in the project, which, of course, included Phillippa.

From there we were all taken to the primary school to meet the children and the school staff. Lined up to welcome us were the excited children, each wearing a smart light-blue smock and holding a cellophane-wrapped rose and an olive branch. Speeches by a member of staff and one child, in well-rehearsed English, were given, before each child, in turn, gave each member of the Quaker party a rose and olive branch. The posters, in English, on the walls told us what our visit meant to the village; there was a deep felt thanks that they were not forgotten, and the joy that the playground gave the children. In an emotionally charged atmosphere, many Friends, including me, were in tears.

Then, with two children, one to each hand of a Friend, the party was conducted down the slope to the Garden. What started as a formal walk, ended in a head-long dash of exuberant joy to the entrance gate. Once inside it was pandemonium, with the children shouting and scrambling over the swings, slides, climbing frames and roundabouts. The whole area had been decked with bunting and balloons; in the doorways of the houses as we passed, stood the mothers dressed in their Sunday best. I was presented with another bunch of wild flowers, picked from the local hillside, which I passed on to Renee. Unfortunately, it all had to come to an end. We carried with us their messages and thanked them, before setting off on the long journey back to Brummana. Once in Beirut, we dropped off Phillippa, Nick and Hind, having said our farewells. After a light supper with the Barmans and Renee, I retired to bed with a temperature. It had been an extraordinary day, one never to be forgotten.

Next morning, I was told that the final talk given in the series on the environment in the Dobbing Hall by Fouad Hamdam, the representative of Greenpeace Mediterranean, had been a great success and well attended. Unfortunately, I was unable to be present, but it seemed to me the series had helped both Friends and local residents to understand the conservation issues in Lebanon. Instead, I had benefitted from a good night's sleep.

We had to make an early start, so after our last breakfast with Renee we joined the others, along with Phillippa and Katia, in the bus. We had so appreciated Renee's warm hospitality for four days. The journey from Beirut over the mountains into the Bekaa was marred by low cloud and rain. On reaching the valley bottom, we turned south-west along a poor quality road towards Ain Aammiq, with the snow-capped Jabel el Barouk to the west. The bus halted, and we alighted, alongside an extensive wetland. Underfoot it was extremely muddy, which made walking difficult. In among the grass and along the water verges were numerous green, croaking male Savigny's tree frogs *Hyla savignyi*; it was difficult to avoid them underfoot. The Aammiq wetland is the last remaining significant wetland in Lebanon, a remnant of much more extensive marshes and lakes that once covered thousands of acres of the Bekaa. In the spring the water comes down from the melting snow on the surrounding mountains. The Reserve is run by a Portuguese foundation called La Roche (The Rock) Trust, a Christian organisation concerned with wildlife conservation. It consists of about 100 acres of mixed reed bed, seasonally open pools and winter flooded pastures, and is an important bird migration site in the spring and autumn, with thousands upon thousands of birds passing through.

Friends were met by Chris Naylor, who with his wife, Susanna, are leaders of a team of volunteers that care for the Reserve. It was hoped, so Chris told us, to create the Reserve into the fourth in Lebanon; negotiations for such a status were being conducted. Certainly, of all the Reserves we had seen or heard about in Lebanon, this seemed to have the most potential. Unfortunately, in an area which lacks water, the wetlands are gradually being drained for agricultural and domestic use. In spite of the cold conditions, several species of bird were present. Coursing over the reed beds was a single marsh harrier *Circus aeruginosus*; both garganey *Anas querquedula* and little grebe *Tachybaptus ruficolis* were present. Feeding in the partially submerged grassland were a few little egrets *Egretta garzetta*, along with a single great white egret *Egretta alba*.

Before moving to the Syrian border, there was time for Friends to visit Baalbek, eating a sandwich lunch on the way. Once there, Katia was in her element as she explained its origins and history, for Roman Baalbek is the most impressive ancient site in Lebanon. My memories of Baalbek, or the 'City of the Sun', were very vague, for I had last visited it in 1944. I was seeing Baalbek as if for the first time, and I was most impressed. The whole complex was much larger than I had imagined and many of the buildings were in a good state of preservation, in spite of generations of human and earthquake destruction. We were shown round the various temples, admiring the still standing massive Corinthian columns of the Temple of Jupiter and the almost complete Temple of Bacchus. The decorated frieze entrance to the latter is a flight of stairs with three landings. It was on these stairs that my parents in the 1950s saw Shakespeare's Julius Caesar, performed by the Royal Shakespeare Company. What an experience it must have been for them! It was mid-afternoon by the time the party left this site where Caesar had founded the Roman Colony.

We parted company with Phillippa and Katia at the Syrian border, having thanked them both, particularly Phillippa, for making our visit enjoyable, interesting and, at times, very exciting. Waiting for us on the other side was Arlen, our Syrian guide for the next twenty-four hours. She took us rapidly through all the border formalities. Arlen Arnekian, an unmarried Armenian woman in her mid-thirties, was a bubbly character with an infectious smile, who spoke good English, but sometime got her metaphores mixed! It was soon obvious that she was a fount of information. Travelling along good roads in a luxury coach, we soon reached the outskirts of Damascus, and, instead of going direct to our hotel, Arlen took us to the sparsely inhabited heights above the City. There, from our vantage point, we looked down on Damascus in the dusk, its roads beginning to twinkle as lighting up time came. It seemed vast, extending to the east as far as the eye could see. By now it was becoming very cold, and I was glad to get back into the coach. We drove into the centre of Damascus and went to the Alaa Tower Hotel Number 5, an odd establishment, occupying the top five storeys of a tower block! The rooms were comfortable, but the public facilities, such as the dining room, were restricted. Unfortunately, Margaret Makins took a tumble on getting off the coach, and was rather shaken up, but recovered enough to join us all for an entirely Arab meal at a nearby restaurant. It was a wonderful end to an interesting day. David and I were pleased, at that stage, how well the tour had gone.

I had a wretched night coughing, in which I also kept David awake. I crept down to breakfast in an overcrowded dining room. Over a light meal, I was, along with the others, introduced to George Chabbour, a Syrian author and civil rights campaigner. He was a longstanding friend of Sydney and Brenda Bailey; Brenda had contacted him the previous evening. I found him an interesting person to have a brief conversation, for it was obvious that he had moved, as did the Baileys, among those involved in the peace process in the Near East. Breakfast over, and luggage fully loaded, we all boarded our luxury coach again. Bubbly Arlen was there to greet us, with ambitious plans for our day in Damascus; these we had to curtail somewhat. However, she was able to show us a great deal. Travelling round the walls of the old City, we came to the Church of St.Paul's, which, according to Arlen, marked the spot where the disciples lowered Paul out of a window in a basket so that he could flee the Jews (Acts 9 v 25). We briefly looked at the Church, before going on to the Eastern Gate where we parked. The majority of the party walked through the old City to the Omayyad Mosque, which I had visited with Tony and Philip Manasseh in 1995, so, along with Margaret Makins, who was still recovering from her fall, I stayed on the coach. I needed to catch up with some sleep.

After an hour, Friends returned to the coach enthusing much about the Great Mosque. The highlight of the morning's activities for me was the visit to the National Museum; by now I had revived sufficiently to go round it. The imposing facade of the museum is a reconstructed Umayyad desert palace entrance of the seventh century C.E. from near Palmyra. Once in the museum, what really attracted my attention were the exhibits from Palmyra itself, especially the reconstruction of an underground burial chamber. Being there, triggered distant memories of my visit to Palmyra in 1955. Like the others, I was impressed by the layout of the museum and felt that the visit was very worthwhile. Again, I returned to the coach, while the others went to the main souk. Finally, we had to leave Damascus and drive to the Syrian-Jordanian border. It was not long before we were at Der'a, where Arlen rapidly took us through the border checks. Our brief visit to Syria had been most enjoyable, and, thanks to Arlen, had gone without a hitch.

Standing on the Jordanian side was Gus. It was good to see him again; he had not changed at all, still full of facts, know-how, charm and humour. Staying on the same coach, we drove on to Jerash, which we reached in the late afternoon. In the early evening light, Gus took us round Jerash, which we had almost to ourselves. I was fascinated by the changing colours of the stone work as dusk approached, and particularly memorable was the sunset behind the Corinthian columns of the portico of the Temple of Artemis.

I was glad when we eventually reached the Manar Hotel on Amman. At my request, David and I were given separate rooms, hoping it would give us both a better night's sleep. Waiting for us in the hotel foyer was Yousef Atieyh, the Atic Tours manager in Amman, who we met in 1996. There was much to discuss, for we were about to complete the second phase of our Quaker study tour. Here, however, we were on familiar ground and, with the help of Gus, were able rapidly to sort out the coming itinerary.

Prior to Friends' visit to Amman, Brenda Bailey had been in contact with the Crown Prince El Hassan of Jordan's office. Both she and Sydney had known the Crown Prince when they were actively involved, on behalf of Quaker Peace and Service, in the Middle East peace process. Unfortunately, the Prince Hassan was not available during the time of our Quaker visit, but he arranged for his Inter-Faith programme coordinator, Mahmoud Mufti, to meet the party. He arrived after supper and told us of his plans for the following day, which consisted of a series of lectures at the Jordanian Institute of Diplomacy. Mahmoud spoke perfect English and, in a subsequent conversation, I learned that he was educated at Millfield School in Somerset, where, as a member of the first fifteen Sidcot School rugby team, I used to visit for matches. At the end of the day I was able to contact Patricia on the telephone - it was good to hear her voice again.

The Institute of Diplomacy was a modern, two-storey building in Amman, built of local stone. Established in 1994 by Royal Decree, it is a higher educational establishment, with academic programmes in diplomatic and foreign service studies. Ushered into a spacious and well appointed lecture room, and sitting at rows of tables under a portrait of King Hussein, Friends were introduced to a series of speakers by the President of the Institute and former

185

Foreign Minister of Jordan, Professor Kamel Abu Jaber. He started the proceedings by talking to us about the 'Dynamics of the Middle East Peace Process', and he was followed by Dr.Walid Sa'adi, former editor of the Jordanian Times on the 'Human Rights in the Iraqi Predicament- Sanctions or Famine?' Following a coffee break, Mahmoud addressed Friends on 'The value and Limitations of Interfaith and Intercultural Dialogue in Peace Building in the Middle East'. Then, Major General Muhammad Shiyyab, now retired from the Royal Jordanian Airforce, spoke on the 'Creation of a Middle East Free of Weapons of Mass Destruction'. The final contribution was by Mr. Rami Khouri, a political analyst and columnist for the Jordanian Times, on 'Civil Society, Democracy and Politics in modern Jordan'. All spoke in English and after each contribution there was an opportunity for questions. By early afternoon it was time to move on, for Friends had been treated to an unexpected occasion, thanks to Brenda. We left with our minds full of facts and our hearts full of hope. Along with Gus, who had been with us throughout the day, we thanked our hosts and were taken back to the Manar Hotel. Mahmoud, meanwhile, arranged for the party to be collected in the evening for a meal.

On returning to the hotel, I discovered that David was not so well, having, I thought, picked up the infective organism from me. I went into the pharmacy next door and bought some antibiotics for him and advised him to start taking them straight away.

Kaan Zaman is a tourist 'hot spot', designed to attract the likes of us to come and spend our money on all sorts of wares and local crafts in a multi-shop complex. Situated at Al-Yadaideh, a district about six miles outside Amman, meant that we had to be taken there by coach. It was dark when we arrived, and after looking round the shops and obtaining a few purchases, Friends were ushered into the restaurant as guests of the Institute of Diplomacy. Walking past food being prepared on open charcoal fires, we were all shown to a long table reserved for us by Mahmoud. In dim lighting, I found myself in a smoked filled cellar-like room, with typical Arab vaulted ceilings. Sitting next to one of our hosts, who originally came from the Caucacus, but now lived in Jordan, and above the noise of the Arab music and the constant babble of talk from others in the restaurant, I had an interesting conversation

186

about life in southern Russia. It was a pleasant meal, in which we had to help ourselves. However, after a while, the smokey atmosphere from the charcoal fires and cigarette smoke got the better of me, and I had to go out into the cool night air to relieve my coughing spasm. As I sat under the starlit sky on a low wall, the spasm settled; eventually, we all returned to the hotel at mid-night.

After a leisurely start to the day, Friends boarded the coach again and were driven eastwards from Amman across the Jordanian deserts. Quite soon the terrain became very arid, with little, or no, vegetation. Bewildering in its size and relentless in its climate, the desert was a place of yellow sand and barren black basalt flintstone outcrops, on a gently undulating plain, unlike anything I had seen before. In earlier times, in this inhospitable environment, the only way across was by camel, but the modern traveller drives along a well-kept tarmac road. Lawrence describes vividly the harsh conditions which he and his entourage had to endure, when crossing such places on their camels. Occasionally there was an Army outpost, a cafe or resting place by the roadside. I noticed a string of high voltage pylons, which seemed to me to be out of place striding out across the desert into the distance. The desert had lost its mystique, with the advance of modern civilisation.

Having passed Qasr Muwaggar, one of the famous Ummayed Desert Castles, we eventually reached another one at Qasr Amra. Muwagger was surrounded by tourists, but there were fewer at Amra, so we stopped to have a look at the building. Built in the eighth century as a luxury bath house, with a sophisticated heating system, it had on its high vaulted ceilings and walls some outstanding frescos, depicting athletic and hunting scenes, along with illustrations of the local wildlife. Gus was in his element describing the restored frescos and the building's layout. As well as an auditorium chamber, Amra was dependent on a deep well, the water being raised by animal power. A harnessed beast, walking in a circle, operated the lifting mechanism. Now, however, like elsewhere in Jordan, underground water levels had dropped considerably or had disappeared altogether. Amra was certainly not a castle, but a place of leisure. As we left, we spotted, sitting on the perimeter fence, a masked shrike *Lanius nubicus*.

187

To reach Shaumari, the driver left the main road and drove along an unmade track, billowing clouds of dust from the behind the vehicle as it did so. I wondered if we were ever going to get to the National Nature Reserve, for the desert route seemed endless. From my front seat vantage point, I saw a small flock of white-tailed plovers *Chettusia leucurus* take off and land nearby.

Ammed, the warden, greeted us with enthusiasm. He liked showing parties round the visitors' enclosure, especially English groups, because, as he said, they liked the birds, and knew something about them. Shaumari National Wildlife Reserve was created in 1975 in the desert some seven miles south of Azraq. Its perimeter mesh fence is eight miles in length, and it is there to keep the goats out and allow desert vegetation to regenerate. Initially, according to Ammed, the habitat was rich, but because of chronic water shortages, it was beginning to deteriorate. The effect of this was that fewer visitors came to Shaumari, resulting in a fall in income. Yet, in spite of these factors, Ammed and his staff were doing their best for the Reserve.

Passing through the main gate and having paid their dues, Friends were taken to the central, three-storey observation tower. Compared with the desert conditions through which we had just travelled, I was aware that there was much more vegetation than I had expected, especially in the large enclosure. From the top storey, along with others, I could see a small herd of Arabian oryx *Oryx leucoryx*, feeding with three Syrian onagers or Asian asses *Equus hemionus*. Both mammal species were part of an international captive-release programme. Elsewhere on the Reserve, as part of the same programme, we could see other enclosures for some of the smaller desert gazelle species, such as the Dorcas gazelle *Gazella dorcas*, as well as for ostriches *Struthio camelus*. There was a considerable migratory movement of both large and small birds through Shaumari that morning. With the help of Ammed, we identified both the golden eagle *Aquila chrysaetos* and the imperial eagle *Aquila heliaca*, and the long-legged buzzard *Buteo rufinus*, along with three species of shrike.

I gleaned considerable information about the Arabian oryx, especially from the small museum on the site. Apart from the camel, it was the largest ruminant in the area and was particularly adapted

188

to living in arid conditions, going for long periods without water. The oryx fed on succulent plants and a variety of grasses, from which it met some of its water needs. This heavily built antelope, with its spectacular thin, long, black, corrugated horns, has a dominantly white pelage and patterned face; it is very conspicuous in its desert environment. With the advent of modern four-wheel drive vehicles, capable of travelling over desert sands, and the development of automatic weapons, the Arabian oryx was hunted to the point of extinction. To the nomadic Arabs, the oryx was, and still is, a traditional hunting trophy, as well as having blood with medicinal properties. By the 1960s, only a small number of Arabian oryx remained in the wild.

It was then that the Fauna and Flora International launched its Operation Oryx, taking wild oryx from Aden, to which were added captive animals from Saudi Arabia and Kuwait. These antelopes were moved to Arizona's Phoenix Zoo, and in a habitat similar to their own were encouraged to breed. The programme proved to be so successful, that captive-released Arabian oryx were released back into the wild in Oman for the first time in 1982. The Shaumari herd, which numbered over 200 animals at the time of Friends' visit, was part of the same programme. Recently, the Jordanians had donated several oryx to the Syrians, so that they could re-stock their desert areas. Unfortunately, the animals at Shaumari are reaching their carrying capacity for the Reserve, and quite soon, provided they are left alone by the nomadic tribesmen, they will release a few into the wild. One of the aims of the Shaumari Centre is to educate the nomadic peoples, so that they will change their attitudes and eventually own and protect their Arabian oryx. Regrettably, at the time of writing, I read in my spring copy of the F.F.I.'s magazine Oryx, that due to a resurgence of poaching in Oman, the 400 wild Arabian oryx in that country have been reduced to 138 still roaming free.

I came away from Shaumari well pleased with what I saw and experienced, and felt there was hope that much of the desert fauna and flora could still be saved, provided the Reserve was adequately funded. For the F.F.I., the oryx story has been counted as one of their earliest successes.

Lawrence of Arabia was captivated by Azraq, for he writes, *'Azraq's unfathomable silence was steeped in knowledge of poets, champions and lost kingdoms'*. For here, among its extensive fresh water marshes, fed by underground springs, he set up his headquarters in 1918 in the old fort. The Quaker party approached it from the south and were taken immediately, by Gus, to the fortress. According the guide books, it was re-modelled in basalt stone in the 13th century CE by Mamluks, on a basic 3rd century CE Roman fort layout. We were surprised at how much of it was still standing, and, on entering the main gate, found before us a large central courtyard. Over the main gate, Lawrence had his room in which he planned his final campaigns and suffered from the extremely cold weather. Gus demonstrated that one of the huge, finely balanced, basalt doors could be moved by an individual. Central to the whole site was a small ancient unadorned mosque. Like the weather in March 1918, we found conditions were cold, and therefore decided to move on into the Druze part of the town.

Passing along some of the dusty, back streets of Azraq, Friends eventually found the remnant of one of its ancient marshes, which once supported thousands upon thousands of migratory birds. Now, due to massive drainage schemes of the underlying aquifer to supply water to Amman and Irbid, many of the marshes had dried up; on some, like the one we visited, the vegetation was badly burnt by extensive fires. The authorities are trying to reverse these destructive trends and restore some of the marshes to their former status. In spite of these findings, wildlife existed, albeit in limited numbers. In among a small reed bed there were night herons *Nycticorax nycticorax,* along with a solitary squacco heron *Ardeola ralloides,* a new species for me, and also a clamorous warbler *Acrocephalus stentoreus.*

The cold winds from the north had been whipping up dust storms, filling the air with irritant particles which made some of us wheeze. I was thankful to get back into the air-conditioned coach and return to Amman for a much needed rest.

The last time I travelled along the King's Highway, I was in a hurry. The aim then had been to get to the D'ana National Nature Reserve in the south of Jordan. This time, however, it was different. In spite of an awfully wheezy night, I, like the others, was keen to

190

set off. We made an early start, heading for Mount Nebo. Situated a few miles south-west of Amman and off the King's Highway, Mount Nebo is prominent on the eastern escarpment of the northern Rift Valley. It was from here that Moses saw the Promised Land, as he looked across the Rift at what is now called the West Bank. Claimed as a Christian site, the Franciscans built the Monastery of Syagha on the foundations of an earlier chapel, dating back to the third or fourth century CE. To get to the Monastery, the Quaker coach was parked in the public car park, and Friends had to walk up a gentle slope to the buildings. On the way, we passed a memorial stone to Moses, on which there was an inscription claiming Mount Nebo as a Christian site. Some of us felt unhappy about this statement, for Moses, so it seemed to us, was an important prophet to all three main monotheistic religions that arose out of the region. On reaching the top, there was no view of the 'Promised Land', for the whole of the Rift was filled with low cloud and mist! Friends ventured into the Monastery, and Gus pointed out a series of excavations and early Byzantine mosaics. The details depicted in the mosaics were magnificent, some of the best in Jordan, we were told. At the far end, there was a simple altar with an apse behind it, from which light poured through modern stained glass windows.

Madaba, a busy ancient Jordanian city, is on the King's Highway and is a regular stopping off point for tourists. Like good tourists, the Quaker party paid a visit to the Chapel of St. Theodore in the Greek Orthodox Church of St. George. We had come to see Madaba's famous, multi-coloured, mosaic map of Palestine dating from the sixth century CE. However, we were not the only party present in the church, so Friends gathered silently in one of the naves in what became a Meeting for Worship, the silence only being broken by the quiet mumblings of the guide of the party in front of us. When it was our turn to look at the map, Gus led us to the Chapel and explained its layout in great detail. The map was of the Holy Land and surrounding areas, and was used regularly by pilgrims to guide them on their way. Considered to be the oldest map in existence, especially in Christendom, it is just under 1,000 square feet in size. Jerusalem is shown in the greatest detail, and many places are labelled. We emerged feeling dazzled, not only by the bright sunlight, but also by what we had seen. As Gus had a planned a busy programme for Friends on that day, there was little time to linger in Madaba, whose history went back over 3,000 years.

In 1996 Gus had been disappointed that he had been unable to show Friends Kerak, but then, unlike this journey, we had been in a hurry to get to D'ana. We parked on a cold March afternoon near the entrance to the castle and, under Gus' guidance, ventured in. The massive stone work was immediately apparent, with its thick walls and solidly built battlements. We went first to a viewing point overlooking the town of Karek, which today is a flourishing community. Below us, floating on an up current of air from the castle's glacis, was a golden eagle *Aquila chrysaetos*. From these battlements, Reynaud de Chatillon, a Crusader knight, who had acquired the castle through marriage, used to throw his enemies to their deaths. The inhumanity and cruelty of some of the Crusaders, all done in the name of Christianity, is, for me, beyond belief. The castle at Kerak was constructed at the beginning of the 12th century CE, and was one of a string of such castles which stretched from Turkey to Aqaba, and defined the eastern borders of the medieval Christian kingdom. It eventually fell to Saladin in 1187 CE after the battle of Hittin, and Reynaud was taken prisoner and executed. To return to the coach, Gus took us through a series of vaulted subterranean passages, and several domestic rooms and soldiers' quarters.

By now, like the others, I was tired of visiting ancient monuments, and was pleased when we were back on the coach heading south. As usual, I sat in the front seat of the coach, the other seat being occupied by different fellow travellers on different journeys. On this occasion I was joined by Kathleen Haines. I asked her if she would help me in the production of this travel journal, by reading and correcting the manuscripts. She told me that she would be only too pleased to do so, and her help has been much appreciated.

Leaving Karek, our route was still along the King's Highway, but at Tafila we turned south east to join the Desert Highway. We reached Petra by late afternoon. Unlike Friends' previous visit, we stayed this time at the Edom Hotel. Still in the process of construction, this hotel was comfortable and served excellent meals, but it was not quite as comfortable, or close to the entrance to the necropolis, as the Petra Hotel and Rest House. We would not, I thought, have the opportunity of watching the horses collecting in the morning. I was glad of the rest before the evening meal.

The wind was still in the north when the Quaker party departed for D'ana Nature Reserve, bringing with it cold air and overcast skies. This time Gus knew precisely where to go. On reaching the car park at the Reserve's entrance, we found the multi-coloured shuttle waiting for us. It looked a bit the worse for wear, but still functional. Everyone managed to find a seat, but on this occasion the shuttle had to make two journeys. I was taken down the slope to the encampment on the first journey, travelling, among others, with Mary Martin. Mary, on descending the metal steps, slipped and caught her wedding ring on a piece of projecting metal. The ring buckled, inflicting deep cuts on both sides of her ring finger. Initially it bled profusely, but one of the Jordanian guides, with great skill, kindly cut off the ring and strapped up her finger. Luckily, on close examination, I found that she had not damaged the flexor tendon. Mary, being Mary, stoically joined us in all that we did that day, in spite of being in pain.

We were introduced to an English speaking guide, who took us along one of the regularly used footpaths. A variety of spring flowers blossomed in profusion, including the endemic purple flowering globularia *Globularium alypum*. However, due to the cold conditions, few birds were to be seen. A pair of griffon vultures *Gyps fulvus* was nesting on a high vertical cliff on the opposite side of a deep valley, and a woodchat shrike *Lanius senator* appeared on a bush next to the footpath. There were no reptiles, and few insects about. Somewhat disappointed, we walked back to the encampment. There, prepared for us in a Bedouin tent, was a wonderful cold meal of Arab food, with plenty of fresh fruit. We sat down and helped ourselves. The meal over and the tables cleared, Friends asked Gus if they could have a period of silent worship; he joined us for what was a new experience for him.

It was time, yet again, to depart; some members of the party decided to walk up the hill to the reception building, the rest travelled in the shuttle. On reaching the top and while waiting for

193

the walkers, David noticed a sudden migratory movements of long-legged buzzards *Buteo rufinus* overhead. In what appeared to be adverse climatic conditions, over a hundred birds flew northwards. We got back to Petra at dusk.

My first concern on reaching the hotel, was to get Mary to a hospital to deal with her injury. Gus ordered a taxi and came with us to the casualty department of the local Government hospital. We were taken to a cubicle and almost immediately a Jordanian doctor, in his mid-forties, appeared. After examining the injury, he collected a stitching trolley, on which was a bottle of neat iodine! With this disinfectant, he cleaned the wound. Mary almost 'hit the roof' on its application, but it proved to be very effective, for the wound remained clean for the rest of the tour. Under a local anaesthetic, a number of stitches were inserted. Mary coped cheerfully. Both of us, with our respective medical trainings, watched with interest all that was going on - it being our first experience of a Jordanian hospital! We thanked the staff and returned, along with Gus, to the hotel. A memorable experience to end the day.

I was still coughing, particularly at night. Room conditions in the hotel were warm, so much so, that I had no idea how cold it was outside. After an excellent help-yourself breakfast, Friends were taken to the entrance of the necropolis. I soon realised I had insufficient warm clothing, but then I had not anticipated such conditions. Gus joined the party and walked with us down the Siq; Brenda Bailey went down in one of the small horse drawn carriage that visitors can hire. Much had changed since the 1996 visit. A paved way had been uncovered at least six feet under the usual walkway and this was now being restored in places. There were no Sinai rosefinches *Carpodacus synoicus* nesting along the rocky ledges of the Siq this year. There were fewer visitors milling round the Treasury, and the skies were overcast, making photography difficult.

Gus showed us round the main sites, as for several of us it was a first visit to Petra. We arrived at an old burial cave, lined with portable white plastic seats which seemed a suitable place to have our picnic lunch, and to get out of the cold wind. Lunch over, Friends settled down for a Meeting for Worship. In the last few days worship had been held in a Greek Orthodox chapel, a bedouin tent, and now, a disused Nebatean burial chamber, showing, yet again, that it was possible in any setting. After Meeting, Friends were left to their own devices, splitting up into small groups to explore. Some, such as Joyce Pickard, climbed up to the tomb known as The Monastery, which looks over the necropolis, whereas David and I, along with the Roberts and the Barmans, walked up to the royal tombs, particularly the Urn tomb, which at one time had been a Byzantine church. Having examined the tomb, David and I wandered on further into the rocky terrain and dried up river beds. Suddenly, I became aware that we had the whole place to ourselves. I felt as if we were coming on Petra for the first time and no one else had been there before. Flying round us were nesting rock martins *Ptyonoprogne fuligula,* and overhead flew fan-tailed raven *Corvus rhipidurus.* We over-turned small boulders to find sheltering under them medium-sized, yellow scorpions *Buthacus sp.* For me, it had been a splendid moment of communion with God as time stood still. But we had to get back to the entrance and David and I were the last to reach the assembly point, ready for the long drive to Aqaba.

Again, the Miramar Hotel provided us all with comfortable facilities. Our room on the third floor overlooked the sea front and the port. Little seemed to have changed since our last visit; the loud, early morning call to prayer from the local mosque woke us at dawn. The day was listed in the itinerary as a 'free day', leaving Friends to do as they wished. Several of us paid a visit again to the Royal Diving Centre down the coast, having caught the bus from the forecourt of the neighbouring hotel. Most snorkled, but weather conditions were not quite as warm as on the previous occasion, and there were fewer fish to see. As before, I explored the compound for snakes and birds; the only thing of note was a passage movement of blackcaps *Sylvia atricapilla* on their way north. By mid-morning Friends decided to return to Aqaba, but, before doing so, to stop off at the Marine Science Station. Like those in the party who had been there on the previous visit, I found it of considerable interest. Many highly-coloured tropical fish were displayed in large fish tanks, but, as it was explained, some were endangered because of the damage done to the coral reefs.

Those Friends who had not come to the Diving Centre, had spent the morning exploring old Aqaba and all came together at the hotel at midday. After a light lunch, we hired two glass-bottom boats and were taken out to the reefs and round the harbour. The day, which had been relatively quiet and relaxing compared with the previous days, ended with a Meeting for Worship in the Board Room of the hotel.

In spite of a wretched night coughing, I decided to join the Quaker tour's day visit to Eilat in Israel. I am glad I did so, for what could have been a difficult time in crossing the border between Jordan and Israel, turned out to be no problem. In some ways we were testing the system, to see if it was possible to cross for the day, with ample time available in Israel. After an arms search and putting our limited hand luggage through an X-ray scanner, the whole party was let into Israeli by security, without our passports being stamped! A young Israeli female security guard commented about my place of birth, but that did not hold us up. Waiting on the other side of the border was an Arab driver, with Israeli citizenship, who spoke excellent English. He took us to the International Bird Ringing Station, but, unfortunately, by the wrong route. We arrived at a hut that had seen better days, and was the raptor ringing station. Our arrival angered the American ornithologist in charge, but he re-directed us.

At the newly-constructed International Centre we were all welcomed by an Indian scientist, currently in charge of the ringing programme. He introduced us to his young volunteer American assistant, whose knowledge of birds was excellent. Apart from Arabian babblers *Turdoides squamiceps* in the surrounding scrub, along with some lesser whitethroats *Sylvia curruca* and house buntings *Emberiza striolata*, there were few birds. However, the American showed us a male woodchat shrike *Lanis senator*, which had been trapped and ringed that morning, explaining to us its migratory route and breeding biology. Before he released it, some of us were able to photograph it. At the time of our brief visit, he pointed out an overhead northward movement of steppe buzzards *Buteo buteo vulpinus* (a subspecies to our British buzzard), accompanied by a single black kite *Milvus migrans*. As a parting thought, our American friend suggested we went to the reservoirs north of Eilat.

It was our original intention to go to the Timna Nature Reserve, but this proved to be too far north, so, instead, Friends agreed to visit the reservoirs. This proved to be very worthwhile. To reach the reservoirs, the driver had to take us north along the main highway to kilometre post number 20, and then turn directly east towards the Jordanian border. Travelling over a dusty track, we parked within walking distance of one of the stretches of water. By now the morning heat was building up. The terrain, sandy and stoney, was sparsely covered with small stunted evergreen shrubs. There were several lizards about, and I found my first elegant gecko *Stenodactylus sthenodactylus* sheltering under a small boulder. On reaching the water's edge, the ornithologists in the party identified a group of greater flamingos *Phoenicopterus ruber* feeding in the shallows, their beautiful pink and white feathers reflecting off the water's surface and contrasting with the arid background. There were a number of spoonbills *Platalea leucorodia* present, as well a raft of shoveller ducks *Anas clypeata*. We lingered a while, taking in the scene before us, before returning to Eilat.

When planning the visit to Eilat, David and I had thought it would be a good idea to visit the Coral Beach Nature Reserve and its underwater observatory, as well as the International Bird Ringing Station; a number of people had recommended it. We arrived over the lunch hour and were able to purchase snacks. Walking across the raised, 300 foot planked gangway over the submerged coral reef to the observatory, I immediately saw a number of very colourful fish, more so than I had seen on the Jordanian side of the Red Sea. The steel, circular observatory, sunk twenty feet into the sea, consisted of twenty strengthened glass observation panels overlooking the coral reefs. To get to the darkened, submerged observation platform, we had to climb down a spiral staircase. The colourful tropical fish swam around us, and we were in a fish hide. We were caged and the animals were free! There were many species to be seen of various sizes, but, on this occasion, no sea turtles or sharks appeared. Symbolically, I thought, mankind was not part of this habitat and was, for once, being caged; the whole place was remarkable, producing a feeling of magic.

Once outside, there was an opportunity to look at some sharks, rays and turtles swimming in several large pools, and to read the exhibition material on the care of the fragile coral reef, on which so many of these aquatic animals depended for their existence. There was a small yellow submarine to carry visitors out into deeper waters, but none of our party chose to take it.

The marine centre was well worth the visit, and a place to come back to in the future. Eilat itself, was not an attractive place; it was too much like the rapidly-expanding seaside resorts that can be found anywhere in the western world, full of expensive hotels, shops and an active night life. Of the two ports on the Gulf I much preferred Aqaba. Crossing back to Jordan was uneventful, and there, to meet the Quaker party, was Gus. So ended another eventful day.

Our last day in Jordan meant travelling back to Amman for an overnight stay at the Manar Hotel, but there was one more place to visit - Wadi Rum. I never get tired of visiting Wadi Rum, its grandeur, beauty, harshness and remoteness never fails to excite me. For some of the party, it was their first visit, and an unforgettable experience. After an early start from Aqaba, we were driven up the Desert Highway before turning east towards the Rum massif. The route and contents of the day was very similar to the 1996 trip, and we had hot, desert-like, conditions. On reaching Rum village and having our coffee break, Friends piled into three hired, four-wheel drive pickup trucks and were driven off at high speed into Wadi Rum. A number of us had brought our red and black keffiyehs and black rope aqals, that had been given to us by the Manar Hotel on our arrival in Jordan. I wore mine and it proved to a most useful garment, keeping out the sun and the dust thrown up from vehicles. The day was the hottest we had experienced so far on this trip. Gus took us to the two Nebatean inscription sites that we had visited in 1996, one of which was the dried up waterway coming from a spring within a cleft in a high rock face. By midday we were all back in our air-conditioned coach, travelling further east to Disi. Soon after leaving Wadi Rum, both David and I noticed an adult lesser spotted eagle *Aquila pomarina,* along with one of its youngsters, perched on two small boulders by the roadside. We were close enough to them for every detail of their plumage to be easily distinguished, so we brought the coach to a halt, and Friends could all get a good view. Above, circling some adjacent cliffs, were black kites *Milvus migrans* and fan-tailed ravens *Corvus rhipidurus*.

There was less to see, with fewer birds in the orchards, and a much reduced welcoming party from the local residents than on our earlier visit to Disi In spite of the dry weather, the reservoir, fed by a local spring, was full. We watched male redstarts *Phoenicurus phoenicurus* and several hoopoes *Upupa epops*, before boarding the coach again to face the long journey back to Amman. I sat glued to the window, watching the miles and miles of desert terrain fly past as we progressed northwards up the modern Desert Highway. From time to time, a desert lark *Ammonanes deserti* would fly away from the roadside verge as the coach approached. We stopped at a highway cafe and were served with an excellent Arab meal. David looked exhausted, and I knew he was looking forward to getting home. We reached the Manar Hotel in good time for our last evening meal together. Next day the Quaker party flew out of Amman and reached Heathrow by mid-afternoon. So ended another Quaker Al Mashrek tour.

I was thankful that we had all returned safely, without a major incident. It had been very different from the previous tour, with so many unforseen experiences. Due to the cold weather conditions, the wildlife content of the tour was much less than we had hoped for, but, all the same, what we did see was of considerable interest. I was glad to be back home with Patricia; my chest was still playing me up and a subsequent X ray showed that I had an infection.

A young starred agama. Drawn by Michael Thompson

CHAPTER X

Epilogue

WHAT IS IT ABOUT Al Mashrek that attracts me so much? I find this a difficult question to answer, as it is complicated by many factors, and every time I go there, I think that journey may be my last. In 1995 Tony Manasseh suggested that I should settle permanently in the Lebanon, and that I had all the credentials of an occidental, that is a westerner who settles in the east. But this has never been part of my thinking, for my family and my roots, which are deep, are in the north of England, particularly in Yorkshire and Cumbria. However, I can always return to the region and, at the time of writing, David and I are planning another Quaker expedition to Al Mashrek in 2000 CE.

I suppose one of the first reasons is that in places, the area is stunningly beautiful, in spite of the damage that mankind has inflicted on it over the centuries. It has everything topographically, from the beautiful Mediterranean Sea, the snow-capped mountains of Lebanon, and the hills of Galilee, to the Rift valley and deserts of Syria and Jordan. My few desert experiences are ones I will always treasure. There are still places I have not visited, such as the Negev in Israel or Mount Sinai in Egypt, but, I hope, that these gaps may be filled in future expeditions. This brings me to my second reason - its wildlife.

My interest in wildlife was triggered when I was a boy roaming the wadis of Mount Carmel, and further nurtured at Sidcot School, when I wandered the Mendip Hills. So, Al Mashrek's fauna and flora have been very much part of my upbringing, and, in many ways, I could have not had a better introduction to the natural world than in this region. Al Mashrek is rich in its wildlife, for it is on the crossroads between the east and west, between Africa, Asia Minor, Europe and Arabia. Every year millions upon millions of birds pass through the area on their spring and autumn migrations. The vegetation is a mixture from all these continents, as is its climate, influenced by land masses and seas. Add to that the different peoples of Al Mashrek, and we have an extraordinary mix.

The history of mankind is to be found here, from early Neanderthal man on Mount Carmel, through numerous civilisations, to the modern states that make up the region today. I was taught history well at Sidcot by John Russell, and was encouraged by my Father to read books other than medical ones, and have always been interested in history, especially relating to the Near and Middle East. So, to visit historical sites, where some of this history was acted out, has been a bonus for me. Out of this region have arisen three of the major world monotheistic religions. Two of them, Christianity followed by Islam, having arisen out of Judaism. Of late, and in this setting, the Jesus of history has became a fascination for me.

I began asking myself questions about him and what he stood for. Much influenced by the Biblical, historical scholarship of E. P. Sanders, Elaine Pagels and Geza Vermes, and helped by frequent visits to Woodbrooke, I realised I was no longer interested in a faith in Jesus, but a faith of Jesus. Much of what orthodox, or establishment, ecclesiastical Christianity stands for, I now find is meaningless, such as a virgin birth or a physical resurrection. Most of what I now read in the four gospels in the New Testament is prophecy historised, and not history remembered. This is often, in a small way, confirmed by the lack of authenticity in some of the 'Jesus' sites I have visited, with others, in the Holy Land. Occasionally, site guides prefix their statements with the words 'supposed place in which'. However, many of the stories in the Hebrew Bible and the New Testament do come alive in my imagination, as I move around the area and imagine them in their supposed settings. My search goes on and I see that all this questioning is a healthy part of my spiritual journey through life. Jesus of Nazareth remains central to my religious life, for he, above all other persons, it seems to me, had a loving relationship with God and showed us what it meant to be in such a relationship. That statement, in conventional Christian terms, excludes me, I think, from being called a Christian.

Quakerism, rooted in Christianity, has been established, in a small way, in Al Mashrek for over one hundred and thirty years It first arrived at the end of the 1860s, with both American and British Friends appearing in Palestine and Lebanon at the same time, with the arrival of Eli and Sybil Jones of New England Yearly Meeting and Alfred Lloyd Fox and Clare Millar of London Yearly Meeting. By 1888, British and American Friends agreed to divide their work, American Friends taking Ramallah and British Friends, Brummana. Besides the two Friends' schools, Friends have continued to work both in Palestine, Jordan and Lebanon, relieving suffering and helping in education programmes. Numbers of both Monthly Meetings have fluctuated, but in recent years have declined. The four families that make up Brummana Monthly Meeting are a closely knit fellowship, dependant on the survival of Brummana High School as a Quaker institution. I felt a small part of that fellowship, following my visit in 1995. In Lebanon, an area of sectarian divide, the Quaker message of 'that of God within each person' and that concept that God cannot be encapsulated in a set of words or a creed, is little understood. The vast majority of Lebanese like their worship and religious life programmed according to a set of deeply held religious doctrines and beliefs, but Friends favour an experiential witness to their spiritual life. Thus, another reason I like going to Al Mashrek is to be with Arab Friends and to support them in their witness.

Ultimately, I suppose, I am drawn to Al Mashrek because it is the land of my birth.

Dinka men loading paddle steamer The Gedid, *Sudan 1944.*
Drawn by JOHN THOMPSON

Appendices

A. Fauna of Al Mashrek

THE ANIMAL LISTS are of those I have observed during my many visits, and are not complete lists for the area, but do show the variety of wildlife present. Subspecies listed when known. (C) indicates specimen collected for South Kensington Natural History Museum in 1952/55 (see Chapter 2). Palestine is the areas under the Palestine Authority i.e. the West Bank and Gaza Strip

1 Amphibians.

Spotted salamander	Salamandra salamandra	Lebanon (C).
Banded newt	Triturus vittatus	Lebanon
Green toad	Bufo viridis	Lebanon, Israel
Savigny's tree-frog	Hyla savignyi	Lebanon
Edible frog	Rana esculenta	Israel.
		5 species

2. Reptiles

Greek tortoise	Testudo graeca	Isreal, Jordan
Swamp turtle	Mauremys caspica rivulata	Israel
Elegant gecko	Stenodactylus sthenodactylus	Israel
Turkish gecko	Hemidactylus turcica	Israel
Fan-toed gecko	Ptyodactylus puiseuxi	Israel, Jordan.
Pale agama	Trapeius pallida	Israel
Starred agama	Laudakia stellio stellio	Lebanon (C), Israel, Jordan
Chamaeleon	Chamaeleon chamaeleon	Lebanon (C).
Bridled skink	Maybuta vittatus	Lebanon (C).
Gold skink	Eumeces schniderii	Lebanon (C)
Ocellated skink	Chalcides ocellatus	Israel
Bosc's lizard	Acanthodactylus boskiana	Jordan
Leopard lizard	Acanthodactylus pardalis	Israel
Green lizard	Lacerta laevis	Lebanon (C), Israel
Sand lizard	Lacerta agilis	Israel.
Menetries's lizard	Ophisops elegans	Lebanon (C).

203

European glass lizard	Ophisaurus apodus	Lebanon (C).
Diced-water snake	Natrix tessellata	Lebanon (C)
Syrian black snake	Coluber jugularis asiana	Lebanon. (C)
Dahl's whip snake	Colubar najadum	Lebanon (C), Israel.
Coin-marked snake	Coluber ravergieri (nummifer)	Lebanon.
Mueller's snake	Micrelaps muelleri	Lebanon (C).
Black-headed snake	Rhynchocalamus melanocephalus	Lebanon (C).
		23 species

3. Birds

Black-necked grebe	Podiceps nigricollis	Israel
Little grebe	Tachybaptus ruficolis	Lebanon.
White pelican	Pelecanus onocrotalus	Israel.
Cormorant	Phalacrocorax carbo	Israel, Lebanon.
Pygmy cormorant	Phalacrocorax pygmeus	Israel.
Squacco heron	Ardeola ralloides	Jordan.
Night heron	Nycticorax nycticorax	Israel, Jordan.
Cattle egret	Bubulcus ibis	Israel, Palestine, Lebanon
Great white heron	Egretta alba	Israel, Jordan, Lebanon.
Little egret	Egretta garzetta	Israel., Lebanon
Grey heron	Ardea cinerea	Israel, Jordan, Lebanon..
Spoonbill	Platalea leucorodia	Israel.
White stork	Ciconia ciconia	Israel, Lebanon.
Black stork	Ciconia nigra	Israel.
Greater flamingo	Phoenicopterus ruber	Israel.
White-fronted goose	Anser albifrons	Lebanon.
Shelduck	Tadorna tadorna	Israel.
Mallard	Anas platyrhynchos	Israel.
Wigeon	Anas penelope	Israel.
Garganey	Anas querquedula	Israel, Lebanon..
Shovler	Anas clypeata	Israel.
Teal	Anas crecca	Israel
Marble duck	Marmaronetta angustriostris	Israel.
Tufted duck	Authya fuligula	Israel.
Osprey	Pandion haliatus	Israel.
White-tailed eagle	Haliaeetus albicilla	Israel.
Black kite	Milvus migrans	Israel, Jordan.
Short-toed eagle	Circaetus galliicus	Israel, Jordan.
Egyptian vulture	Neophron percnopterus	Israel, Jordan.
Griffon vulture	Gyps fulvus	Israel, Jordan, Lebanon..
Marsh harrier	Circus aeruginosus	Israel, Lebanon
Hen harrier	Circus cyaneus	Israel.
Levant sparrowhawk	Accipter brevipes	Israel, Jordan, Lebanon..
Buzzard	Buteo buteo	Israel, Jordan.

204

Steppe buzzard	Buteo buteo vulpinus	Israel.
Long-legged buzzard	Buteo rufinus	Israel. Jordan, Lebanon.
Honey buzzard	Pernis apivorus	Israel.
Golden eagle	Aquila chrysaetos	Israel, Jordan, Lebanon.
Imperial eagle	Aquila heliaca	Jordan.
Bonelli's eagle	Hieraeetus fasciatus	Jordan.
Lesser spotted eagle	Aquila pomarina	Israel, Jordan, Lebanon.
Steppe eagle	Aquila nipalensis	Israel.
Red-footed falcon	Falco vespetinus	Jordan.
Kestrel	Falco tinnunculus	Israel, Jordan, Lebanon.
Lesser kestrel	Falco naumanni	Israel.
Hobby	Falco subbuteo	Lebanon, Syria.
Chukar	Alectoris chukar	Israel, Jordan.
Black francolin	Francolinus francolinus	Israel.
Moorhen	Gallinula choropus	Israel, Jordan.
Coot	Fulica atra	Israel, Jordan, Lebanon.
Common crane	Grus grus	Israel.
Black-winged stilt	Himantopus himantopus	Israel.
Spur-winged plover	Hoplopterus spinosus	Israel , Lebanon.
White-winged plover	Chettusia leucurus	Jordan.
Redshank	Tringa totanus	Israel.
Greenshank	Tringa nebularia	Israel.
Green sandpiper	Tringa ochropus	Israel.
Common sandpiper	Actitis hypoleucos	Israel.
White-eyed gull	Larus leucophthalmus	Jordan.
Black-headed gull	Larus ridibundus	Israel, Jordan, Lebanon.
Mediterranean gull	Larus melanocephalus	Israel, Lebanon
Lesser-blackback gull	Larus fuscus	Israel, Jordan, Lebanon.
Common tern	Sterna hirundo	Israel.
Sandwich tern	Sterna sandvicensis	Lebanon.
Black tern	Chlidonias niger	Israel.
Caspian tern	Sterna caspia	Jordan.
Sand partridge	Ammoperdix heyi	Israel.
Quail	Coturnix coturnix	Jordan.
Stock dove	Columba oenas	Jordan.
Rock dove	Columba livia	Israel, Jordan.
Turtle dove	Streptopelia turtur	Israel, Jordan.
Collared dove	Streptopelia decaoto	Israel, Jordan.
Palm dove	Streptopelia senegalensis	Israel, Jordan, Palestine, Syria, Lebanon.

Ring-necked parakeet	Psittacula krameri	Jordan.
Cuckoo	Cuculus canorus	Israel, Jordan.
Little owl	Athene noctua	Jordan.
Alpine swift	Apus melba	Israel, Jordan, Lebanon.
Little swift	Apus affinis	Israel.
Swift	Apus apus	Israel, Jordan, Lebanon, Syria.
Kingfisher	Alcedo atthis	Israel.
Smyrna kingfisher	Halcyon smyrnensis	Israel, Jordan.
Lesser pied kingfisher	Ceryle rudis	Israel.
Hoopoe	Upupa epops	Israel, Jordan, Lebanon.
Bee-eater	Merops apiaster	Israel.
Blue-cheeked bee-eater	Merops superciliosus	Jordan.
Little green bee-eater	Merops apiaster	Israel.
Roller	Coracias garrulus	Israel.
Syrian woodpecker	Dendrocopos syriacus	Israel.
Skylark	Alauda arvensis	Israel, Lebanon.
Crested lark	Galerida cristata	Israel, Jordan.
Desert lark	Ammomanes deserti	Israel, Jordan.
Calandra lark	Melanocorypha calandra	Israel.
Sand martin	Riparia riparia eilat	Israel, Lebanon.
Rock martin	Ptyonoprogne fuligula	Israel, Jordan.
Crag martin	Ptyonoprogne rupestris	Lebanon.
House martin	Delichon rubra	Israel, Jordan, Lebanon.
Red-rumped swallow	Hirundo daurica	Israel, Lebanon.
Swallow	Hirundo rustica	Israel, Jordan, Lebanon.
Red-throated pipit	Anthus cervinus	Israel.
Water pipit	Anthus spinoletta coutelli	Israel.
Pied wagtail	Motacilla alba alba	Israel, Jordan, Lebanon.
Yellow wagtail	Motacilla flava feldegg (black-headed)	Israel, Lebanon.
	Motacilla flava flava (blue-headed).	Israel.
Yellow-vented bulbul	Pycnonotus xanthopygos	Israel, Jordan, Lebanon.
Nightingale	Luscinia megarhynchos	Israel.
Bluethroat	Lusinia svecica svecica	Israel, Jordan.
Blackstart	Cercomela melanura	Israel, Jordan, Lebanon.
Stonechat	Saxicola torquata ? armenica	Jordan.
Black redstart	Phoenicurus ochruros	Lebanon.
Redstart	Phoenicurus phoenicurus	Israel, Jordan.

Wheatear	Oenanthe oenanthe oenanthe	Israel, Lebanon.
Black-eared wheatear	Oenanthe hispanica melanoleuca	Jordan, Lebanon.
Isabelline wheatear	Oenanthe isabellina	Jordan.
Desert wheatear	Oenanthe deserti	Israel, Jordan.
Mourning wheatear	Oenanthe lugens	Jordan.
Pied wheatear	Oenanthe pleschanka	Jordan.
White-crowned black wheatear	Oenanthe leucopyga	Jordan.
Blue rock thrush	Monticola solitarius	Jordan.
Blackbird	Turdus merula syriacus	Israel, Jordan, Syria, Lebanon.
White-throated robin	Irania gutturalis	Lebanon.
Robin	Erithacus rubecula	Israel, Lebanon.
Reed warbler	Acrocephalus scirpaceus	Israel.
Clamorous warbler	Acrocephalus stentoreus	Israel, Jordan.
Sedge warbler	Acrocephalus schoenobaenus	Israel.
Cetti's warbler	Cettia cetti	Israel.
Scrub warbler	Scotocera inquieta	Israel, Jordan.
Graceful warbler	Prinia gracilis	Israel, Jordan, Lebanon.
Garden warbler	Sylvia borin	Israel.
Whitethroat	Sylvia communis	Israel, Jordan.
Lesser whitethroat	Sylvia curruca	Israel, Jordan, Lebanon.
Blackcap	Sylvia atricapilla	Israel, Jordan, Lebanon.
Sardinian warbler	Sylvia melanocephala	Israel.
Orphean warbler	Sylvia hortensis	Israel.
Chiffchaff	Phylloscopus collybita	Israel.
Willow warbler	Phylloscopus trochilus	Israel, Jordan, Lebanon.
Goldcrest	Regulus regulus	Israel.
Spotted flycatcher	Muscicapa striata	Lebanon.
Palestine sunbird	Nectarina osea	Israel, Jordan.
Arabian babbler	Turdoides squamiceps	Israel.
Penduline tit	Remiz pendulinus	Israel.
Great tit	Parus major	Israel, Lebanon.
Great grey shrike	Lanius excubitor	Israel, Jordan.
Lesser grey shrike	Lanius minor	Israel.
Woodchat shrike	Lanius senator	Israel, Jordan.
Masked shrike	Lanius nubicus	Israel, Jordan.
Syrian jay	Garrulus glandarius atricapillus	Israel, Palestine, Syria.
Rook	Corvus frugilegus	Lebanon.
Hooded crow	Corvus corone sardorius	Israel, Palestine, Lebanon.
House crow	Corvus splendens	Jordan.
Raven	Corvus corax	Israel.

Brown-necked raven	Corvus ruficollis	Israel, Jordan.
Fan-tailed raven	Corvus rhipidurus	Israel, Jordan.
Tristram's Grackle	Onychognathus tristramii	Israel, Jordan.
Starling	Sturna vulgaris	Israel, Jordan.
House sparrow	Passer domesticus	Jordan, Lebanon.
Dead Sea sparrow	Passer moabiticus	Israel.
Spanish sparrow	Passer hispaniolensis	Jordan.
Chaffinch	Fringilla coelebs	Israel, Lebanon.
Syrian serin	Serinus syriacus	Jordan, Lebanon.
Linnet	Acanthus cannabina	Israel, Jordan.
Goldfinch	Carduelis carduelis	Israel, Jordan, Lebanon.
Greenfinch	Carduelis cholris chlorotica	Israel, Jordan, Lebanon.
Trumpeter finch	Bucanetes githagineus	Jordan.
Sinai rosefinch	Carpodacus synoicus	Jordan.
Corn bunting	Miliaria calandra	Israel.
House bunting	Emberiza striolata striolata	Israel, Jordan.
Cretzschmar's bunting	Emberiza caesia	Jordan.
		166 species

4. Mammals

Eastern European hedgehog	Erinaceus concolor	Lebanon.
Egyptian friut bat	Rousettus aegyptiacus	Isreal.
Greater horseshoe bat	Rhinolphus ferrumequinum	Lebanon.
Kuhl's pipistrelle	Pipistrellus kuhlii	Lebanon.
Ruppell's sand fox	Vulpes ruepellii	Jordan.
Golden jackal	Canis aureus	Lebanon.
Egyptian mongoose	Herpestes ichneumon	Israel.
Rock hyrax	Procavia capensis syriaca	Israel.
Ibex	Capra ibex ibex	Israel.
Cape hare	Lepus capensis	Israel.
Arabian oryx	Oryx leucocoryx	Jordan.
Syrian onager	Equus hemionus	Jordan.
		12 species

Other mammals not seen, but evidence of them from sign, track and trail.
Red fox (Vulpes vulpes), gazelles - possibly Dorcas gazelle, wild boar (Sus scrofa), Indian crested porcupine (Hytrix indica), lesser mole rat (Spalax leucodon) golden spiny mouse (Acomys russatus), Persian squirrel (Sciurus anomalus) and social vole (Microtus socialis)

208

B. Flora of Al Mashrak

This flora list was compiled by Hugh Maw, with the help of Pat Alexander, on the 1996 tour and is roughly in the order the plants were seen.

1. Flowers

Blue shrubby cromwell(Lithodora fruticosa), Honeywort(Cerinthe major), Golden henbane (Hyoscymus aureus), Corn marigold(Chrysanthemum segetum), Crown daisy(Chrysanthemum coronarium), Field marigold(Calendula aevensis), Syrian thistle(Notobasis syriaca), Holy milk thistle(Silybum maritimum), Mountain tulip(Tilipa argensis), Tassel hyacinth(Muscari cornosum), Naples garlic(Allium neapolitanum or Allium subhirsutum), Bermuda buttercup or Cape sorel(Oxalis pes-caprae), Italian arum(Arum italicum), Sea rocket(Cakile maritima), Bug orchid(Orchis coriophopra), Greater butterfly orchid(Plantanthera chlorantha), Yellow bee orchid(Ophrys lutea), Rough poppy(Papaver hybridum), Corn poppy(Papaver subpiriforme), Navelwort(Umbilicus intermedius), Thorny broom(Callictome villosa or spinosa), Lupin (Lipinus pinosus), Lupin(Lupinus micranthus), Hairy yellow vetchling(Lathyrus sp.), Wild pea (Pisum elatius), Turban buttercup anemone(Ranunculus asiaticus), Common anemone(Anemome coronaria), Pheasants eye or Summer adonis(Adonis eastivalis), Stinging nettle(Urtica dubia), Roman nettle(Urtica pilulifera), Prickly starwort(Salsola kali), Ramping fumatory(Fumaria capreola), Wild migonette(Reseda lutea), Montpellier milk vetch(Astragalus monspessulanus), Annual yellow vetchling(Lathyrus annus), Blue scarlet pimpernel(Anagallis arvensis), Common mallow(Malva nicaensis), Narrow leaved cistus(Cistus monspeliensis), Sage-leaved cistus(Cistus salvifolius), Alexanders(Symrnium olusatrum), Persian cyclamen (Cyclamen persicum), Sea bindweed(Calystegia soldanella), Pale blue lobellia sp., Narrow-leaved crimson clover(Trifolium augustifolium), Hairy flax(Linum pubescens), White henbane(Hyoscyamusal bus), milkworts(Polygala sp.), yellow rockrose(Cistus sp.), periwinkle(Vinca sp.), French lavender(Lavendula stoechus), Toothed lavender(Lavendula dentata), Sage clary(Salvia officionallis), Jerusalem sage(Salvia hierosolymitana), Bears breeches(Acanthus mollis), Etruscan honeysuckle(Lonicera sp.), Common scabious or Carmel daisy(Scabiosa prolifera), yellow daisy(Pallensis spinosa), White daisy(Annacyclus clavatus), Milk thistle(Silybum marianum), Bristly hollyhock(Alcea setosa), Hollow-stemmed asphodel(Asphodelus fistulosus), Rough dogstail grass(Cynosurus coloratus), Winter wild oat (Avena sterilis), Field swod lily(Gladiolus italicus), Afternoon iris or barbary nut(Gyandiris sisyrinchium), Virinia stock(Malcolmia crenulata), Papyrus or paper reed(Cyperus papyrus), Giant fennel(Ferula communis), Jerusalem surge(Euphorbia hierosolimitana), sorrel(Rumex sp.), Pellitory of the wall(Urticacae sp.), Stonecrop(Sedum sp.), Star clover(Trifolium stellatum), Yellow chamomile(Anthemis chamomile), Mountain knot grass(Paronychia argentea), Musk storksbill(Erodium moschatum), Bugle(Ajuga chamaepitys),

Square-stemmed bugloss(Anchusa strigosa), Spiny bears breech(Acanthus spinosus), Fly orchid(?sp.), Anatolian orchid(Orchis anatolica), spiny restharrow(Ononis antiquorum), Large blue alkanet(Anchusa azurea), Striped pink vetch camelthorn(Alhagi graecorum ?), Shrubby globularia(Globularia alypum), rue(Rue chalapensis), White aphodel(Asphodelus albus), Yellow star of Bethlehem(Gagea commutata or pendcularis), Sad stock (Matthiola fruticulosa), sweet alison(Globularia maritima), Large disc medick(Medicago orbicularis), Hop trifoil(Trifolium tormentosum), Birdsfoot trefoil(Ornithopus compresus), Silky bindweed(Convolvulus stachydfolius), Borage(Borago officionalis), Buttonweed(Cotula coronopifolia), Maidenhait fern(?sp.), Thistle(Ptilostemon stellatus), Ground thistle or dwarf saw-wort(Rhaponticum pusillum), snapdragon(Antirrhinum ajus), veined vetchling(Lathyrus pseudocicera), red-horned poppy(Galcium aleppicum), Morning glory(Ipomea sp.), Ramping fumitory(Fumaria capreolata), Summer savoy(Satureja thymbra), Spiked thymbra(Thymbra spicata), Maltese cross(Ricotia lunaria), Goats beard(Geropogon hybridus), Desert storksbill(Erodium touchyanum), Dotted willow(Lavatera punctata), mallow-leaved bindweed(Convolvulus altheodes), Pink mustard(Erucaria hispanica), Field mustard or charlock(Sinapis arvensis), Three horned stock(Mattheola tricuspidata), Desert fagonia(Fagonia mollis), Iberisan thistle(Centaurea iberica), Nerved-calyx stachys(Stachys neurocalcina), Desert spike(Eremostachys lacineata), Chian bugle(Ajiga chia), Lesser celandine(Ranunculus ficaria), Milk vetch(Astragalus macrocarpus), Yellow water lily(Nuphar lutum), Galilee mullein(Verbascum galileum), Bishops weed(Ridolfia segetum), Sun spurge(Euphorbia helioscopia), Desert broomrape(Cistanche tubulosa), Jericho oxeye(Asteriscus pygmaeus), Launaea daisy(Launaea augustifolia), Jaffa grounsel(Senicio joppensis), Sow thistle(Sonchus cleraceus), Oriental garlic(Allium orientale), Mayweed chamomile(Anthemis leucanthemifolia), Southern daisy(Bellis silvestris), Crown flower(Artedia squamata), Tordylium(Tordylium aegyptiacum), Narrow-leaved asphodel(Asphodelus tenuifolius), Green arum(Arum hygrophilum), Common reed(Phragmites australis), Cyprus cane(Arundo donax), Nepeta (Nepeta curviflora), Alkanet(Alkanna strigosa), Centaury(Centaurea cyanoides ?), Podonosoma (Podonosoma syriaca), Hyacinth squill(Squilla hyacinthoides), Judean bugloss(Echium judaeum), Tassel grapehyacinth(Leopoldia comosa), Great figwort(Scrophularia rubricaulis), Hottentot fig(Carpobrutus edulis).

149 species

2. Trees and shrubs, some wild, some cultivated.

Oleander(Nerium oleander), Carob tree(Ceretonia siliqua), Camel's foot(Bauhinia sp.), Acacia spp.(karoo & retinoides), Desert cistus, Castor oil(Ricinus communis), Indian bean tree(Catalpa bignonoides), Tamarisk (Tamarix sp.), Eucalyptus(Eucalyptus camaldulensis & other spp.), Judas tree(Cercis siliquastrum), Storax(Styrax officinalis), Strawberry tree(Arbutus andrachne), Aleppo pine(Pinus halepensis and other spp.), Oaks (Quercus spp.), Junipers(Juniperus oxycedrus & phoenicea), Turpentine tree(Pistacia terebinthus), Desert white broom(Retama raetam), Shrub tobacco(Nicotania glauca), Yitran(Thymelea hirsuta), Wild fig(Fiscus sp.), Sycomore fig(Ficus sycomorus), Cytisus(Cytisus triflorus), Cistus(Cistus silviaefolius), Prickly pear(Opuntia maxima), Thorney burnet(Sarcopterium spinosum), Bougainvillea(Bourgainvillea ?glabra), Pomegranate(Punica granatum), Wild & cultivated olive(Olea europaea), Hibiscus(Hibiscus rosa-sinensis), Lantana(Lantana sp.), Caper(Capparis spinosa).

C. Participants of Quaker Tours and Middle East Yearly Meeting.

1. Woodbrooke on the Road Holy Land Tour 1990.

John Adamson,	Mary Armstrong,	MauriceArnold
Tina Day	Annie Elliott	Charlotte Fellows
Michael Fellows	Anne Fletcher	Alison Forrester
Harvey Gillman	DavidGray	Yvonne Grundy
Jacky Kulkarni	Peggy McGeoghegan	Marion McNaughton
Hugh Maw	Daphne Maw	Denise Neale
Rachel Neill	Janey O'Shea	Ruth Pilkington
Rosemary Quested	Martie Rafferty	Joyce Rawlings-Davies
Elizabeth Roberts	Kate Roberts	Colin Somerville
Dilwyn Spence	Sheila Squibb	Kurt Straus
Michael Thompson	Patricia Thompson	Ruth Wheatman
Barbara Wilson		

2. Middle East Yearly Meeting held at Brummana 1994

Corinne B.Johnson	Floresca Karanasou	Paul Lalor
Tony Manasseh	Henry Selz	Jean Zaru
Jan Ramaker	Patricia Thompson	Michael Thompson
Ralph Wadge	Jean Wadge	John Scott
Marjorie Scott	Renee Baz	Sami Cortas
Najwa Cortas	Joseph Abu Khalil	Shatha Abu Khalil
Anna Kennedy	Albert Abu Khalil	Amal Abu Khalil
Juhaine Abu Khalil	Heather Moir	Nasri Khatar
Andrew Clark	Sabah Baz	Hilary Baz
Rabi' Baz		

3. Middle East Yearly Meeting held in Amman, Jordan 1995
(incomplete list).

Tony Manasseh	Philip Manasseh	Jean Zaru
Violet Zaru	Selim Zaru	Sami Cortas
Najwa Cortas	Renee Baz	Phillippa Neave
Paul Lalor	Retha McCuthen	Hans Weening
Jane Tod	Henry Selz	Nasri Khater
Michael Thompson	Amal Abu Khalil	Junaine Abu Khalil
Raymond Ayoub	Anna Kennedy	Yvette

Three American Quaker couples with children, working for non-Quaker agencies.

211

4. The Quaker Natural History Tour 1996

Patrick Alexander   Brenda Alexander   Alison Bush
Rosemary Day   David Gray   Jean Grudgings
John Harvey   Jane Harvey   Hugh Maw
Stan Murrell   Joyce Pickard   Hugh Roberts
Elizabeth Roberts   Ann Strauss   Michael Thompson
Moira Thomson

5. Quaker Middle East Study Tour 1998

Patrick Alexander   Brenda Alexander   Brenda Bailey
Ben Barman   Candia Barman   Alison Bush
Peter Fox   Sheila Fox   Kathleen Haines
John Harvey   Jane Harvey   David Gray
Jean Grudgings   Margaret Makins   Marjorie Malik
Mary Martin   Bill Matchett   Judy Matchett
Joyce Pickard   Hugh Roberts   Elizabeth Roberts
David Solloway   Stella Solloway   Michael Thompson